This is a comparative study of the role of English and French towns in feudal society in the middle ages. Professor Hilton challenges the view that 'a town is a town wherever it is', and takes issue with the perception of the medieval town as the harbinger of capitalism.

Differences between English and French feudalism are taken into account; but these differences, as well as those between English and French medieval towns, existed within sufficiently similar contexts to justify the kind of comparison pioneered by Marc Bloch in his *Seigneurie française et manoir anglais*. Medieval France was much larger than medieval England, and contained a far larger number of towns. French town populations were bigger than those in England, although it is possible that England had a higher proportion of small market towns. Comparisons are made between the feudal presence within the towns of both countries, and between their urban social structures. Conflicts arising from urban demands for freedom and autonomy are examined, together with frictions between various levels of society, such as mercantile elites, craft masters, journeymen, the unskilled and marginals. Finally, the mercantile domination of English town governments is contrasted with that acquired by lawyers and officials in late medieval French towns – the 'trahison de la bourgeoisie', as one French historian has described it.

In bringing together much material which dissolves old categories and simplifications in the study of medieval towns, Professor Hilton provides an important new perspective on medieval society and on the nature of feudalism.

Past and Present Publications

English and French towns in feudal society

Past and Present Publications

General Editor: PAUL SLACK, *Exeter College, Oxford*

Past and Present Publications comprise books similar in character to the articles in the journal *Past and Present*. Whether the volumes in the series are collections of essays – some previously published, others new studies – or monographs, they encompass a wide variety of scholarly and original works primarily concerned with social, economic and cultural changes, and their causes and consequences. They will appeal to both specialists and non-specialists and will endeavour to communicate the results of historical and allied research in readable and lively form. This series continues and expands in its aims the volumes previously published elsewhere.

For a list of titles in Past and Present Publications, see end of book.

English and French towns in feudal society

A comparative study

R. H. HILTON

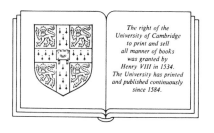

The right of the
University of Cambridge
to print and sell
all manner of books
was granted by
Henry VIII in 1534.
The University has printed
and published continuously
since 1584.

CAMBRIDGE UNIVERSITY PRESS

Cambridge New York Port Chester
Melbourne Sydney

Published by the Press Syndicate of the University of Cambridge
The Pitt Building, Trumpington Street, Cambridge CB2 1RP
40 West 20th Street, New York, NY 10011-4211, USA
10 Stamford Road, Oakleigh, Victoria 3166, Australia

First published 1992

Printed in Great Britain at the University Press, Cambridge

A cataloguing in publication record for this book is available from the
British Library

Library of Congress cataloguing in publication data

Hilton, R. H. (Rodney Howard), 1916–
     English and French towns in feudal society: a comparative study/
R. H. Hilton.
          p.   cm. – (Past and present publications)
     Includes bibliographical references and index.
     ISBN 0 521 41352 4 (hardcover)
     1. Cities and towns. Medieval–England.   2. Cities and towns,
Medieval–France.   3. Feudalism–England.   4. Feudalism–France.
5. Social structure–England–History.   6. Social structure–France–
History.   I. Title.
HT115.H55   1992   91–12206
307.76′0942′0902–dc20   CIP

Library of Congress cataloguing in publication data

UP

ISBN 0 521 41352 4 hardback

To Jean Birrell

Contents

Preface

This book is rather a risky venture. Most of my research on medieval social and economic history has been agrarian rather than urban, and my recent ventures into urban history have been concerned with small market towns rather than with big cities. Amongst other aims, I have tried in this book to justify the 'small town' theme as being an important feature of urban history.

My main purpose, however, has been to consider the role of the town within feudal society, as will, I hope, become clear from chapter 1 onwards. This is a specific theme and, while it has to be considered in the general context of the history of medieval towns, there are many aspects of urban history which will not be dealt with in detail. These include both the general and particular economic developments within towns; the patterns of international and regional trade; the economic relationships between the towns and their rural hinterland; not to speak of urban constitutional and political development. These and other aspects of medieval urban history will, of course, be an important context to my main theme. And, while emphasising the towns' relationships with the feudal social formation, I will attempt to convey some feel for medieval town life.

I have developed the Anglo-French comparative theme, because of my interest in France and in French history. If my documentary research into medieval English urban history has concentrated on the study of the small town economy and society, all of my work on French towns has been confined to secondary sources – monographs on specific towns and articles on various themes in urban history, general surveys of urban history. The historiography of French urban history is very rich and I cannot claim to have made a complete coverage. If I did, I would never get round to writing even a small book.

Introduction

The medieval England whose towns I am considering had virtually the same boundaries as those of contemporary England. The same is true of France, with one major exception. The county of Flanders was a fief of the French monarchy, though, as in the case of many other counties and duchies, by no means dominated by the Capetians or the Valois. Most of the county of Flanders is in modern Belgium. Some of the most important towns of medieval Europe were contained within it – Ghent, Ypres, Bruges, as well as many smaller urban centres. The Flemish towns were commercially and industrially to the forefront of the economic, social and political development of northern Europe, especially in the late thirteenth and fourteenth centuries. As historians such as J. Lestocquoy have shown, they are most appropriately compared with the towns of northern Italy.[1] I have therefore taken the view that they were not characteristic of French urban development. In spite of the wealth of primary and secondary material on them, I have not included them in my comparative study.

On the other hand, Provence was not part of the medieval French kingdom until the end of the fifteenth century. Unlike Flanders, however, it was similar in economy and social structure to an important French region – Languedoc – and contained urban centres which have been well studied by French historians. I have therefore included it in my comparative study.

My coverage, even given these omissions and inclusions, cannot be claimed to be complete. I have read as much on French towns as – so far – possible, and also on English towns. I will certainly have to continue. However, given the fact that I am considering a specific

[1] *Les villes de Flandre et d'Italie sous le gouvernement des patriciens (XIe–XVe siècles).*

theme, as well as attempting a comparative perspective, I may perhaps be forgiven some omissions.

ENGLAND AND FRANCE: A USEFUL COMPARISON?

The value of comparative historical studies has been accepted in principle for many years. The same phenomena studied in different countries are often quite differently documented, so that the better evidence for one country will help to understand similar features in another country or countries. For example, the agrarian history of medieval England is much better documented than that of most other European countries, and if used with care may throw light on problems elsewhere than in England. France and England are sufficiently close and yet sufficiently different to make comparisons worthwhile, as Marc Bloch showed in his Sorbonne lectures, published after his death under the title *Seigneurie française et manoir anglais.*[2]

Marc Bloch began his lectures by drawing attention to the contrast in his day – that is in the 1930s – between the enclosed countryside of England and the open fields of northern France, between the advanced capitalist farming of England and the still predominantly peasant agriculture of France. He sought for the origins of this contrast as far back as the middle ages. As far as English and French urbanism is concerned, I do not intend to have a similarly contemporary starting point. If I have in mind a perception of a significant and historically conditioned divergence, it goes back rather to the early modern period when England embarked, more quickly than France, on the road to capitalism. France, as Fernand Braudel insisted in his *Identité de la France*, was then backward economically, in spite of its size, wealth and political power.[3] It is not that I am suggesting that it was simply a contrast in urban developments which produced these divergent economic and social histories, but that an exploration of comparable urban histories in the two countries may well throw light, not merely on post-medieval developments, but on the problems concerning the way in which the towns fitted into feudal societies.

France and England in the middle ages were different from each other, but not too different to be usefully comparable. In spite of the

[2] Paris, 1960.   [3] Vol. II.

destructive wars waged by England on French soil in the fourteenth and fifteenth centuries, the two countries had intermeshed socially and politically for hundreds of years. For example, it is clear that there had been close commercial relationships between the Anglo-Saxon and Frankish states. This was strikingly illustrated by the famous correspondence at the end of the eighth century between Offa, king of Mercia, and Charlemagne, in which the latter complained about the length of woollen cloaks imported from England.[4] Contacts other than commercial must have been even earlier. The Anglo-Saxon missionaries in the seventh and eighth centuries not only had a considerable impact on the pagan Germans but also exercised influence throughout the Frankish kingdom. The Venerable Bede, a Northumberland monk, was sufficiently well known beyond the boundaries of the Northumbrian kingdom, for his *Ecclesiastical History* (*c.* 731) to establish a chronological system which was adopted throughout western Europe. And, as is well known, the Northumbrian scholar, Alcuin, was an important member of the circle of intellectuals at Charlemagne's court, beyond which his influence spread when he became abbot of the monastery of St Martin at Tours. The English Channel was no barrier to Anglo-Frankish/French relations – including those with Normandy, which, though leading to conflict in 1066, must have been close.[5]

This Norman conquest of 1066 had obvious and long-lasting consequences. The English aristocracy was largely replaced by the Normans and their various allies, so that for nearly four centuries the English ruling class was as much francophone as anglophone. The Norman and Angevin kings were lords of Normandy and of much of western France until the early thirteenth century, and then, although losing Normandy, Anjou and Poitou, controlled Gascony until the middle of the fifteenth century. The Anglo-Norman language continued to be the language of the English law courts throughout the middle ages. English barons and knights were involved, along with their Norman, Angevin and Gascon counterparts, in the administration of the French lands of the kings of England.

[4] F.M. Stenton, *Anglo-Saxon England*, p. 20.
[5] See D. Wormald, 'The Age of Offa and Alfred' and 'The Ninth Century' in J. Campbell, ed., *The Anglo-Saxons*; and H.R. Loyn, 'The Overseas Trade of Anglo-Saxon England' in *Anglo-Saxon England and the Norman Conquest*.

There were, of course, sharp contrasts. Although Normandy, Brittany, Picardy and the Ile de France were very similar geographically to lowland England, Mediterranean France, and indeed most parts of France where the *langue d'oc* was spoken, were very different.

The size of France and of its population also contrasts with that of England, but this also means that for our purposes more comparative material is available. The French population in the thirteenth century may have been three times that of England. In 1316, 227 *bonnes villes* of France were represented in an assembly summoned by the king, whereas the analogous urban representation in the English parliaments at about the same time was between eighty and ninety towns.[6]

The great number of towns within the boundaries of modern France has provided French historians with a fine opportunity to develop the study of medieval urban history. There are not only many monographs dealing with individual towns, but studies of urban development in regions such as Brittany, Languedoc and Provence. To these may be added many studies of specific features of urban development such as Petit-Dutaillis' history of the communal movement, or Coornaert's study of the gilds. Nor are large, up-to-date syntheses lacking, such as the *Histoire de la France urbaine* edited by G. Duby.[7] This abundance contrasts with the lesser attention given to medieval urbanism by English historians, at any rate in the inter-war period. There were some innovative writers in the late nineteenth and early twentieth centuries, such as Alice Stopford Green, whose *Town Life in the Fifteenth Century* was broader than the title implies. James Tait's *Medieval English Boroughs* and *George Unwin's Gilds and Companies of London* were also works whose value remains.[8] More recent generalisers about the medieval English town have not always matched the achievements of their predecessors, though Susan Reynolds' *Introduction to the*

---

[6] B. Chevalier in the index to *Les bonnes villes de France aux XIVe et XVe siècles*, lists the 240 French towns; the English towns represented varied very much in numbers. The figure mentioned was normal, but 'at one time or another', between 1294 and 1337, as many as 140 towns might have had to send representatives – T.F.T. Plucknett, 'Parliament 1327–36' in E.B. Fryde and E. Miller, eds., *Historical Studies of the English Parliament*, I, p. 217.

[7] E. Coornaert, *Les corporations en France avant 1789*; C. Petit-Dutaillis, *Les communes Française. Caractères et évolution des origines du XVIIIe siècle*; G. Duby, ed., *Histoire de la France urbaine, II, La ville mediévale*.

[8] A.S. Green, 2 vols., London, 1894; J. Tait, Manchester, 1936; G. Unwin, London, 1908.

History of Medieval English Towns provides good coverage of most of the themes of urban history.[9] There have also been a number of good studies of individual towns.

There are various reasons for the relative shortage of work on English medieval urban history (as compared with that for the early modern period), admirable though some of it has been, and continues, to be. One obvious reason is the relatively small number of English towns. The other is that, compared with the sources for agrarian history, those for medieval urban history are much less abundant. This may be one of the reasons why scholars with a general interest in the economic and social history of the middle ages tended to be attracted to the history of the estate and manor rather than to that of the town. Lords and peasants have received more attention than artisans and merchants. A comparison of English and French towns in the context of their respective feudal societies could certainly be of interest to English urban historians as well as to their French opposite numbers – and to any historians of the European middle ages.

[9] Oxford, 1977.

1. *The town and feudalism:*
preliminary definitions

A TOWN IS A TOWN WHEREVER IT IS?

What was a town? A preliminary definition, however general, may be useful. The definition need not attempt to cover all towns from antiquity to the twentieth century, but only those of medieval, feudal society. One of the problems is that even medieval towns varied greatly in size and function, from small market towns with even fewer than 1,000 inhabitants to great cities, like Paris, with more than 100,000. A useful definition may, then, be rather what was *not* a town than what was. In effect, the town has to be distinguished from its rural hinterland and not, as some historians have tended to do, to be assimilated into the agrarian economy and society.[1]

The first point to be made is that the town, great or small, was the location of permanent market activity, not only at a weekly chartered market, which the lords of many villages also obtained in the thirteenth century. Second, and this is crucial, the inhabitants of the town did not, in contrast to those of the village, produce their own means of subsistence, even though they might have small vegetable plots, vineyards or even meadows. Their main activity was devoted to manufacture and trade, from which the bulk of their income was derived. The essential feature of towns, large or small, was occupational heterogeneity in an economy which produced, bought and sold commodities other than those necessary for subsistence, that is, mainly agricultural products.

The existence of a permanent market and of occupational heterogeneity might seem to be sufficient to define the medieval town very broadly, but many historians would probably wish to add at

[1] Already criticised in 'Towns in English Feudal Society' reprinted in my *Class Conflict and the Crisis of Feudalism.*

least an institutional dimension. This usually included the possession by the town's inhabitants of certain basic liberties, without which their special function could not be properly fulfilled. They would at least need freedom of status and tenure, freedom of movement and freedom of access to the market. Even if it were argued that a settlement with a market and an occupationally heterogeneous population should be assumed to be a town, one would expect that the grant of at least elementary liberties usually followed the economic development implied by the first two conditions, and would provide an extra indicator of urban status.

The role of the town in medieval feudal society has been perceived in many different ways, over the years, both by historians and sociologists. Some sociologists, in particular, have been tempted to assimilate the medieval town, like medieval feudal society, into a generalised pre-industrial or 'traditional' era in human history. In their long term perspective of pre-industrial history, they have perceived a duality between town and country, from the ancient world onwards, and conceived 'the city' as an unchanged social essence whose economy, society and ethos were always and necessarily specific to a model of urbanism, whatever the overall social formation.

This concept of 'the city' as an entity independent of the context of the wider society is reflected in the views of Louis Wirth in his famous article, 'Urbanism as a Way of Life'.[2] Not all sociologists, of course, ignored the historical context. One has only to remember Max Weber's book on *The City*, a work with many illuminating perceptions of medieval urbanisation.[3] G. Sjoberg's *The Preindustrial City* emphasises the varying economic, social and political contexts of pre-industrial cities. Unfortunately, he over-generalises pre-industrial society. For him, the whole pre-industrial world is divided into 'folk' and 'feudal' social formations, defined in a manner unrecognisable by historians. His elaborate theorising, however much he preaches to those (especially historians) presumed to be ignorant, is of little use in dealing with real feudalism.[4]

On the whole, historians have been less all-embracing in their perception of the pre-industrial town. Nevertheless, there have been elements in their work which, to a greater or lesser extent, include the concept of the unchanging town:country duality. Even Fernand

---

[2] *American Journal of Sociology*, 44, 1938.
[3] Trans. D. Martindale and G. Neuworth.   [4] New York, 1960.

Braudel, in his *Capitalism and Material Life*, writes 'A town is a town wherever it is',[5] a statement sufficiently influential to be taken as the title of an introductory section of the collected papers printed in *The Pursuit of Urban History*.[6]

Henri Pirenne's theory concerning the revival of urbanisation in the early middle ages initiated a very influential interpretation of urban development which could also imply the city's identity, specific to itself, separate from the social formation within which it was contained. As is well known, he believed that true urbanisation in the medieval period began with the revival of long distance trade, which he supposed to have been ruptured in the Mediterranean as a result of the activities of the Moslems in the Carolingian era. Once this threat had disappeared, itinerant merchants dealing in (mainly) luxury commodities could settle down at suitable, and often fortified, places on international trade routes – and thus laid the basis for the growth of the great commercial centres of medieval Europe.[7] Fruitful though much of Pirenne's work on medieval towns has been, his version of early medieval urbanisation has been severely questioned, not only conceptually but empirically.[8] His critics have insisted that the de-urbanisation of the Roman Empire and the diminution of Mediterranean and European trade began long before the Arab conquests. And although a significant revival of international trade did occur in the late tenth and early eleventh centuries, it was not the itinerant merchants who became the ruling bourgeoisie of the growing towns. As many historians, from Lestocquoy to Hibbert, have shown, these urban patriciates were mainly composed of local landowners and feudal officials, often from families of the lesser nobility.[9]

Pirenne's writing on urban history, unlike that of some of the theorists mentioned above, does, however, pose the critical question of the role of the bourgeoisie in feudal society. Did the bourgeoisie, whatever its origins, become an anti-feudal social force in the central period of the middle ages? In the twelfth and thirteenth centuries in particular, a number of towns obtained elements of self-government, jurisdictional exemption from outside feudal courts, and facilities

---

[5] Trans. M. Kochan, p. 373.   [6] D. Fraser and A. Sutcliffe, eds., p. 3.

[7] See his *Medieval Cities: their Origins and the Rebirth of Trade*.

[8] See, for example, the articles collected in A.F. Havighurst, ed., *The Pirenne Thesis. Analysis, Criticism and Revision*.

[9] J. Lestocquoy, *Les dynasties bourgeoises d'Arras*; J. Hibbert, 'The Origins of the Medieval Town Patriciate'.

for the admission of outside servile immigrants. I will consider the details of these privileged towns later, but the general issue is, of course, of considerable importance. If towns were 'non-feudal islands in the feudal seas',[10] and if their economic, social and political interests were in conflict with the interests of the feudal ruling class, then one would expect them to be a driving force in the transition from feudalism to capitalism, long distance generators of the bourgeois revolution. Such an interpretation of the urban role would also, of course, enforce the concept of a 'dual' society, in which the towns constituted an alien element within the social order of agrarian feudalism.

In fact, the concept of the separateness or antagonistic role of the medieval town within feudal society has now been much eroded. Standard texts on urban history are adjusting to a new standpoint, as in Hohenberg and Lees' *Making of Urban Europe 1000–1950*, in which they recognise that 'urban histories are inseparable from the histories of the economic, social and political systems of which they are part'.[11] However, the single-minded pursuit of urban history naturally involves a concentration of what seems to be specific to the town. For the historian of feudal society as a whole, what is needed is an examination not only of the role played by towns in feudal society, but of the extent to which the economic, social, political and ideological structures of feudalism are found in town as well as in the country.

WHAT WAS FEUDALISM?

We must, of course, recognise that there are different ideas about what is 'feudalism'. The traditional interpretation defines it in terms of the relationships between different strata of the landowning class. The determining features are the lord–vassal relationships, concretely manifested in the granting from on high of landed fiefs to clients, retainers and relatives, in return for homage, military service, aid and counsel.[12] Although this could imply a fairly tightly organised pyramidal structure, as was found in the Norman

---

[10] M.M. Postan, *The Medieval Economy and Society*, p. 212.

[11] Cambridge, Mass., 1985, pp. 2, 19.

[12] F.M. Stenton, *The First Century of English Feudalism, 1066 to 1166*, very well describes the feudo-vassalic aspect for England. For France, see F.L. Ganshof, *Feudalism*, trans. P. Grierson. Marc Bloch, *Feudal Society*, trans. L.A. Manyon, presents a more wide-ranging view.

monarchy in post-conquest England, from the king down through the barons to the knights, the model usually implied a decentralisation of power. It was the private jurisdictions of barons, bishops, abbots and knights, with a concomitant fragmentation of power, which was seen as one of the chief characteristics of feudalism. The economic basis of landed estates worked by a subordinated peasantry was recognised, the peasants being seen as analogous at the bottom of the social heap, because of their dependence on their lords, to the knights or barons higher up the social scale. They were seen as the base of the pyramid of mutual duties and obligations.

This interpretation – or description – of medieval feudalism contains much that is demonstrably true. It also fits in with a perception of urbanism primarily defined in terms of a by-product of long-distance trade in luxury goods. Towns, in order to develop as trading centres, needed basic liberties of tenure and status which would allow their burgess populations to engage freely in buying and selling on the market. In order to avoid the interference and impositions of the feudal landlords, they needed, as we have said, to be as free as possible from seigneurial jurisdiction, to be justiciable in their own town court and, if possible, to be able to appeal to what could be regarded as 'public' rather than 'private' authority. The public authority was thought of, in terms of this particular interpretation of feudalism, as the monarchy. The ideal town, therefore, would be one ruled by its own burgesses, free from interference by feudal potentates and protected by the monarch or the nearest equivalent of public authority, such as the counts or dukes of major territories. Such an interpretation would seem to fit in well with the urban communal movements of the twelfth century. It is also an interpretation which assumes that the monarchy as public authority was non-feudal.

Our picture of towns in feudal society may be somewhat different if we define feudalism as a social formation within which the lord–vassal relationship, emphasised in the traditional interpretation, was certainly important, but without being determinant.[13] As a social formation, the first aspect of feudalism is the level of technology, which meant that the basic unit of production was small scale, the peasant holding based on the family labour force normally

---

[13] See my entry, 'Feudal Society' in T. Bottomore *et al.*, eds., *A Dictionary of Marxist Thought*.

reinforced by at most one or two servants. Most productive activity was agricultural. The ruling class, including the feudal monarchies, was a landowning class. In varying degrees, at different times and in different places, some landowners might attempt the direct cultivation of home farms or demesnes by using labour services from peasant holdings or the hired labour of smallholders. But demesne production generated a minor and always uncertain proportion of the total income of the landowning class. That income was mainly derived by a transfer of as much as could be obtained of the surplus product of the peasant holding. This could take the straightforward form of rent in kind or in money or, as previously mentioned, in labour. It could also be taken as profits of private jurisdiction, including *banalités* such as compulsory grinding of corn at the lord's mill, baking in the lord's oven, pressing grapes in the lord's wine press, all at a cost to the tenant. The extraction of rent and other dues was done by various forms of direct and indirect coercion.

The coercion was legitimised for a large number of peasants by the institution of juridical serfdom. There was a considerable variation in the proportion of servile to free peasants from region to region, in both England and France. It must also be recognised that many supposedly free peasants had to give rents and services to their landlords which had the taint of servility. For many people in the upper ranks of feudal society, the peasants, the *rustici*, were thought of as servile, even though legally they were not. Whether serfdom was a continuation of ancient slavery, by the provision of holdings for slaves (*servi casati*), from which they provided their own means of subsistence, or whether it resulted from the enserfment of once-free peasants, it had a profound effect on the medieval mentality. Perhaps the most important effect was on the enserfed peasants themselves. For them, 'freedom' became a compelling social aim. From the earliest period of enserfment to the sixteenth century, that 'bondmen' should be made free retained its ancient resonance.[14] Hence, although conflicts between kings and barons and between various levels of the landowning class were an essential feature of feudal politics, the principal social relations in this primarily agrarian society were between landlord and tenant. These relationships led to conflict, both at the local and at higher levels, but only occasionally well documented.

[14] See my *Bond Men Made Free*.

The main features of the two definitions of feudalism just outlined are largely based on evidence from the eleventh century onwards. The chronology of feudalisation in Anglo-Saxon England and Frankish Gaul before the eleventh century is a matter for dispute among historians.[15] The answer, to some extent, depends on whether one considers feudo-vassalic relationships among the landowning class to be essential in the definition of feudalism. In this case, it is possible to argue convincingly that there might have been a rapid development of such relationships around the year 1000, even though not, as some have insisted, a 'feudal revolution'. If the broader definition of feudalism as a social formation embodying a mode of production based on a class relationship between landlords and peasants is accepted, an earlier arrival of feudalism may be posited.

What was the social formation which preceded feudalism? The mode of production determining ancient society is often assumed to have been based on slavery. However, recent writings are inclined to stress, even at the height of the Roman imperial system, but certainly in the later empire, the greater numerical importance of peasant producers than of slaves. The existence of slavery is not denied, but its exploitation is not regarded as the main source of private or public wealth. The state and its ruling class was based on the appropriation of the surplus produced by the working population, peasants in greater numbers than slaves, in the form of tribute or tax, the peasants in the later empire being of varying legal status but almost all subordinated to landowners. In this case, feudalism, characterised by a relationship between peasant producers and landowners with surplus transferred in the form of rent, could be argued to have developed as the tax-gathering state collapsed, perhaps as early as the sixth century.[16]

In sharp contradiction to this interpretation, some historians argue that western Europe was a slave society (*société esclavagiste*) until the end of the tenth century. There is little doubt that the 'barbarian' invasions of the Roman Empire, and wars between barbarian tribes, did result in much enslavement. The various Germanic law codes from the early sixth century onwards also make clear that slavery was part of the social structure. Slaves were not

---

[15] P. Bonnassie, 'The Survival and Extinction of the Slave System in the Early Medieval West (Fourth to Eleventh Centuries)'. G. Bois, *La mutation de l'an mille: Lournand, village mâconnais de l'antiquité au féodalisme.*

[16] C. J. Wickham, 'The Other Transition: from the Ancient World to Feudalism'.

only acquired in war. Slavery was also a punishment for grave offences.[17]

The problem is, however, whether the presence of a number of slaves is compatible with a feudal society. Was not England at the time of Domesday Book a feudal society? According to this survey, about ten per cent of the recorded population were slaves, although they were soon to become servile tenants. What proportion of the population had to be slaves in order to distinguish a slave from a feudal society? Would slaves be exploited *en masse* on big demesnes, or would they exist in ones and twos on the holdings of wealthy peasants? At what stage would the settlement of slaves on holdings from which they would provide their own and their families' subsistence represent the end of a slave economy?

Another problem is that there is very little statistical evidence. Literary sources indicate that big demesnes in the Auvergne could be worked either by slaves or by peasant tenants owing labour services – the latter being characteristic of big, ninth century estates elsewhere (such as that of St Germain des Prés in the Ile de France) in the Carolingian period. The estate of St Bertin in Picardy in the ninth century provides evidence of a somewhat more complex situation. Tenants owing labour services had slaves of their own, who did their demesne labour services, as well as (presumably) working on the tenant's holding. There were also some demesne slaves. But the numbers of peasant tenants, including a good number of *servi casati*, considerably outnumbered the slaves – eighty-five to fifteen per cent.[18]

It would seem sensible to recognise that the social formation, in both Frankish Gaul and Anglo-Saxon England, was 'feudal' rather than 'slave', well before 1000 and certainly in the Carolingian period. Furthermore, it seems dubious to assume that the transition from ancient to feudal society was quickly achieved by any sort of revolutionary act, analogous to the revolutions characterising later transitions.

Whether one defines feudalism in the narrow sense as a system of lord–vassal relationships among members of the landowning class,

---

[17] Bonnassie, 'The Survival', cites much detail from the various 'barbarian' law codes. The Anglo-Saxon law codes are typical. See F.L. Attenborough, *The Laws of the Earliest English Kings*; A.J. Robertson, *The Laws of the Kings of England from Edmund to Henry I.*

[18] G. Fournier, *Le peuplement rural en Basse-Auvergne durant le haut moyen âge*, pp. 201–16; R. Fossier, *La terre et les hommes en Picardie jusqu'à la fin du XIIIe siècle*, pp. 208ff.

or as a mode of production, another question must be answered. Was the feudal system, as P. Sweezy designated it,[19] based on a natural economy, producing use values? Could it only be transformed by the introduction of trade and commodity production from outside? No one would wish to deny that much that was produced, whether on the peasant's holding or on the lord's demesne, never went through the market. Nevertheless, simple commodity production additional to production for subsistence was a characteristic feature of feudal societies. Trade in basic commodities was to be found in markets and small towns as early as the eighth century as far apart as Anglo-Saxon England and the Basse-Auvergne in France, not to speak of most Mediterranean countries.[20] It was not only that peasants needed to market agricultural surpluses in order to acquire such commodities as salt and manufactured goods. But, in addition, the landed classes required ever-increasing quantities of cash for military and luxury expenditure. Their pressure on the rural and urban populations for rent and tax in cash increased, and the proportion of the commodities which the peasants produced for exchange rather than for consumption also increased.

The basic producers in feudal societies were subjected to a multiplicity of demands of which rent in whatever form was the most prominent. But the increasing demands of another generation of tax-gathering states considerably increased the burden, especially from the late thirteenth century onwards. This raises again the problem of how the monarchical state should be regarded. Should one regard the 'public authority' of the monarchies as non-feudal? C. Petit-Dutaillis wrote an important comparative study of England and France from the eleventh to the thirteenth centuries, in which he designated the monarchies as 'feudal monarchies'.[21] This is a correct description, whatever one's definition of feudalism. However much the kings of England and of France may have attempted to extend their political and jurisdictional control over the territories of their vassals, they did so as competitors within a feudal society. They regarded themselves as a public authority, but in no way sought to undermine the essence of the feudal order. This is so obvious as to

---

[19] See his contribution to *The Transition from Feudalism to Capitalism*, intro. R.H. Hilton.
[20] Suggested by H.P.R. Finberg in his edition of *The Agrarian History of England and Wales*, I, Part 2, p. 392; and by Fournier, *Le peuplement*, pp. 127–200.
[21] *The Feudal Monarchy in France and England*, trans. E.D. Hunt.

be almost banal. Their domains were managed in the same way as those of feudal landowners. Their family inter-connections were with the higher ranks of the feudal nobility. However much they may have used elements from the petty nobility in state administration, they depended essentially in war and peace on the high nobility. In so far as the monarchies appeared to be in conflict with baronial interests, on close examination it often appears that there was rather an internal conflict of noble factions, with the monarchy involved with one of them. Thus, when we discover the monarchical presence in the towns, we must not assume in any way that it represented an antagonism to feudalism as a socio-political system.

Another element in the medieval social order of particular relevance to the towns was the church. Historians of the middle ages, as well as medieval thinkers, have regarded the church as an order of society somewhat distanced from feudal interests, rather as has been thought of the monarchy. It is a grave error to separate the church from feudalism. Apart from the fact that churchmen constructed the 'three estate' social theories which justified the feudal order – 'l'imaginaire du féodalisme', as Georges Duby describes it[22] – the hierarchy of the church, as well as its economic base, reflected that of the lay element in the feudal order. Whatever their social origin – and it was normally aristocratic – the archbishops, bishops, cathedral chapters, monks and nuns constituted part of the landowning aristocracy. Their estates were organised in much the same way as those of the lay nobility, if often more efficiently. Their income was derived from peasant rents and services, from jurisdiction, from the profits of fairs and markets and from urban property rents. And, in both countries, the parish tithes of agricultural produce, which were supposed to go to the parish priest, were in various ways appropriated by the big ecclesiastical landowners. The church was by no means immune from the class conflicts of feudal society which, for the most part, emerged from peasant resistance to seigneurial demands. In fact, both in England and in France, some of the earliest peasant rebellions were directed against church landowners.

The long-lasting peasant protests, referred to as *coniurationes* and *conspirationes*, against the attempts by their lords to increase customary rents and services, are found in many Carolingian edicts and capitularies as far back as the late eighth century. The edict of

---

[22] *Les trois ordres ou l'imaginaire du féodalisme.*

Pîtres in 884 insisted on the performance of labour services by 'coloni tam fiscales quam ecclesiastici', a sure indication that these supposedly free peasants – *coloni* – had been refusing to perform them. A particular example is found earlier at Antoigné, a possession of the abbey of Corméry in the Loire valley. The brief evidence for this is in a written act of Pepin I of Aquitaine in 828. In 996, there was a general rising of Norman peasants against the deprivation of their common rights in woods and fisheries, indicating the persistence of peasant discontent. Much more detailed accounts of struggles by the peasants become available as a result of better documentation in the twelfth century. One example is that of Rosny-sur-Bois, near Paris, which lasted from 1180 until 1246, once more against a church lord, the wealthy abbey of Ste Geneviève. This has been described by Marc Bloch, the matter at issue being a claim by the peasants for freedom.[23] Similar protests by English peasants are rarely documented before the thirteenth century, but by then they frequently involved conflict with ecclesiastical and particularly monastic lords. Such lords, like their lay counterparts, usually asserted what they considered to be their rights against their unfree tenants. Sometimes a more ideological expression of opinion emerges from the mouths of the monastic landowner. Around about 1280, the wealthy abbot of Burton-on-Trent, during a dispute with his villeins (serfs), said that they owned nothing but their bellies. After a dispute in the early 1270s between the abbey of Leicester and its tenants at Stoughton, concerning the deprivation of their freedom around 1200 by an earlier abbot, the peasants were dismissed by the king's justices to whom they had appealed. One of the monks wrote a derisory poem describing the conflict, ending by saying, 'What should a serf do but serve and his son after him? He will be purely a serf and will not have freedom. Judgement at law proves this as well as the royal court.'[24]

URBAN CLASSES – A PRELIMINARY VIEW

Much of the conflict in feudal society, and that which is best known, resulted from competition for land and power within the upper

[23] For Antoigné, see *Bond Men Made Free*, p. 66; for Rosny-sur-Bois, see the English translation of Bloch's article in S.L. Thrupp, ed., *Change in Medieval Society*.
[24] R.H. Hilton, 'Lord and Peasant in Staffordshire in the Middle Ages', in Hilton, *The English Peasantry in the later Middle Ages*, p. 23; Hilton, 'A Thirteenth Century Poem on Disputed Villein Services', in Hilton, *Class Conflict and the Crisis of Feudalism*, p. 110.

ranks of society. But if we accept that the main division, and
therefore area of conflict, was between two classes, namely the ruling
landowning aristocracy, lay and ecclesiastical, and the peasantry, a
re-evaluation of the idea that the towns were the leading element in
anti-feudal movements will need to be made. If towns were not, by
their very nature, anti-feudal entities, were the divisions within
feudal society reflected in them? How different from those of the
countryside were urban classes and class relationships?

One fundamental difference, of course, was that the urban
artisans did not, like the peasants, produce their own means of
subsistence, although many urban artisans did in fact have small
plots and gardens within or just out of town.[25] Nevertheless the
artisan workshop, like the peasant holding, was an enterprise based
on a family labour force with only two or three additional persons
– an apprentice, one or two journeymen – just as many peasant
households had one or two servants. Below the artisans, whether
masters, apprentices or journeymen, there were many unskilled
workers, as well as beggars, prostitutes and other marginals. A
constant flow of rural immigrants sustained the numbers of the
artisans and retail traders, as well as of the unskilled workers and
marginals. It was an influx almost impossible to measure. It was
partly due to the higher mortality of the urban population, as well
as to the attractions of urban life. But even though rural immigration
cannot be reliably quantified, there are indications from the number
of people with surnames indicating a rural origin that in some of the
expanding urban centres in the late thirteenth and early fourteenth
centuries, at least a third of the tax-paying inhabitants were recent
immigrants, and probably an even higher proportion further down
the social scale.[26] We can only guess what was their influence on
town life.

If we move above the mass of artisans, small shopkeepers and
other petty traders, do we then find a class which is clearly separate
from, and antagonistic to, the main structures of feudal society?
Studies of medieval towns have clearly designated the nature of their
ruling class. Wealthy leading masters of craft gilds occasionally
obtained a minor voice in town government. In some areas, the
lesser nobility and officials with legal training might have a greater
share (increasingly in the case of the latter), and there was always

[25] A. Higounet-Nadal, 'Les jardins urbains dans la France médiévale'.
[26] A survey of some of the evidence is in P. McClure, 'Patterns of Migration in the
Later Middle Ages: the Evidence of English Place-name Surnames'.

some inter-penetration of landowning and mercantile interests. But for the most part, the urban ruling class was mercantile. Given the importance of small-scale craft production, they *were* concerned with its internal social, even 'political' organisation, as one can see in the control of the craft gilds. But they were hardly at all concerned with its internal economic organisation, even when the 'putting out system' developed. They were only concerned with buying and selling. The richest of them bought and sold commodities of international trade. Others dealt in money as changers and lenders. The two groups often overlapped. Lower down the social scale, though still above the artisanate, were merchants involved in local and regional trade. If any of these people could be described as capitalists, they were merchant capitalists. But can the interests of merchant capital be described as being in any way antagonistic to the feudal order?

Given the intermeshing interests of the feudal landed aristocracy and the feudal monarchies with those of merchant capitalists, it would seem that there could not be any such antagonism, in spite of the lofty social disdain which some aristocrats had for the money makers. The landed aristocracy was, of course, very interested in money, down to the last halfpenny extracted in rent from their peasants. Every aspect of their style of life, from the furs, the fine woollen cloths and silks with which they clothed themselves, to the wines, spices and other luxury foodstuffs on which they feasted, and to their manor houses and castles, could only be acquired by spending money. As a class, the aristocracy constituted an essential market for the goods provided by the merchant capitalists. And given the overspending by the aristocracy, not merely on luxury but on war, they, and the state powers which in the last resort represented their interests, also constituted a permanent demand for the services of the moneylenders.

In general terms, then, it would seem that, far from being an antagonistic element within feudal society, towns would be one of its essential constitutive components. Feudal societies, however, were no more simple than capitalist societies, so we must examine the many specific variations not only in feudal–urban relationships, but also in the internal ordering of the towns themselves. In particular, we must consider the actual socio-political presence of the feudal ruling class in the urban scene, whether at the level of the market towns or of the larger centres.

ENGLISH AND FRENCH FEUDALISM

Before we examine the towns it may be well to consider, if only briefly, the main differences between English and French feudal societies.[27] The similarities considerably outweigh the differences, even if one looks as far away from England as Provence. In both countries the overwhelming majority of the population was rural, and most were peasant cultivators. The core of the peasantry in both countries consisted of producers with enough land to provide for the subsistence of the family, with sufficient surplus for transference in the form of rent (labour, kind, money) to the landowner – and in taxation to the state. At different periods and in different places, as a result of varying economic and demographic conditions, there would be a greater or smaller proportion of smallholders below the core peasantry, who would have to engage in labour for lords or richer peasants, or other by-occupations, in order to make up for the inadequacy of their holdings. Higher up the social scale there would be rich peasants, whose holdings would be more than adequate for subsistence and who would produce for the market, not merely to acquire products which could not be produced on the holding, but to engage in the accumulation of land, livestock and so on. In both countries there were, as one would expect, variations as between primarily arable areas and those where pastoral production predominated. The chief difference in crops grown was that, as far north as the Laonnais in France, but hardly at all in England, vineyards and wine production were developed. And in Mediterranean France, olive trees had been providing oil since ancient times.

The similarities between English and French social structures can be traced back to the ninth century at least, even though the documentation of peasant conditions is rather scanty in these early years. Nevertheless, both the surviving estate surveys, of which the *Polyptique* of Irminon of the Parisian abbey of St Germain des Prés is perhaps the most famous, and the occasional Carolingian capitulary, indicate a peasantry on the big estates many of whom were unfree, or at best dependent, and subject to heavy obligations, especially labour services. There were still peasants with less heavy obligations on these big estates, and, of course, in less heavily

---

[27] This is a very big subject. For a brief consideration, see Hilton and Jacques Le Goff, 'Féodalité and Seigneurie in France and England' in D. Johnson, F. Bédarida and F. Crouzet, eds., *Britain and France: Ten Centuries*.

seigneurialised areas, but the general tendency, as we have seen, was for the peasantry of one-time free status to be merged into a position of dependency on landowning lords with the serfs, who were the descendants of slaves who had been allotted family holdings (*servi casati*).[28] There are no complete estate documents from Anglo-Saxon England, but it is clear that the old image of a predominantly free peasantry before the Norman conquest cannot be maintained. In the ninth and tenth centuries there were big estates belonging to lay and ecclesiastical lords, not to mention those of the Wessex and other Anglo-Saxon kings. A charter of about 900 indicates that peasants on the estate of the church of Winchester at Hurstbourne on land granted to it by King Alfred, paid heavy rents in money and in kind as well as labour services on the lord's demesne. A fuller document, reflecting conditions in the late tenth century (the *Rectitudines Singularum Personarum*), probably on estates of the bishop of Worcester, indicates heavy obligations, including labour services owed by those who were, in effect, servile tenants, and also the familiar stratification of peasant society between the well-to-do, the middling and the smallholding peasantry.[29] Slavery probably lasted longer in England than in France, but the slaves in Domesday Book which, as we have mentioned, constituted nearly one tenth of the recorded population, were soon to become unfree tenants, probably of smallholdings. Slaves were not as profitable to their owners as were servile tenants.

There were obviously a lot of regional differences within each country, for instance in the proportions of free to servile tenants. The pressure on peasants, especially for labour services, tended to slacken in the eleventh century in France and in the twelfth century in England, as a result of the decline of the direct cultivation of the demesnes. In the Ile de France and to the north and east, in the late twelfth and thirteenth centuries, peasant communities asserted themselves and fought for – or bought – freedom of status and elements of autonomy from their lords. By this time, however, there began to develop important differences in the legal status of the French and English peasantries. The survivals of juridical serfdom were slight and scattered in France, although the development of the *seigneurie banale* implied the jurisdictional subjection to the lords of

---

[28] Marc Bloch's articles on serfdom, collected in his *Mélanges historiques*, II, remain essential reading in spite of later criticism. See also Duby's very important *The Rural Economy and Country Life in the Medieval West*, trans. C. Postan.

[29] Finberg, *The Agrarian History*, pp. 453 and 512ff.

many families which were in theory of free status.[30] In England there had been an economic and social development which contrasted with that of France. Although the direct cultivation of the demesnes had declined in England in the twelfth century, as compared with what we can see in Domesday Book, there was a reversal of this situation on a scale which did not exist in France. Large estates, both lay and ecclesiastical, saw the revival of the direct cultivation of the demesne with a consequent need for labour services from the peasantry. This was at the heart of an intensification, rather than, as in France, a dwindling of serfdom. A powerful aristocracy was backed by a strong monarchy which, while willing to guarantee the rights of well-to-do freeholders, helped the landowners to deprive the customary tenants or villeins of their freedom of status. In many parts of England by the end of the thirteenth century, well over half of the peasant population was juridically servile, subject to seigneurial jurisdiction and with only rare access to the royal courts. Those classic features of servile status – heriot, merchet and tallage – were commonly found in the English villages.[31]

England, a much smaller country than the whole kingdom of France, was controlled by a more powerful feudal monarchy, though it should not be supposed that this strong state was the result of the Norman conquest. It was taken over by the Normans, having been created, especially during the wars against the Scandinavian invaders, by the kings of Wessex, notably Alfred, in the ninth century. It was preceded by the strong Mercian kingdom of the eighth century, especially during the reign of Charlemagne's contemporary, Offa. But was it a feudal monarchy? To a certain extent, this depends on one's definition of feudalism, a matter which we have already raised. The mobilisation of a military force by the imposition on landowners of the duty of providing a quota of knights for the king's service, linked with the sub-enfeoffment of land in return for military service, through a hierarchy of great, lesser and smaller lords, as was completed between 1066 and the mid-twelfth century, did not exist in that form before the conquest. Nor did it exist in such a neatly hierarchical arrangement in France.

Nevertheless, before 1066, the English social structure should be described as feudal. As we have seen, it was based on a dependent peasantry, whose rents and services maintained a highly diversified

---

[30] Duby, *The Rural Economy*, Book 3, chapter 2.
[31] Hilton, *The Decline of Serfdom in Medieval England*.

landlord class – as was the case in France. There were earls, heads of wealthy aristocratic families, and other lay landlords of lesser wealth, down to the thegns who were lords of villages (or even less) – antecedents of many of those who in the twelfth and thirteenth centuries would be known as knights. In addition, there were wealthy landowning bishops and abbots who controlled great estates, freed from undue lay influence since the reforms of the tenth century. As in post-Carolingian France, it was the lay and ecclesiastical aristocracy which provided the ruling cadres at the level of the shire (county in France), and – especially the ecclesiastics – had private jurisdiction over their estates. One should also probably not exaggerate the difference between Anglo-Saxon military mobilisation and that regarded as properly 'feudal'. The word 'feudum' (fief) may not have been used, but the vassals of the king and lords did in fact do military service for lands received, as E. John pointed out many years ago.[32]

England after 1066 had its earls, barons, bishops and abbots with vast estates, but these estates tended to be scattered. Coherent duchies and counties, as in France, did not exist, except (marginally) on the frontiers of Scotland and Wales. The wide scattering of the aristocratic estates is shown in Domesday Book. One of the wealthiest of the Norman expropriators of the English landowners was the count of Meulan, whose considerable estates (793 manors) were distributed over Cornwall, Buckinghamshire, Devon, Dorset, Northamptonshire, Somerset, Sussex and Yorkshire. Earl Roger of Montgomery, nearly as wealthy (544 manors), held his lands mainly in Shropshire, but also in eleven other counties, down as far as Sussex. The earl of Chester (Ranulf III), at the beginning of the thirteenth century, was also earl of Lincoln and lord of the Honours of Leicester and Lancaster. His contemporary, the famous William Marshal, had a fief as far north as Cartmel (Lancashire) and family holdings in two midland and four southern counties, not to speak of his scattered acquisitions resulting from his marriage to the daughter of the earl of Pembroke. In the late thirteenth century, the Clare earls of Gloucester, one of the richest landed families, not only had the lands of their family honours of Gloucester, Clare (Suffolk) and Tonbridge (Kent), but also various other acquisitions. Their manors were scattered throughout some twenty counties, from the midlands

[32] E. John, *Land Tenure in Early England*; see also his contribution to Campbell, ed., *The Anglo-Saxons*.

to the south-east. This scattered distribution of feudal estates continued throughout the middle ages.

In the tenth, eleventh and twelfth centuries, the Capetian monarchy, although claiming suzerainty over France west of the Rhône (and of Alsace and Lorraine), still only had control over its domain in the Ile de France, with a wider indirect influence over a number of bishoprics and abbeys beyond. The great dukes and counts had, in effect, what were independent principalities, of which the duchies of Aquitaine, Brittany, Normandy and Burgundy, and the counties of Toulouse, Flanders and Champagne were the most important. After the marriage, in 1152, of Eleanor of Aquitaine to Henry Plantagenet, count of Anjou, later to become king of England (1154), the whole of western France, except for Brittany, from Normandy to Gascony, came under the control of the English monarchy.

Within the royal, ducal and comital domains, as well as those of the great ecclesiastics, there was, as in England, a hierarchy of feudal landowners, barons, castellans, knights and lords of villages, though in France, the castellany was a more important intermediate element in the feudal hierarchy than in England.[33] All acquired powers of jurisdiction, not only over their tenants but over all inhabitants of their lordship (*seigneurie banale*). *Haute justice*, that is, jurisdiction over cases for which there was death penalty for the guilty, was not enjoyed by petty lords, but nevertheless was found much lower down the social scale than in England, for, in spite of the considerable jurisdictional powers that lords of manors in England had over their unfree tenants, the king monopolised *haute justice*.

The centrally-controlled law courts in England were matched by relatively sophisticated royal financial and administrative apparatuses, with effective locally-based officials. By the thirteenth century, the Capetian monarchy was developing similar institutions, though primarily on the royal domain rather than throughout the kingdom. Because the English lay and ecclesiastical nobility was not able to develop regional powers to the extent found in France, it pursued its political interests at the centre. However much elements among the baronage might oppose royal policies, they had to do so at the national level. Their aim was to control the king, his court and his administration, not to set up rival states of their own. However

---

[33] Duby, *The Chivalrous Society*, trans. C. Postan.

'constitutional' the monarchy became – and this must not be exaggerated – it remained a strong, and for its era, a centralised feudalism. The centralisation of the French monarchy was greatly delayed. When it came, it had much to do with the military response which it had to make to the rival claims of the feudal kings of England, lords of Aquitaine, although the French kings had already begun a policy of using uncertain successions to various duchies and counties to create appanages for their kindred. These changing features of the two feudal monarchies were not without their effects on the character of their towns.

2. *The feudal presence in towns*

TOWNS IN THE TRANSITION FROM ANCIENT TO FEUDAL SOCIETY

One of several problems facing a historian attempting to interpret urban social and economic structures in terms of the feudal social formation within which they were located, is that of the chronology of feudalism. The problem cannot be ignored when more and more evidence is appearing that the de-urbanisation of post-Roman society (say from the fifth century onwards) has been exaggerated – partly because of the emphasis which has been put on the urban expansion of the eleventh century. What was the social formation which followed the collapse of the ancient world? It certainly was not the 'fief–vassal' aspect of feudalism which developed from the tenth century onwards. But if the broader definition of feudalism is accepted, as primarily a social formation determined by the exploitation of a dependent peasantry by a ruling class of landowners – far removed both from a 'slave mode of production' (if ever predominant) and from the tax-gathering Roman imperial state – then we may find its early manifestations at least by the sixth century, though as shown in chapter 1, there are some difficulties in defining the social formation of the early Frankish and Anglo-Saxon kingdoms. Nevertheless, some consideration of the nature of towns in this transitional period is needed before examining the feudal presence in towns in the central period of the middle ages.

The theory that there was no urban revival until the eleventh century, whether attributed to the economic revival (especially in agriculture), beginning in the tenth century or to the effect of long-distance trade in luxury goods for the aristocracy, implies a collapse of the towns of the late empire resulting in a de-urbanised western

Europe during the dark and early middle ages. There was, indeed, a severe reduction in town populations and in urban areas from the end of the third century. From the late empire until the eleventh century, there was a succession of setbacks to economic and social stability. These included invasions by Germanic tribes in the late and immediately post-Roman period; by Moslems, especially from north Africa and Spain, in the eighth to tenth centuries; and by Scandinavians (Vikings) in the ninth and tenth centuries. It may well be that these invasions were less destructive than contemporary (mostly monastic) sources have suggested. Germanic peoples such as the Ostrogoths, the Visigoths, the Lombards, the Franks and the Anglo-Saxons eventually settled down, and in various ways achieved a synthesis with the Roman and post-Roman societies which they penetrated or conquered. After the defeat of the Moslem raid from Spain, in Poitou in 732, subsequent Moslem raids on the north Mediterranean coasts, though disturbing, were not of lasting significance. The Vikings undoubtedly created considerable havoc, but many of them settled and were absorbed into the existing social structures, in England as well as in northern Frankia.

In questioning the traditional view of the devastating effects of the Germanic and Scandinavian invasions of western Europe, we must not imply that life was tranquil for the majority of the population. Then and later, a necessary feature of feudal society was that of violent competition between the lords of land, in search of booty and still more land.[1] Its ethos was military, and if the pillaging of peasants by feudal warriors should be stressed in the early middle ages, let us remember that the later formation of supposedly stable feudal states did not end warfare and plunder at the expense of peasants and of urban populations.

In the so-called 'dark ages', towns continued to exist, even if no longer resembling their Roman predecessors. An important feature of towns in France, as we shall see, though perhaps less so in England, was the influence on post-Roman urbanisation of various types of ecclesiastical institutions.

The continuing urban network in France was to a considerable extent based on existing episcopal cities. These continued as centres of power, as well as fulfilling the economic functions of the town as a market centre and a focus of artisan production. This is hardly surprising since the Christian ecclesiastical organisation had been

---

[1] G. Duby, *The Early Growth of the European Economy*, trans. H.B. Clarke.

based on the secular Roman diocesan network. Furthermore, their significant urban role was in no way dependent on a network of international trade routes. They were, economically, regional market centres and no less significant for that. By the end of the eighth century, there were, in Carolingian Gaul, a hundred and twenty-nine metropolitan and episcopal cities. England, much smaller, of course, had only seventeen sees, four in the north and thirteen in the south.[2]

Within the boundaries of present-day France there would obviously be differing chronologies of urban decline and revival. The county of Provence was still well urbanised in the fourth century, especially where there were cathedral churches, baptisteries and dwelling places for the bishops and cathedral clergy within the city, with cult centres on the city outskirts. They did not escape, however, the damage caused, not only by barbarian but also Moslem raids, until the tenth century. Further north, an urban recovery based on the diocesan network was later in developing. A feature emphasised by J. Lestocquoy was the foundation of sanctuaries and monasteries outside the cities, which inevitably attracted people in service occupations who followed the monks and other clergy. An early foundation outside the walls of Auxerre was by the bishop, St Germain (429–48), of an oratory which became the abbey of St Germain, followed by two other extra-mural abbeys. By the end of the sixth century, Tours, in the Loire valley, had a cathedral and two other churches within its walls, seven other churches, two baptisteries and five monasteries outside the walls. By the seventh century, large monastic foundations, such a St Rémy at Reims, St Bénigne at Dijon and St Germain at Paris, were adding to the clerical demand for all forms of transported commodities, a demand already well established by the episcopal network.[3]

The cathedral cities, or diocesan centres, were places for the collection of royal or imperial taxes and, as such, focal points for the concentration of transferred rural wealth. They were also the locations of the lords of rural estates, whose profits also came into the city. These not only included the bishops and the cathedral chapters, but also monastic foundations, both within the city walls

---

[2] For the metropolitan and episcopal cities of Carolingian Gaul, see Duby, ed., *Histoire de la France urbaine*, I, *La ville antique*, pp. 126–7. Part 5 of this book (by M. Fixot) discusses towns between the seventh and ninth centuries. English dioceses and their bishops are listed in *The Handbook of British Chronology*, Royal Historical Society.

[3] P.-A. Février, *Le développement urbain en Provence de l'époque romaine à la fin du XIVe siècle*; J. Lestocquoy, 'Le paysage urbain en France du Ve au IXe siècle'.

and in *bourgs* outside. These would generate minor suburban populations but also, as gathering places for worshippers from beyond, would become trading places and markets as well as fairs. It is not surprising, therefore, that markets and fairs were in existence by the seventh century. It is even suggested that many of the fairs might have begun in pre-Roman times at pagan cult centres.[4] After Christianisation, they were turned into Christian cult centres, the Christian saints' days being altered to pre-Christian cult dates. Many of these fairs were taken over by ecclesiastical institutions and yielded considerable profits from tolls. Such were the Lendit fairs outside Paris, the Pierre-Levée fair at Poitiers, the Champ à Saille fair at Metz and that at Beauvray near Autun. The links of fairs and markets with the episcopal network was confirmed in 744 in the Capitulary of Soissons, which laid down that there were to be official markets in the cities, presided over by the bishops' officials. More and more of these cities were setting up mints for the production of silver coins, even as early as the Merovingian period.

The bishops did not rule unchallenged in the early medieval urban network. With varying success they had to face up to the rivalry of counts and viscounts, semi-feudalised imperial officials (who were also powerful landlords) especially in the south-east. Before the ecclesiastical reforms of the eleventh century, the problem was partly resolved by the fact that the counts and the bishops tended to come from the same predominant landed families of a region. At the end of the tenth century, the viscount of Béziers and Agde, in Languedoc, left the city of Agde and its bishopric to his wife, and the city of Béziers and its bishopric to his daughter, so that both, through her marriage, came to the counts of Carcassonne. In Provence, the family of the viscounts of Marseilles held the bishopric between 965 and 1073. When episcopal appointments were, to a certain extent, removed from lay control, there resulted a certain fragmentation of authority, so that a city could be divided between separate lay and ecclesiastical jurisdictions.[5]

The economic aspects of the concentration of cathedral, bishop's palace, chapter house and monasteries in the diocesan cities are fairly obvious. For example, quite apart from the cathedrals, with their bishops and canons, there were in the high middle ages at Arles, some eleven monasteries or nunneries; at Marseilles there

---

[4] A. Lombard-Jourdain, 'Y-a-t-il une proto-histoire urbaine en France?'.
[5] Duby, 'Les villes du sud-ouest de la Gaulle'; F. Vercauteren, 'La vie urbaine entre Meuse et Loire du VIe au XIe siècle'.

were about half a dozen or more, founded during the same early period. They were not simply centres of worship but contained numbers of well-endowed ecclesiastics with their servants, constituting a demand for services and supplies. Would this imply a population of artisans, shopkeepers and chapmen who would also settle there? Or are we to assume that great landowners, especially the monastic, not only satisfied their own consumption needs by goods brought in from their estates, but also had a variety of artisans and even merchants as retainers within the ecclesiastical precincts or in domanial centres elsewhere on the estate? It is sometimes suggested that in act the two scenarios are not incompatible.

There is abundant evidence that the episcopal cities in France had an urban and commercial function by the eighth century. In spite of the relatively small size of the cathedral city network in Anglo-Saxon England, three English examples of market activity in cathedral cities throw some light on these places as centres of trade.

Canterbury in the ninth century had as its main focus the cathedral and the nearby abbey of St Augustine, outside the walls. There was a dense concentration of houses around the cathedral, a market to the east of it and a cattle market on the street leading to Dover. Surviving charters bear witness to a considerable market in landed property in the ninth century, the property bought and sold being urban plots, very often with appurtenant cultivated land outside the city and with pasture rights for pigs (a well known urban animal) in the city's woods. We must bear in mind that a land market necessarily reflects more general market activity. This is illustrated by the fact that urban property in Canterbury was ten times the value of rural property of similar size.[6] In the same period, the episcopal city and re-fortified *burh* of Winchester, with its cathedral and three religious houses, had a similar land market. Street names indicated specialist artisan areas – Shieldworkers street, Tanners street, Fleshmonger street, Cheap (that is, market) street.[7] Another episcopal city, away from the populated south-east, Worcester, in the ancient kingdom of the Hwicce, had a land market in the ninth century. There were one or more commodity markets, over which the bishop got the right to levy fines on dishonest traders,

---

[6] N.P. Brooks, *The Early History of the Church of Canterbury: Christchurch from 597 to 1066*, chapter 2, 'The Urban Setting: Anglo-Saxon Canterbury'.
[7] M. Biddle, ed., *Winchester in the Early Middle Ages*, Part 5.

in a charter from the king's representatives, the ealdorman Aethelred and his royal wife Aethelflaeda.[8]

Anglo-Saxon England has also produced many other types of evidence which indicate very strongly that its economy was by no means simply a 'natural' one, nor particularly backward in urbanisation. England, like much of western Europe, had its 'dark ages', though not entirely dark, given chronicle evidence such as that of Bede and others. However, as far as towns and markets are concerned, it must be accepted that coins from English mints seem not to have been used in exchange transactions between the early fifth and the early seventh centuries,[9] even though some towns may have survived as centres of political and especially ecclesiastical authority. The exchange of goods by barter may have taken over. There was, however, a quick recovery of commercial activity from the seventh century onwards. This seems to have resulted from an English participation, together with Frisia, in international trade with continental Europe, especially those parts near to the Rhineland trade routes. At the same time England, like France, was plagued by wars between what we might call small pre-feudal states, as well as (later) by Scandinavian invasions. This resulted in the fortifying of centres of authority, to which the name *burh* was applied, emphasising originally its function as a place with walls, but eventually, as *borough* to become identified with urban functions.

Perhaps too much emphasis has been placed, in the past, on the purely military function of the *burhs*. The fortification of these places between the seventh and the ninth centuries coincided with the favourable trade balance and the consequent import of silver to pay for exported wool, cloth and slaves, and the emergence of trading places on or near the coast, such as Norwich, Fordwich, Ipswich, London, Sandwich and Southampton. Imported silver was minted into pennies under strict central control. There is some disagreement about the total amount of silver minted, but one estimate of coin in circulation around the year 1000 is about 20 million pennies (not to speak of coin exported as Danegeld).[10]

There was a clear coincidence in Anglo-Saxon England between the emergence of the pattern of *burhs* and of mints. It could be argued that mints would naturally be located in safe places, but

---

[8] H. B. Clarke and C. C. Dyer, 'The Early History of Worcester'.

[9] P. Spufford, *Money and its Use in Medieval Europe*, Part 1, chapter 1; R. Hodges and B. Hobley, *The Rebirth of Towns in the West AD 700–1050*, p. 70.

[10] Spufford, *Money*, p. 97.

urbanisation was not simply a product of trading activity, but of a concatenation of social, economic and political factors. There are many indications in the records that markets were located in the royal administrative centres which became *burhs*, and that it was assumed that the existence of a mint implied the presence of a market. For various reasons, including a decline, in the tenth century, in the Frisian trade, as well as a shortage of mined silver, there was a fall in the amount of coin in circulation in western Europe. It has been argued that even earlier, in the ninth century, Viking and Saracen raids had put an end to the 'false dawn of a "monetary economy"', the true dawn having to wait until the 'commercial revolution' of the thirteenth century. Be that as it may, there is still enough evidence that urban development in the early middle ages may have been underestimated.[11]

By the 1060s, there were eighty-seven mints under royal control. Some thirty of these only operated from time to time, but the full-time mints in the fifty-six other *burhs* (or boroughs), ranged from London, where there were more than ten moneyers at work, to some twenty-five smaller towns where there was one permanent moneyer. By the time of the compilation of Domesday Book (1086), there were 112 boroughs and forty-four markets. This figure has been criticised for including places without genuinely urban charac-teristics. Nevertheless, there were certainly some seventy sizeable towns inhabited by burgesses holding their houses either from the king or from lords of the region. The forty-four markets were additional to those which we can assume to be normal for a borough. About half of the boroughs were in the counties south of the Thames (as were half of the non-burghal markets), a significant increase since the period around 900, when the Burghal Hidage listed twenty-nine, but then, of course, the emphasis was on the military aspect.[12]

There were, of course, market centres whose reason for being was by no means simply as centres of ecclesiastical demand, but there was a clear contrast in the early middle ages between the majority of French towns, episcopal cities with constellations of abbatial *bourgs*,

[11] *Ibid.*, p. 47.
[12] D.M. Metcalf, 'Continuity and Change in English Monetary History, 973–1086'; Hodges, *Dark Age Economics: the Origins of Towns and Trade*, citing D. Hill, 'Trends in the Development of Towns during the Reign of Ethelred II' in Hill, ed., *Ethelred the Unready*; H.R. Loyn, 'Towns in late Anglo-Saxon England' in P. Clemoes and K. Hughes, eds., *England before the Conquest: Studies Presented to Dorothy Whitelock*.

and the Anglo-Saxon *burhs*, controlled by the monarchy. Taking the present boundaries of France, there were, as we have seen, many more towns than in England, and many were also probably bigger. Calculations of French urban populations in this early period are very uncertain. Cautious estimates suggest eighth-century populations of 1,000 to 6,000 before a contraction in the late eighth and ninth centuries. English urban populations cannot satisfactorily be estimated before the mid- to late eleventh century – Canterbury 6,000, Gloucester 3,000, Worcester 2,000. Larger populations of many towns in France, compared with those in England, are found throughout the middle ages, though some French regions may have been less urbanised than England.[13] There was, however, another feature of medieval urbanisation in which England was, perhaps, somewhat less backward – the generation of market towns.

SMALL TOWNS AS FEUDAL FOUNDATIONS

The theory that early medieval urbanisation was primarily determined by the commercial activity of merchants dealing in long-distance trade is no longer tenable. Long distance trade did exist, as did mercantile faubourgs close to centres of feudal power. Large towns at convenient places on trade routes were also developing, partly because they *were* on trade routes, but equally importantly because they were at points where upper class demand for luxury commodities was conveniently focussed. But the relationship between towns and feudal society must be sought at all levels of the urban continuum. The market town, where peasant producers or small-scale intermediaries received cash in return for agricultural commodities, was as important as the larger town where that cash, having become the income of the ruling class, was spent on the goods of international trade. The market town was important as part of the whole circuit of exchange relationships. The larger towns, cities and metropolises were, of course, qualitatively different from them in terms of economy, society and culture, but the necessity

[13] Duby, ed., *Histoire de la France urbaine*, I, pp. 522–4. Fixot is uncertain, though inclined to overestimate. The uncertainties are indicated by the suggestion that Poitiers might have had either 4,000 or 10,000 inhabitants in the seventh to ninth centuries. The Domesday Book evidence is the firmest available for the size of eleventh-century English towns. However, it involves guessing at the multiplier from houses to people. See S. Reynolds, 'Towns in Domesday Book' in J.C. Holt, ed., *Domesday Studies*, for the most recent generalisations.

remains – to explore the relationships between towns and feudal society at all levels.

A problem poses itself with regard to the small town as the starting-point of those exchange relationships which are so necessary, if not all-sufficient, for medieval urbanisation. Some urban historians dismiss the market town as an important feature of urbanisation on the grounds that it is in fact no more than a village containing a market. There were, of course, villages containing markets, usually held no more than once a week. These remained villages rather than towns because the great majority of their inhabitants were cultivators, providing their own means of subsistence. But, as we have seen, it is an accepted definition of a town that it is a place with an occupationally heterogeneous population. Following this definition, we can designate many places as market towns, rather than as villages, because one finds in them twenty or thirty non-agricultural occupations and a minority of cultivators.[14] The former include those who service the market itself, especially the victualling trades. But we find, too, a range of crafts producing goods in leather, metal, wood and cloth, which are essential, not only for the townspeople, but for the cultivators in the surrounding countryside. The factors precipitating the growth of market towns can be quite diverse – the market itself in a convenient location for buyers and sellers; a religious institution creating both a demand for various commodities as well as supplying agricultural commodities from its estate; a lord's fortress doing the same. Administrative centres, not to speak of cathedral cities at the centre of dioceses, were bound to contain markets. And here, of course, we are moving to the secondary sort of town, already mentioned, where money income is spent rather than generated in the first place.

In England and France in the middle ages, the market town seems to have become as much a part of feudal society as the manor or the fief. Perhaps this is why some enthusiasts of the urbanisation process refuse to accept it as genuinely a town. As we have seen, urban markets were numerous in Anglo-Saxon England, and in Carolingian and post-Carolingian France. Although most of these were situated in towns of some size, it can be shown that in pre-conquest England – and in France before 1000 – many markets were in smaller but nevertheless recognisably urban centres. If we consider the central period of the middle ages, from the eleventh to the fourteenth centuries, the classic era of feudal social formation, market towns are clearly an essential element in the urban networks. Further to this, they owed their existence, as institutions, to feudal lords who were their founders and who profited from them. By the beginning of the fourteenth century, there were nearly 400 small boroughs or market towns in England, the vast majority founded by lords whose agents presided over the borough courts.[15] The counting of these small boroughs is virtually complete because of the way in which the English feudal monarchy generated documentation through its central administrative processes; and also because of the survival of a great deal of the documentation of the feudal estates, of which the market towns were considered to be a part.

The documentation of small towns in France is somewhat uneven, as one would expect, given the size of the country and the late survival of provincial autonomy. Nevertheless, we have no reason to suppose any great contrast with England. R. Latouche, many years ago, drew attention to the early foundation of *bourgs* in the eleventh century, in the county of Maine.[16] These were mainly creations of religious institutions, and were in part due to the movement for the extension of cultivation, since most of the original inhabitants were cultivators. They were attracted by offers of freedom of tenure, but were subject to the jurisdiction of the founding lord. But the *bourg* was also the location of a market and fair, from the tolls of which the lord of the *bourg* would profit, as well as from the rents and the *banalités*. Latouche only mentions about sixteen of these foundations in Maine, but L. Musset made a much wider investigation into the foundation of *bourgs* in Normandy. Here again there was an important element of promotion of rural settlement by offering the advantages of burgage, that is free, tenure to the burghal population. Some 140 *bourgs* were founded between the eleventh and the thirteenth centuries. Half of them were 'purely rural', but the other half were market centres.[17]

In Brittany, there were fifty-seven new town foundations in the

[15] M. Beresford and H.P.R. Finberg, *English Medieval Boroughs: a Handlist*.

[16] 'Un aspect de la vie rurale dans le Maine aux XIe et XIIe siècles: l'établissement des bourgs'.

[17] L. Musset, 'Peuplement en bourgages et bourgs ruraux en Normandie du Xe au XIIIe siècle; Musset, 'Foires et marchés en Normandie à l'époque ducale'; F. Pilette, 'Les bourgs du sud du Pays d'Auge du milieu du XIe au milieu du XIVe siècle', adds a further fourteen to the Norman total.

tenth and eleventh centuries. In the small county of Forez (west of Lyons) in the twelfth and thirteenth centuries, twelve new market towns were added to the three old Gallo-Roman *vici* (Feurs, Roanne, Moingt). One of the market towns, Montbrison, grew and became the capital of the county. In Provence, in addition to the seven bigger cities of the county, there were, by the end of the thirteenth century, sixty-five *bourgs*. And in two other regions, fourteenth-century figures indicate a previous growth of small towns, which, in addition to being market centres, had begun to develop cloth manufacture. In Languedoc, in addition to the five main centres of Toulouse, Carcassonne, Limoux, Béziers and Narbonne, Philippe Wolff counts seventy-one smaller towns, mostly in the west. In French Flanders, in addition to the bigger towns of Arras, Douai, Lille and St Omer, Espinas lists forty-four smaller centres of trade and manufacture.[18]

Another aspect of small town development to which attention should be drawn is the foundation of *bastides* in the south-west of France. They were founded by Capetian kings of France, by dukes of Aquitaine who were also kings of England and by prominent lords, such as Alphonse de Poitiers, count of Toulouse and brother of Louis IX of France. Sometimes they were founded as *paréages*, that is, in co-operation with a local lord who would share the profits and jurisdiction of the *bastide*, as well as deriving prestige from collaboration with a king. Their proliferation in areas disputed between the French and English kings (the latter, of course, being vassals of the former, as dukes of Aquitaine) has led some historians to see them as primarily military in function, especially since some of them were surrounded by walls. This view was effectively dismissed by J.-P. Trabut-Cussac in 1954.[19] His detailed study demonstrated that by no means all bastides were fortified, that fortification was done mainly on the initiative of the burgesses many years after their foundation, and that military threats did not arise from Anglo-French disputes but from rapacious feudal lords of the region.

---

[18] H. Bourde de la Rogerie, 'Les fondations de villes et de bourgs en Bretagne du XIe au XIIIe siècle'; E. Fournial, *Villes et économie d'échange en Forez: XIIIe–XIVe siècles*; E. Baratier, *La démographie provençale du XIIIe au XIVe siècle*; P. Wolff, 'La draperie en Languedoc du XIIe au début du XVIIe siècle' in Wolff, *Regards sur le midi médiéval*; G. Espinas, *La draperie dans la Flandre française au moyen âge*, II.

[19] 'Bastides ou forteresses: les bastides de l'Aquitaine anglaise et les intentions de leurs fondateurs'.

The reasons for foundation were economic and political rather than military. The king–dukes, in particular, were making up for their lack of demesne estates in Aquitaine and attempting to develop positions of power and influence, even when sharing the lordship of a *bastide* with a local lord or lords. As with seigneurial boroughs in England or *bourgs* elsewhere in France, a *bastide* could also be a source of profit. So settlers were tempted by the offer of urban franchises – freedom of status, tenure and commerce, privileges in the fairs and markets, protection against arbitrary feudal demands, an element of self government, to mention only a few of the chartered privileges.

There were as many as thirty-five clauses in the foundation charter of the *bastide* of Beaumont-en-Périgord. This was founded in 1272, on behalf of Edward I of England, by his seneschal in Guyenne, Lucas de Thanay. It was in association (*paréage*) with the prior of St Avit Seigneur, the abbot of Cadouin and the lord of Biron. Most of the clauses of the charter concerned freedom from obligations to the lords, such as tallage, *gîte* and so on; but also very detailed spelling-out of other freedoms guaranteeing no seigneurial interference in any sphere of personal or family life; or in property or other transactions. Punishments were specified for crimes and misde-meanours, from which the lords profited. Jurisdiction was only in the court of the *bastide*, and the lords' officials were supposed to swear before the *prud'hommes* of the town to observe its customs. There was to be a Tuesday market and a number of fairs at fixed dates, again with profits from tolls on certain transactions going to the lords. The *bastide* was sufficiently profitable for Henry le Waleys, a London vintner, several times mayor of London and once of Bordeaux, to take it on farm for twenty years in 1284 – along with other *bastides*.[20]

The profitability of the *bastides* was probably dependent more on the market than on profits of jurisdiction. In fact, the market, as the town plans of surviving *bastides*, such as Beaumont-en-Périgord itself, Montflanquin, Montpazier, and Ste Foy – demonstrate, was much more their defining characteristic than walls and fortified gateways. They were much involved with the developing wine production, as the era of their burgeoning – the last four decades of the thirteenth century – would suggest.

[20] L. Testut, *La bastide de Beaumont-en-Périgord 1272–1789: Etude historique et archéologique,* chapter 6.

The view, expressed by Chédeville, that *bastides* were simply *bourgs ruraux* is hardly tenable. Like many small French towns, their inhabitants had land outside the town, especially vineyards, as well as being involved in the wine trade. However, the seigneurial incomes, as pointed out with regard to the twenty-five *bastides* of thirteenth-century Périgord, derived from rents, sale taxes, market tolls and the profits of jurisdiction, suggest that most of the *bastides* deserve to take their place in the urban hierarchy. It cannot be supposed that all *bastides* survived as market towns, but both P. Wolff and M. Beresford agree in calculating that there must have been about five hundred founded in southern France between the early thirteenth century and the beginning of the Hundred Years War. Their contribution to low-level urbanisation cannot have been negligible.[21]

Some of the evidence regarding the *bourgs* of the north-west provides early indication of the motivation of their founding lords, and of their subsequent function. Around 1070, the abbey of Marmoutier acquired two *bourgs* (St Sauveur and St Guingabois) from the lord of Chateau-du-Loir in Maine. The charter making the grant emphasises not only the market function, in insisting on freedom of trade in the *bourgs* and their hinterland, but the right of the abbey to take the toll revenue at the markets and fairs. Brittany's *bourgs* had organised grain markets with the lords taking the toll profits on market transactions – Moncontour, for example, quoted by Leguay in his work on the urban network in Brittany; and Donges, cited many years ago by Bourde de la Rogerie. Donges also compares interestingly with the *bourgs* in Maine granted to Marmoutier. It was given by viscount Frioul in the second half of the eleventh century to the monks of Donges. They were to have all market tolls except those on Wednesdays which went to the viscount, with whom they shared the fair tolls equally.[22]

The market towns of twelfth- and thirteenth-century England may have been more uniform institutionally than those in various parts of France – the burgage tenure of Normandy was not found in

---

[21] Duby, ed., *Histoire de la France urbaine*, II, p. 196; A. Higounet-Nadal, ed., *Histoire du Périgord*, chapter 5; Wolff, *Histoire de Toulouse*, p. 120; Beresford, *New Towns of the Middle Ages*.

[22] A. Bouton, *Le Maine. Histoire économique et sociale des origines au XIVe siècle*, pp. 286–9; J.P. Leguay, *Un réseau urbain au moyen age: les villes du duché de Bretagne aux XIVe et XVe siècles*, chapter 13; de la Rogerie, 'Les fondations', p. 75.

the market towns of central and southern France as the defining features of burgess status. In England, the new boroughs (market towns) tended to have foundation charters containing the privileges to be found in the larger royal boroughs. The origin of these privileges is still a matter of dispute. Were they insular copyings of burgess tenure and borough privileges already found in eleventh-century Europe, transmitted perhaps by the adoption of the laws of Breteuil? Musset's insistence on the originality of Norman burgage tenure has been disputed. J. Boussard is inclined to suggest that the boroughs and burgages of mid-eleventh-century England may have preceded the Norman *bourgs*, and even that the laws of Breteuil may have been influenced from England rather than vice versa.[23]

Whatever the chronology, the small town franchises in feudal urban foundations in England have remarkable similarities with the European urban franchises. Whether or not burgess status was tenurial or personal, it implied freedom and an absence of all charges with servile implications: rents were paid in money – there were no labour services; there was a borough court, presided over by the lord's steward and it was only in this court that the burgesses were justiciable, apart from *haute justice* in the royal courts; burgesses could engage in retail trade without paying toll, and tolls paid by incoming merchants went to the lord; there was usually at least a weekly market and an annual fair; the burgesses could elect their own officials – under the eye of the steward – one or two bailiffs, a collector of moneys, constables and ale-tasters; and delinquents of various sorts were presented to the court by juries chosen from the burgesses. All the profits of the court went to the lord. The point is perhaps worth making, that although the borough privileges listed above seem consistent with European urban franchises in general, in the proceedings of the courts of seigneurial boroughs which have survived in some numbers, the business strongly resembles that of the manor courts, except for tenurial issues. The interests and the profits of the lord are always present.[24]

This is not surprising. Lords did create boroughs for philanthropic reasons. They were well aware that markets were necessary for their

---

[23] J. Boussard, 'Hypothèses sur la fondation des bourgs et des communes en Normandie'.

[24] For the components of typical borough charters, see A. Ballard, ed., *British Borough Charters, 1042–1216*; the application of the charter of a larger town (Hereford) to the small seigneurial borough of Halesowen is discussed in Hilton, 'Small Town Society in England before the Black Death'.

agricultural tenants to get money in order to pay rent. They also knew that the market itself was profitable, not to speak of the exercise of jurisdiction and the collection of urban property rents. It was in their interest to establish a permanent community of traders and artisans rather than an ephemeral village market. Such communities of traders and artisans serving the local economy would have established themselves in any case. As we have seen from the evidence of some small French towns, the lords could expect to make a profit in promoting simple commodity production. The bishop of Durham, who was the direct lord of five small boroughs in county Durham (in addition to the cathedral town of Durham itself), preferred to farm out the borough profits. In the fourteenth century, Bishops Aukland, for example, was farmed for £26.13.4, the profits collected from the farmer being from the market toll, the borough court, the toll of ale, two mills and a common oven. Farming was not always chosen as an option. Even the relatively modest lords of the borough of Newmarket, on the Suffolk–Cambridgeshire border, preferred to collect their profits direct, consisting of property rents (including rents of market stalls), profits of the borough court and toll revenue, especially from two fairs. These examples could be multiplied many times in all the English counties.[25]

These small boroughs formed an essential network for the generation of commercial activity; their burgesses had the basic privileges of urban populations throughout Europe; they were completely integrated into the feudal social formation. But, of course, as we shall see, whatever the analogy of small borough or *bourg* privileges with those of the bigger towns in England and France, it cannot be assumed that the social structure of the smaller towns was simply a small-scale match of that of bigger towns, such as cathedral cities or regional centres. As already emphasised, it is not a question of a rural element in the population (and in any case did not big towns like Toulouse, Montpellier, or Lyon contain a large number of peasants?). These market towns had populations divided among non-agricultural occupations, in victualling and in various manufacturing crafts. Many households pursued more than one occupation. Petty traders, especially female – hucksters – were nu-

[25] M.H. Dodds, 'The Bishop's Boroughs'; Peter May, *Newmarket, Medieval and Tudor*, chapter 4.

merous, dealing mainly in agricultural products. The richer burgesses could equally well be prosperous craftsmen or small-scale merchants. They were hardly powerful enough to impose on the petty traders and craftsmen the regulatory systems found in the bigger towns.

As we have mentioned, the evidence from the documents of a relatively centralised monarchy, together with those surviving from a large number of lay and ecclesiastical estates, gives us a body of consistent information about the small seigneurial boroughs in England. Owing to the claim by the English crown to regalian rights over the foundation or legitimation of existing markets and fairs, charters simply granting markets and fairs to the founders of what gradually grew into small market towns are the most numerous in the chancery records. Other charters make it clear that some lords envisaged the establishment of a permanent borough community from the outset, not simply an organic growth encouraged by the presence of a licensed market. They calculated that the grant of recognised urban privileges would attract settlers and encourage the immediate establishment of such a community.

A charter granted in 1220–33 to the 120 men of Macclesfield in Cheshire, by Ranulf Blundeville, earl of Chester, was confirmed in 1261. It granted them a 'free borough'; the right to form a gild merchant; exemption from tolls other than on salt; the right to be justiciable only in the borough court; reasonable amercements; the normal burgage rent of 12d. a year; and freedom to alienate burgage tenements. Feudal control was emphasised by restriction of rights in the nearby forest, where they were not allowed to pasture their pigs; control by the lord over their choice of a reeve from their own ranks; only the lord's corn mill to be used on payment of a multure of one twentieth; and the lord's monopoly of the town's oven. The burgesses of the new town of High Wycombe (Buckinghamshire), originally founded by King John, obtained after various disputes between feudal claimants, a charter from the successful lord, Alan Bassett, in 1226. This gave them the whole borough, with the rents of the burgages, the markets and fairs, and all things pertaining to a free borough. This included the right to have a gild merchant, which gave the burgesses a monopoly of the market, especially in linen and woollen cloths and in dyestuffs. They paid a fee-farm of £30 a year for these privileges.[26]

[26] C.S. Davies, A History of Macclesfield, pp. 7–9; L.J. Ashford, *A History of High Wycombe from its Origins until 1880*, pp. 14–20.

At an uncertain date in the middle of the thirteenth century, the earl of Gloucester founded the small borough of Thornbury, within the Gloucestershire manor of the same name, where there had already been a market at the time of Domesday Book. He granted to it the borough privileges of Tewkesbury (Gloucestershire), which earlier earls had already granted in the twelfth century. These vary slightly from those of Macclesfield and elsewhere, but were in the same mould. The burgage tenements were to be heritable and freely alienable; servile dues, such as heriot, tallage and merchet, were not to be demanded; the burgesses were to be free of market tolls; they could exclude outsiders from the borough community; were subject only to the borough court; could nominate their own officials; and could devise their property by testament. The men of Halesowen, an old settlement within a large Shropshire (now Worcestershire) parish of the same name, were given permission, sometime in the 1260s, by their lord, the Premonstratensian abbot of Halesowen, to borrow what they wished from the privileges granted in 1215 to the royal borough of Hereford. These were in the usual mode, giving burgesses freedom of tenure and status; their own borough court (presided over, as in all seigneurial boroughs, by the lord's steward); freedom from tolls; monopoly of trade; and the right to form a gild merchant. The Halesowen burgesses did not bother to set up a gild merchant, since the monopoly of the market and freedom from toll became a privilege specifically defined as appurtenant to burgess status,[27] sometimes referred to as the liberty of the borough. Similar burghal privileges are to be found in a large number of small market boroughs, mostly granted in the thirteenth century.

THE FEUDAL ELEMENT IN BIGGER TOWNS

It is hardly to be doubted that the bigger towns – those of, say, 3,000 or more inhabitants – would differ qualitatively as well as quantitatively from the market towns of fewer than 2,000 inhabitants. But to what extent did this distance them from the feudal social order? First let us consider again some differences between towns in

[27] For Thornbury, see Finberg, *Gloucestershire Studies*, p. 66; Hilton, 'Lords, Burgesses and Hucksters'; and Hilton, 'Low Level Urbanisation: the Seigneurial Borough of Thornbury in the Middle Ages' in Z. Razi and R. Smith, eds., *The Manor Court and Medieval English Rural Society: Studies of the Evidence*. The Tewkesbury charter is in the *Calendar of Patent Rolls* 1927–41, pp. 424–6. For Halesowen, see note 24 above.

England and France. The most obvious difference would seem to be that in the central period of the middle ages, over seventy per cent of the bigger English towns were royal boroughs, a proportion only a little smaller than at the time of the compilation of Domesday Book (1086). This does not imply any distancing of these towns from the feudal social formation, since the English monarchy was a feudal monarchy. Furthermore, there were other features of these English royal boroughs which emphasise the degree to which they were imbedded in the feudal structure – and for which there is ample evidence in Domesday Book.[28]

Most of these towns in 1066, that is 'in the time of King Edward', to use the phrase of the Domesday commissioners, paid an annual farm of which, in most cases, two thirds went to the king and one third to the earl of the shire. The earl would, of course, be a great landed magnate, but at the same time was regarded as an official of the crown. By 1086 things had changed. Most of the towns no longer paid 'the third penny' to the earl, and the total amount of farm due to the king had considerably increased – often more than doubled. Oxford, for instance, paid £60 the king in 1086, as compared with £20 to the king and £10 to the earl in 1066; the comparable totals for Dover were £54 in 1086, as against £18 in 1066; or Lincoln, £100 in 1086 as against £30 in 1066. This was not due to any increase in urban prosperity. Many towns had suffered from devastation, often deliberate, at the hands of the conquerors. It was simply an increase in the rate of exploitation.

The descriptions of the seventy or so sizeable towns in Domesday Book are very complicated. They are also often – perhaps usually – incomplete. Nevertheless, the information provided makes it clear that in addition to varying numbers of burgesses directly dependent on the king, a large number were the tenants or retainers of a variety of feudal lords. The description of the borough very often includes the names of the lords and the number of tenanted properties within the borough walls. Also, not infrequently, information is found in the descriptions of what have sometimes been described as 'contributory manors'. These were the rural manors of lords to which their borough tenants paid the rent for their town property,

---

[28]   There is a vast literature on Domesday Book. For the most recent comprehensive survey in a series of articles, see Holt, ed., *Domesday Studies*. Domesday Book was first published in 1783, and completed in 1816 (Record Commission, London). The texts are for the most part published in the *Victoria History of the Counties of England*; and more recently, with English translation, by John Morris, ed.

rather than directly to the lord. They were certainly not manorial tenants in the normal sense. It was once thought that they lived in the borough on garrison duty, including upkeep of the town wall, owed to the king by the lord of the manor. Their role, however, was not usually described, as it was in the Oxford entry, where tenants both of the king and of various lords held 'mural houses' and were obliged to do wall repair when called upon. It now seems more probable that the burgesses contributory to manors occupied borough houses as much to act as agents of the lord on the borough market or to store manorial produce, as for military duty.

The number of these 'contributory burgesses' was quite considerable. The Domesday entry for Gloucester gives very scanty information about only fifteen lords owning houses with an uncertain number of tenants, almost certainly below fifty. But in the Gloucestershire manorial descriptions there are seventeen manors to which eighty-two burgesses of Gloucester were attached, the manorial lords being the king, nine lay and five ecclesiastical magnates. Another listing of Gloucester burgess' rents was made around 1100. It refers to 300 burgesses in 1066 who were tenants of the king. Only 196 survived the conquest, but by the date of this listing there were twenty-five feudal landlords (including six bishoprics and abbeys) with 291 burgess tenants. Unfortunately, neither Domesday Book nor the 1100 return tells us how many burgess tenants, other than those of the king, there were in 1066.

The Domesday Book entry for Warwick is quite specific about the town's connection with the contributory manors. The king has 113 houses in his demesne and the 'barons' (specifically so-called) have 112. A list is then given of the 'barons'. Three of them were bishops; two were abbots and there was a small monastery; the rest were lay persons, some of high status, such as the count of Meulan, Earl Aubrey of Northumbria and Hugh of Grandmesnil. Many were not, such as 'Christina' and 'Luith the nun'. Their urban properties (*masuras*) are said to be appurtenant to the lands which they held outside the borough. There were ten of these rural manors with appurtenant dwellings and two with appurtenant burgesses.

These late eleventh-century boroughs, as we have seen, owed farm to the king, usually collected by the town reeve and handed over to the sheriff. The borough court, apart from its judicial function, was also a body through which the interests of the leading, that is, the richer burgesses, were represented. Inevitably, the responsibility of the burgesses for their contribution to the various revenues which made up the farm, would be an important element in generating common action, even before formally acknowledged town ruling bodies existed. Burgesses already had freedom of status and tenure and although some of them would have some agricultural land, their primary economic interests were commercial. They not only participated in the commodity market, but also in a market in urban landed property. The rents (sometimes called 'landgable') which they paid to the king or to other lords – usually not more than about 6d. per property per year, were much smaller than the economic rents of sub-tenancies, which could be in teens of shillings.

This disparity between landgable and the economic rents generated by the land market is well illustrated by the survey of Winchester around 1110 – near enough in date to Domesday Book in which there is not a Winchester entry.[29] Economic rents and rent charges proliferated and brought profit to urban merchants. Does this mean that 'it makes little economic, social or political sense to describe the urban community in feudal terms' (F. Barlow)?[30] The same author, almost simultaneously, tells us that in this royal borough 'the bishop was a landlord of exceptional authority'. There were other fiefs than that of the bishop: those of the prior of the cathedral chapter; of the abbot of Hyde; of the abbess of Winchester; and of the abbesses of Wherwell and Romsey. The income from the land holdings of these lesser fiefs was not great compared with that of the bishop, but the overall feudal–ecclesiastical presence should not be ignored.

To return to Domesday Book: the ownership of landed property in the boroughs by feudal magnates is almost universal. At Oxford, among others, there were the archbishop of Canterbury, the bishops of Winchester, Lincoln, Bayeux and Coutances, and the abbots of St Edmunds and Abingdon. (The abbot of St Edmunds also had his own borough of Bury in Suffolk.) In Leicester, various lords had contributory burgesses to their manors, and Hugh de Grandmesnil, sheriff of Leicester, had 110 houses and two churches. At Lincoln, there were several feudal lords with some urban property, and the bishop, Remy, had nearly one hundred houses over at least sixty of which he is specifically stated to have jurisdiction. The fact that the king was direct lord of many boroughs whose agents (such as the sheriff) collected the various components of urban revenue and

---

[29] Biddle, ed., *Winchester*. This volume contains the 1110 survey (the Winton Domesday).   [30] *Ibid.*, 'Introduction to the Winton Domesday', p. 8.

rendered the farm, should not make us ignore the important element of feudal property and power in 1086.

While the powerful presence of the feudal–ecclesiastical land-owners is found in both France and England, it was even more predominant in French than in English towns. We have already indicated the vastly greater number of cathedral towns in France than in England. In some important cathedral cities the economic, social and political power of the bishop was a striking demonstration of what we may call ecclesiastical feudalism. Narbonne in Languedoc provides an interesting example. It was a place of some 25,000 inhabitants, sharing with Orléans and Strasbourg in the early fourteenth century the fifth place in order of size after Paris.[31] Like many other towns, it was divided into two, the city itself and the adjacent *bourg* of St Paul. In the second half of the twelfth century, as in many other cathedral cities, the Capetian monarchy was supporting the archbishop against the counts and the viscounts. In 1157, the king granted (or confirmed) to the archbishop of Narbonne control over the metropolitan church, its towers and all its dependencies within the city. He was also given half of all the tolls, as well as the duties on salt; most of the mills on the river; lordship over the abbey of St Paul in the *bourg*; over abbeys and villages in the rural hinterland; the castle of Fontjoncouse; and jurisdiction over the *bourg* and elsewhere in the suburbs. In other words, the archbishop had domanial and other possessions relating to the city, an important part of urban jurisdiction and half of Narbonne's revenues. As at Narbonne, bishops in other Languedocian cities, such as Uzès, Nîmes, Lodève and Agde, were strengthening their feudal powers against the lay lords, appropriating jurisdiction, tolls and stallage.[32]

Also significant was the very large number of French towns which comprised constellations of *bourgs*, often under ecclesiastical lordship, surrounding the city or castral town. M. Berthe, writing in 1976 about the county of Bigorre, presented these constellations of four to six *bourgs* in such towns as Tarbes, Bagnères, Lourdes, Ibos and Vic as 'une structure assez originale'.[33] These developed elsewhere, as we have seen, in the early middle ages. In fact, it was

[31] Duby, ed., *Histoire de la France urbaine*, II, p. 191.

[32] A. Dupont, *Les cités de la narbonnaise première depuis les invasions germaniques jusqu'à l'apparition du consulat*, pp. 563ff.

[33] M. Berthe, *Le Comté de Bigorre au bas moyen âge*, chapter 4.

a general phenomenon. Paris had seven 'urban nebulae' on the right and left banks of the Seine around the Ile de la Cité. Poitiers was surrounded by five extra-mural suburban *bourgs*. Other towns had separate seigneurial sub-divisions. Reims was divided between the three lordships of the archbishop, the cathedral chapter, and the abbot of St Rémi. Marseilles consisted of three towns – the bishop's, the cathedral chapter's, and that of the *vicomte* (the port). Le Mans, outside the city, had two monastic *bourgs*. Tours was divided into six lordships of which the most important were ecclesiastical – the cathedral chapter and the two religious houses, St Martin and St Junien. Many towns, like Narbonne, had at least two feudal sub-divisions – Périgueux, for example (the cathedral town and Puy St Front), though Puy St Front was itself 'une ville polynucléaire', composed of four distinguishable groupings, as, for instance, around the lord's castle and mint.[34]

Many medieval English towns also had separate feudal jurisdiction, such as we have found in Domesday Book, especially the episcopal cities. Durham, chief city of a palatinate in the war-ridden north, consisted of the bishop's borough and a cluster of suburbs which acquired borough status, similar to the constellation of *bourgs* in some French towns. New and Old Olvet had as lord the hostillar of the cathedral priory; the priory sacrist was the lord of the 'old borough' or Crossgate; and the Kepier Hospital was the lord of St Giles.[35] In general, this clustering of separate suburban jurisdictions was not common in the larger English towns, though an occasional seigneurial suburb did exist. More frequent were the often conflicting jurisdictions, exercised over the tenants of (mainly ecclesiastical) lords within the walls of the borough or city whose governing burgesses were directly responsible to the crown. The properties owned by the lord could be grouped within specific areas – near the cathedral close, for example – but they could also be scattered among houses whose tenants were subject only to borough

[34] Much is written about medieval Paris. R. Cazelles, in the *Nouvelle histoire de Paris 1223–1380*, discusses the many ecclesiastical jurisdictions; Lombard-Jourdain has recently shown the developments on the Right Bank in *Aux origines de Paris: la genèse de la Rive Droite jusqu'en 1223*. Other relevant works are: R. Favreau, *La ville de Poitiers à la fin du moyen-âge*; P. Desportes, *Reims et les Rémois*, pp. 71–3; V.L. Bourilly, *Essai sur l'histoire politique de la Commune de Marseille*, chapter 1; Bouton, *Le Maine*, pp. 286–9; B. Chevalier, *Tours, ville royale 1256–1520*, chapter 1; Higounet-Nadal, *Périgueux aux XIVe et XVe siècles: étude de démographie historique*; Higounet-Nadal, ed., *Histoire du Périgord*, p. 100.

[35] See Dodds, 'The Bishop's Boroughs' in note 25; and M. Bonney, *Lordship and the Urban Community: Durham and its Overlords 1250–1540*, especially chapter 4.

jurisdiction. We have already noted the ecclesiastical magnates of Winchester, three of whom had exempt jurisdictions. In York, the archbishop, the cathedral chapter, the abbey of St Augustine and a number of smaller landlords claimed jurisdiction, market tolls and exemption from city taxes.[36]

At Worcester, the cathedral chapter was the owner of urban tenements, over which it held jurisdiction. The same situation held good in other towns which were not cathedral centres but where there were rich abbeys. Coventry, which was beginning to emerge in the fourteenth century as one of the most important of the English towns, was still divided into two jurisdictions, the earl of Chester's half and the half of the cathedral priory (of the diocese of Coventry and Lichfield, where the bishop was located). The priory acquired the jurisdiction of the earl's half around 1250. This thriving centre of cloth manufacture did not become an enfranchised borough until 1355. At Chester, the earl had an urbanised jurisdiction around his castle, whose inhabitants (glovers, skinners, bakers and the like) were not considered to belong to the town. He also had five mills on the river Dee at which all the town's inhabitants had to grind their corn and pay multure. The rich abbey of St Werburgh owned a quarter of the city property, a market and a fair, from which it took the tolls, a court of jurisdiction over its tenants and a mill on the Dee. Another substantial landowner was the nunnery of St Mary, whose tenants were exempt from civic duties (jury service, murage and other taxes, watch), did suit to the abbess's court and, if fined in the earl's court, the fines went to the nuns. Gloucester, a county town, had to accept the powerful feudal presence of the Benedictine abbey of St Peter, and of the Augustinian canons of Lanthony.[37]

---

[36] For ecclesiastical franchises in York, see Edward Miller, 'Medieval York'.

[37] The spread of the cathedral chapter's urban tenements is well illustrated in H.J. Bloom, ed., *Original Charters Relating to the City of Worcester in Possession of the Dean and Chapter*. The matter of jurisdiction is largely ignored in M.O. Carver, ed., *Medieval Worcester: an Archaeological Framework*; and in Alan D. Dyer, *The City of Worcester in the Sixteenth Century*. The complicated and much disputed history of Coventry before incorporation is summarised by P.R. Coss, ed., in his introduction to *The Early Records of Medieval Coventry*. This edition includes the Coventry section of the 1279–80 Hundred Rolls (ed. E.L.T. John), in which the physical and jurisdictional divisions of the city are described in detail. For Chester, R.H. Morris, *Chester in the Plantagenet and Tudor Periods*, is still essential. For Gloucester, see C.E.W.O. Fulbrook-Leggatt, *Anglo-Saxon and Medieval Gloucester* and Holt, *Gloucester: an English Provincial Town during the Later Middle Ages*. For the social and political role of St Peter's Abbey, Gloucester, and Lanthony Priory, see Hilton, *A Medieval Society: the West Midlands at the End of the Thirteenth Century*.

Early medieval London, like Paris, had separate private jurisdictions, known by the Anglo-Saxon term 'soke', some lay and
some ecclesiastical. These were beginning to disappear in the
thirteenth century. But even as late as 1275, there were nineteen
sokes, mainly ecclesiastical. More important than the sokes inside
the walls of the city was the extra-mural settlement at Westminster.
In legal terms this was a manor given to the abbey of Westminster,
transformed after the eleventh century not only by the location there
of a royal palace, but also by the increasing presence of the
institutions of royal government. It soon became like a small town,
with a service sector, providing not only for the needs of the abbey
but for royal officials and visitors. While unique as a developing
centre of government, in many ways it resembled an extra-mural
bourg under the seigneurial control of a wealthy religious house.[38]

Only a few towns, like Bury St Edmunds, St Albans and
Cirencester were entirely the fiefs of their monastic lords. And some
royal boroughs had become mediatised since 1086. By 1130,
Leicester, Chester, Warwick, Reading and Bath were placed under
the lordships of the earls of Leicester, Chester and Warwick, the
abbot of Reading and the bishop of Wells, respectively.

Some other changes occurred after 1086. As we have noted, by the
thirteenth century, the principal feudal presence in the towns tended
to be that of ecclesiastical rather than lay lords – bishops, cathedral
chapters and religious houses. The ecclesiastical lords were already
prominent at the end of the eleventh century, but their urban
possessions increased, probably due to the considerable transfers of
lay property to abbeys and to other ecclesiastical institutions, both
by pious grant and sale. It would seem that the ecclesiastical bodies
were more interested in urban property than were the lay lords.

So medieval English, as well as French, towns were also riddled
with feudal jurisdictions. The chief contrast with France in the
central period of the middle ages was that the Norman and
Plantagenet monarchies retained a general control over the bigger
towns. Whatever the jurisdictional rights held by lords over their
urban tenants, the borough court presided over by crown officials

---

[38] For London sokes, see F.M. Stenton, 'Norman London: an Essay' in D.M.
Stenton, ed., *Preparatory to Anglo-Saxon England*, and C. Brooke and G. Keir,
London: the Shaping of a City; A.G. Rosser, 'The Essence of Medieval Urban
Communities: the Vill of Westminster 1200–1540'; Rosser, *Medieval Westminster
1200–1540*.

had overall control, a control which passed to the burgesses when urban franchises were acquired from the twelfth century onwards.

We will conclude this chapter with a more detailed comparison of two cathedral cities, which will both illustrate the theme of the feudal presence in towns, and the contrasting – and changing – role of the English and French feudal monarchies.

Norwich and Lyons were already important urban centres by the thirteenth century, and both experienced economic expansion in the later middle ages, Norwich as a textile manufacturing centre, and Lyons as a focus of international trade and finance.

Norwich was the principal town of the densely populated county of Norfolk, and had been an episcopal city since 1096 when the East Anglian see was transferred from Thetford. It was an inland port on the river Yare and the location of a royal castle, of which the prominent Anglo-Norman family, the Bigods, were the constables. The castle was the centre of a separate feudal jurisdiction in the middle of the city, until the mid-fourteenth century. But it was the fee of the wealthy Benedictine cathedral priory which was the largest, and most contentious, separate jurisdictional area in the city. Outside the walls were other feudal–ecclesiastical jurisdictions. That of the nunnery of Carrow was the most important, followed by those of the abbeys of Wendling and St Benets Hulme. All were in conflict with the citizens. In addition to their separate jurisdictions, the cathedral priory and the nuns of Carrow had fairs from which they took considerable profits from tolls and stallage. The priory had two fairs in the city, at Pentecost and Trinity, which involved the suspension of the city's right to collect tolls within its boundaries. The nuns of Carrow had their fair in September. The Magdalen Hospital also had a fair in July. The most violent of the many battles between the citizens and the men of the Priory was in 1272, at the priory's Tombland fair, over the rival jurisdictions of town and priory.

In spite of the considerable feudal–ecclesiastical presence, Norwich was a royal borough. The citizens were given a charter of franchises in 1158, the farm of the borough in 1194. A framework of autonomous government was developed, characteristically narrow and oligarchic, including the acquisition of county status in 1403. This widened the jurisdictional area of the city and intensified its conflict with the holders of feudal–ecclesiastical jurisdictions. The city's internal politics were complex and riddled with conflict, involving, among other things, the intervention of the lay landed nobility of the county, some of whom were members of the urban oligarchy's Gild of St George. It is worth noting that, although this was a royal borough, when there were conflicts between the city and the cathedral priory, the Crown tended to support the priory.[39]

Lyons was divided by the river Saone between the Holy Roman Empire to the east and the kingdom of France to the west, but the lord of the whole city was the archbishop whose jurisdiction was shared by the cathedral chapter. By the beginning of the fourteenth century there were nine other monasteries and colleges of canons, with property and jurisdiction in and out of the city – not to speak of Templars, Hospitallers, five major orders of friars and several minor orders. A French historian has described it anachronistically as 'une véritable république cléricale'! It would be better described as a complex feudal–ecclesiastical city state. Its feudal character was further emphasised by the exclusive recruitment of the cathedral canons from the noble families of the Lyonnais. The joint archiepiscopal–cathedral chapter jurisdiction of the 'church of Lyons' was sometimes dominated by the archbishop, but more often by the cathedral chapter. The 'church', as the effective ruling body of the city, had an elaborate structure of government. There were not only the separate ecclesiastical and secular courts, but also a variety of seigneurial rights, mainly economic in character – rents, entry fines, market profits, the mint, tallage – all of which required the existence of a considerable body of officials.

As would be expected, the unprivileged bourgeoisie of Lyons regarded with some anger the enjoyment by much smaller towns in the Lyons region of charters of franchise, and agitated against the cathedral chapter in particular. Their communal movement, opposed by the archbishop, the pope and the king of France in the thirteenth century, was nevertheless strengthened in the 1290s. Then, in 1312, the king of France annexed Lyons. At first, he also annexed the church of Lyons' jurisdictional control, but in 1320 gave it back to the archbishop. In the same year, the archbishop gave a charter, of rather limited character, to the citizens. The charter recognised a degree of autonomous government, but without judicial powers, by

---

[39] The best source of material for Norwich is W. Hudson and J.C. Tingey, eds., *Records of the City of Norwich*, 2 vols. The introductions to the two volumes, covering political history and economic history, are still indispensable, as is the collection of source material. See also Hudson, ed., *Leet Jurisdiction in the City of Norwich*. See also the *Victoria History of the County of Norfolk*, II, for the political history.

elected consuls – drawn, as one would expect, from a limited group of patrician families.

The settlement of 1320 gave to those subject to the archbishop's jurisdiction the right of appeal to the French crown. During the fourteenth and fifteenth centuries, the archbishop's powers declined, as those of the consuls and the crown increased. By the middle of the fifteenth century, as in most French towns, the consular government of the bourgeoisie was being diminished and royal officials, especially lawyers, were taking over the governing role.[40]

In comparing Norwich and Lyons, it should be emphasised that perhaps the most important contrast was that which was to be found between English and French towns in general – a very great difference in population size. If we are to believe calculations currently available, Lyons at the beginning of the fifteenth century may have had 30,000 inhabitants, whereas Norwich is supposed to have had between 5,000 and 6,000. It is very likely that the Norwich figures, based on the poll tax returns of 1377, with a third added for children under fourteen (untaxed), are considerably underestimated. Nevertheless, it is unlikely that they would be at all near to the Lyons figures.[41]

Norwich, by the 1520s, had become the next richest city in England after London. In 1377, its population was fourth after London, and its wealth in 1344, sixth. Its ranking order in England, therefore, must have compared fairly well with that of Lyons among French towns, so a general comparison is not altogether inappropriate. What is to be emphasised is the much greater feudal–ecclesiastical presence in Lyons, by no means immediately eliminated by its annexation by the French crown. Norwich, as a royal borough, obtained early autonomy for its bourgeois elite. The

---

[40] The general history of medieval Lyons is in A. Kleinclausz, ed., *Histoire de Lyon*, I. The quotation above is from P. Pouzet, on 'Gouvernement de l'Eglise', III, chapter 1. Kleinclausz deals with the high middle ages (II); IV, 'La Commune', is by J. Déniau (up to the late fifteenth century). See also R. Fédou, 'Regards sur l'insurrection lyonnaise de 1269', and Fédou, 'Le cycle médiéval des révoltes lyonnaises'.

[41] For English population figures, see W.G. Hoskins, *Local History in England*, Appendix, 'The Ranking of Provincial Towns, 1334–1861'; for Lyons, see Déniau in Kleinclausz, ed., *Histoire*, p. 270. Medieval English population estimates have been thrown into confusion since Derek Keene showed that the early-fourteenth-century estimates of London's population should be trebled. This conclusion is based on the detailed research for a project which he has directed, *The Social and Economic History of Medieval London* (Economic and Social Research Council).

bourgeois elite of Lyons, though rich enough to be able to fill official posts in the ecclesiastically dominated city, had virtually no period of general control of their city – until they assimilated themselves into the royal officialdom, which took over in the second half of the fifteenth century.

3. *Urban social structures*

It is often assumed that conflicts in the middle ages between feudal lords or institutions, such as monasteries, and the urban bourgeoisie arose from a clash of incompatible class interests, anticipating later conflicts leading to 'bourgeois revolutions'. The intensity of some of the conflicts between feudal powers and urban communities over rival jurisdictions or over the franchises which towns demanded of their lords, cannot be denied. However, the rivalry between feudal magnates over claims for land and jurisdiction could be equally intense. It is essential, therefore, in considering the problem of urban–feudal antagonism, to come to some conclusions about the urban class structure so as to see how it fitted within the wider social formation. As we have seen, a substantial majority of English market towns, and some larger towns, were under the lordship of feudal landowners. Those under royal control were still subject to a monarchy correctly described as 'feudal'. Private feudal lordship over towns was even more widespread in France. In both France and England, towns were riddled with feudal jurisdictions, mainly ecclesiastical. Both countries were governed by a landowning ruling class, certainly by no means homogeneous, and full of internal contradictions, but nevertheless, together with its monarchies, recognisable as having a common economic and social function and interest.

SMALL TOWNS

Let us first go into further detail about the social structure of the market towns, so many of which, as we have shown, in both France and England, were founded by feudal lords. As we have seen, lords benefited financially from their boroughs, as they did – quite differently – from their rural manors. So we must pose again the question – were these simply rural *bourgs* with no urban characteristics? The surviving documentation is uneven, but the presence in most of these new boroughs of a high proportion of men and women engaged in non-agricultural craft and service occupations is striking, as is the central role of the market in the small borough's social and economic life. The market town of Linton, in Cambridgeshire, had a burgess population without being formally endowed with borough privileges. But in 1246, it had a market and fair, and by 1279, a range of fifteen or more craft and trading occupations – cobblers, smiths, potters, tanners, tailors, merchants, bakers, brewsters, barbers, fellmongers, and so on.

High Wycombe, in the middle of the thirteenth century, had a similar range of twenty or more craft and service occupations, including a small linen and woollen cloth manufacturing element. By the fourteenth century, Thame in Oxfordshire had about twenty-five non-agricultural crafts, some specialising in textile production and glass making. At Newmarket, even in the supposedly depressed conditions of the fifteenth century, there were thirty-six stalls, and seventy-two shops in the market, where butchers, drapers, rope-makers, mercers, tanners, shoemakers and others sold their wares. Much of the trade was, of course, in agricultural produce brought in by peasants from the surrounding countryside. This situation is also described in quite different documentation. The goods designated for sale at Alcester, a small town of Roman origin in Warwickshire, in a charter for a second market in about 1274, included meat, live animals, fish, poultry, dairy produce and grain, as well as linen and woollen cloth, iron goods, leather goods, baskets, hides, wool, salt and spices.[1]

Some of these market boroughs may have had populations of up to about 1,000 before the Black Death. The well-documented boroughs of Thornbury and Halesowen probably did not exceed this figure. Each had small textile industries producing woollen and linen cloths. The majority of their borough inhabitants also had non-agricultural occupations. At Halesowen in the early fourteenth century, only seventeen per cent had land in the large manor which surrounded the borough and from which most of the borough

---

[1] For Linton, see J.H. Clapham, 'A Thirteenth Century Market Town'; for Thame, *Victoria County History of Oxfordshire*, VII; for Newmarket, P. May, *Newmarket, Medieval and Tudor*, chapter 5; for Alcester, *Victoria County History of Warwickshire*, III.

population was drawn. A survey of 1322 for both the borough and manor of Thornbury shows that very little agricultural land in the manor was held by burgesses, a situation confirmed by the fact that only a small number of cases in the records of the borough court implied agricultural interests. In other words, their function was characteristic of the small market boroughs scattered throughout England; first, to provide centres where peasants could sell their surplus products to obtain cash, to pay rent and tax, and thus to provide a major element in the cash income of their lords and the state; second, to enable the peasants to buy basic manufactured commodities; and third, to sustain a range of small-scale artisans and food-processors to service both the market itself and the immediate locality.

Borough court rolls, if sufficiently continuous and detailed provide evidence about the social composition and inter-relationships within the small town community. Borough courts were summoned with varying frequency, but some met monthly. A considerable amount of court activity was recorded, ranging from presentments of peace-breakers to litigation about debt and trespass. Many names, both of residents and outsiders, occur: suitors to the court, whether in attendance or excused; jurors, presenting offenders, making sworn statements, or inquiring into matters of interest to the lord or to the burgesses; offenders; litigants; and pledges providing security. Their occupations are either stated or deducible from their reported activities. This information allows us to have a reasonably certain idea about the families which formed the ruling elites. The adult members of these families regularly attended the court sessions and acted as pledges, whether chosen by neighbours who needed them as securities for court attendance, payment of fines and so on, or (more often) appointed by the court. A remarkably high proportion of them became jurors, and it was from these jurors that the borough officials were chosen by the lord's steward who presided over the court – chosen, no doubt, after consultation with the leading burgesses.

The court records of Halesowen begin in 1272 and continue throughout the middle ages.[2] In the late thirteenth and early fourteenth centuries, a wide spread of families provided jurors and officials (reeves, cachepols, constables, ale-tasters, supervisors of

---

[2] The court rolls of the borough of Halesowen are in the Birmingham Reference Library (BRL 346512 onwards).

ordinances). During this period there were many immigrants, a substantial majority being women. Some were transient, others settled down. The regularity and frequency of court activity by members of resident families enables us to identify those which became established and 'respectable'. Of about a hundred such families recorded in the first half-century of the court roll evidence, only twelve did not provide jurors or officials, though only one third of the jurors were chosen to serve for longer than three years. It was from this smaller group that the officials were chosen. Even so, it constituted a reasonably broad elite, for in these small towns there was no small class of rich merchants, and there was not much social differentiation among the craft masters and the retail traders. The occupational structure was, of course, predominantly non-agricultural, that is, petty merchants dealing in local commodities, craftsmen and craftswomen (including makers of linen cloth), victuallers such as butchers, bakers and brewers. There was also a tendency for many families to engage in more than one occupation. Most households brewed ale and sold what was surplus to family requirements. Butchers grew flax for the linen trade, as did shoemakers and dyers. On the whole, the retail traders, mostly in grain, malt and agricultural products, tended to be more prominent among the jurors and officials than the manufacturing craftsmen.

Thornbury also has a series of court records, beginning in 1324, and, like those of Halesowen, continuing until the sixteenth century.[3] But it is a much more broken series, and although there is a lot of evidence of the same sort of local activity in the surviving records, the gaps make estimates about established families less reliable. Nevertheless, it is fairly certain that the families which provided the jurors and officials in the early fourteenth century were about a quarter of the estimated total numbers of families. They constituted a fairly broad elite, though perhaps a little narrower than that at Halesowen. They seem to have been predominantly involved in retail trade, and the victualling element was important – butchers, bakers, fishmongers and innkeepers. They also dealt in grain and malt at the local fairs. It is of some interest that these leading families seem to have had little interest in the local woollen textile industry. In the early sixteenth century, John Leland visited Thornbury on his well-known tour, and commented that the town had once been

---

[3] The court rolls of the borough of Thornbury are in the Staffordshire County Record Office, D. 641/1/4E/2 onwards.

much occupied in clothing, though in his time quite idle.[4] In the fourteenth-century court records, there are many indirect references to textile components in various households, such as woollen yarn for spinning, finished and unfinished cloth, as well as direct reference to dyeing and to persons identified as textile craftsmen. But none of the officials, jurors and others from the elite families seem to have had any interest at all in the cloth industry. One suspects that it was either producing purely for local consumption, or was perhaps peripherally involved in the Bristol textile trade.

As one would expect, these small towns were not so structured as were the bigger urban centres. Although the borough court and borough officialdom tended to be dominated by representatives of the better-off families, there was less of a social gap between them and the rest of the borough population than one finds between the mercantile elites of the big towns and the craft producers. Although there are a few references to apprenticeship, there were no separate craft organisations and no sets of regulations controlling craft production. Although the sort of confrontation which is well known at manorial level between lords and peasants, over rents, services and legal status, hardly existed, there were remnants of such conflicts. In Halesowen, for example, the abbot, lord of the town, in the early fourteenth century attempted to extract dues and services (such as unpaid labour) from free burgesses. But more generally, it was intervention by the lord or his officials which caused trouble, such as interference with the election of court officials or attempts to control innkeepers, brewstresses and tapsters.

The fortunate survival of the borough court records of some of the small English market towns provides evidence for their social structure and economic activities. Such evidence is not found for the small towns of medieval France. Some of these, especially in the south, have left another type of abundant documentation, namely, the records of local notaries. These register a wide range of contracts or agreements between individuals. They include sales and purchases of goods, loans, marriage agreements, wills, purchase or letting of real property and so on. Directly and indirectly, they provide evidence about individuals, their occupations, their property and their personal relations, even though the evidence inevitably leaves chronological gaps – if registers have been lost – and is only

---

[4] L. Toulmin-Smith, ed., *The Itinerary in England*, V.

cautiously quantifiable. Nevertheless, they do illuminate the characteristics of smaller towns.

A good example is the small port of Berre on the Etang de Berre,
near Aix-en-Provence, with access by canal to the Mediterranean.[5]
Its lord was the count of Provence. It was not until the late
fourteenth century that the town could choose two syndics as its
representatives. Other feudal landowners had property in the town
and the town fields – the abbeys of St Victor of Marseilles and of
Silvacane near Avignon, the house of the Hospitallers of the Order
of Malta at Calissane, as well as families of the local petty nobility.
As a fishing port and a producer of salt, it had certain special
characteristics, but apart from those, it had most of the features of
the average French market town. There were many peasants living
in the town engaged in arable farming and vine cultivation, some of
them quite well to do *laboureurs*. There was an important population
of craftsmen, producing woollen and linen cloth and canvas. Much
of the wool came from local sheep flocks. There was a leather
industry whose leading craftsmen were shoemakers. There were
masons and other building craftsmen, carpenters and smiths.
Butchers were important, linked with, or themselves being, owners
of livestock.

Separate from the craftsmen were merchants and drapers, none,
of course, big dealers in international trade. It was from their ranks
that the syndics were chosen. It is clear that in spite of some links
with Marseilles and the Mediterranean, and although there were
some ship owners, mariners and fishermen among the population,
craft production was predominantly for the local market, and even
the richest merchants hardly went beyond. Perhaps the most
interesting feature, and no doubt characteristic of many other
market towns, was the multiple occupations of individual households. Almost all families, and especially the craftsmen, had
vineyards and small plots outside the town. Craftsmen doubled up
their craft occupations with various forms of retail trade, especially
in consumables such as fish. Berre was a local market town very
closely linked with the arable and pastoral hinterland. Like so many
other small towns it was an essential link in the commercial circuit.

Another market town which is fairly well documented was St
Symphorien-sur-Coise, in the hills to the west of Lyons. It was
smaller than Berre (around one as against two thousand inhabi-

---

[5] Jean Birrell, 'Berre à la fin du moyen âge'.

tants). Its lord was a local castellan, but it was taken over by the crown in 1322. Many of the inhabitants were tenants of the chapter of St Jean, a dependency of St Jean of Lyons. The survival of a large number of wills as well as of lists of tenants of the chapter has made possible an analysis of the social structure, not unlike that of Berre, in spite of the contrast between the mountain and the Mediterranean backgrounds. This small town was the focus of service and manufacturing crafts, which were not found in the purely agricultural villages of the region. As at Berre, the textile and leather trades were in the lead. About a quarter of the population seem to have been peasants, and most of the artisans and petty traders had either gardens or small arable plots. Commerce on a local scale was also carried on by people from the families of craftsmen, but there also emerged from local families a number of professional people, such as notaries.[6]

St Symphorien was probably very similar to the eight or so small market towns of the county of Forez nearby. They too were based on castellanies, and their populations ranged between one and two thousand. Among other resemblances to the English market towns, which we have considered, they were granted by the counts of Forez and other lords of the county a number of rights by charter. These included freedom of status and tenure, freedom from arbitrary elements of feudal jurisdiction (though there was no self-governing urban jurisdiction), freedom of trade and some exemptions from market tolls. The elements of self-government – six *prud'hommes* chosen from the urban elite – were hardly greater than at Berre, as the *prud'hommes* seem to have had no role beyond their responsibility for collecting the not inconsiderable seigneurial dues. There is not much information about the economic and social structure, but there seem to have been the usual service and craft occupations serving the region, partly stimulated, too, by the fact that Forez and its county town, Montbrison, were on a main north–south trade route. The tradesmen and craftsmen of one of the market towns, St Germain de Laval, were probably typical, butchers, tanners, shoemakers, potters, wool merchants, cheesemongers, money changers, ironmongers, salt merchants and so on.[7]

---

[6] M.-T. Lorcin, 'Une bourgade artisanale des Monts du Lyonnais aux XIVe et XVe siècles'.

[7] E. Fournial, *Les villes et l'économie d'échange en Forez aux XIIIe et XIVe siècles*.

LARGER TOWNS

In analysing the social structure of the larger towns, it will be necessary to focus in detail on the two main classes, the artisan producers and the primarily mercantile elites. The large towns had a much greater variety of roles than the market towns, as one would expect, not only as political and administrative centres, not only as centres of long-distance trade, but also containing large and varied populations with many diverse requirements for goods and services. The social mix, therefore, would go beyond that of the many craft occupations and of greater or lesser mercantile activities. Before concentrating, therefore, on the social structures developing from craft production and mercantile activities, we will consider other social groupings to be found in the larger towns.

Big towns in both France and England contained many inhabitants whom we would now classify as 'professionals', and who would be found, if at all, only in small numbers in market towns. There would be a varying number, according to the size and function of the town, of officials in administrative posts. Since literacy was an obvious requirement in administration, whether of municipal government, of feudal powers both lay and ecclesiastical, of law courts or even of craft and mercantile organisations, many of these officials would be clerics, mostly below priestly status. In addition, there would be many other lesser clergy linked with ecclesiastical functions in parish churches and especially in the service of chantries. Nor should we forget the secular canons of cathedral chapters and of other collegiate churches, not to speak of the friars whose presence, according to J. le Goff, was a measure of the degree of urbanisation.[8] In university cities, of which Paris is the outstanding example, there would be a large population of students, who would be clerics. They might also be found in towns without universities as such, but with cathedrals and similar schools.

Lawyers were necessarily important in the bigger towns, whether as pleaders in courts or as legal advisers (like modern solicitors) who would also draw up contracts. The notaries in areas where Roman law provided the basis of the legal system were very prominent, especially in Languedoc and in Provence. Professional money changers and money lenders might not be numerous but would be an important professional element. In big towns which escaped the

---

[8] 'Ordres mendiants et urbanisation dans la France médiévale. Etat de l'enquête'.

anti-semitic policies of the English and French monarchies, there might be important Jewish communities. And, as has been recently illustrated in Provence, medical doctors were important even in medium-sized towns.[9] Nor should we forget, in considering the ambience of the bigger towns, that they had many visitors who were lodged at various hostelries. The landlords often combined their function as inn-keepers with those of commercial intermediaries or brokers. In the fourteenth century, there were seventy hostelries in Toulouse, providing about six hundred beds which would each take two or three people – this in a city with a population estimated at 25,000. By the middle of the fifteenth century, in the smaller city of Aix-en-Provence there were twenty-seven hostelries with between two hundred and two hundred and fifty beds, taking two people each.[10]

More numerous than the professionals and outside the recognised structures of craft production and commercial activity, was the numerically incalculable population known as the 'marginals', to whom we have several times referred and whose special significance in the large towns must be emphasised here. Many of them may have been unskilled workers, ranging from water-carriers to labourers on building sites. Many of them may very well have been a good deal more stable an element low down in the social hierarchy than is generally assumed for 'marginals', but they are not easily counted. Many of the 'marginals' were probably rural immigrants, some transient, others who might settle down as unskilled workers. They too are hardly countable and mostly appear in the judicial records. Such people were not, of course, unknown in small market towns, but were much more important numerically in the big cities which offered a variety of attractions for displaced villagers.

The judicial records also, as one would expect, demonstrate the existence of an, again uncountable, professional or semi-professional criminal element of thieves and burglars, an inevitable consequence of poverty, of extreme social inequality and of alienation from established social structures. Some of them only appear occasionally, others were organised in more or less permanent groups.

Finally, and by no means the least important of those thought of

[9] M. Hébert, ed., *Vie privée et ordre publique à la fin du moyen âge: études sur Manosque, la Provence et le Piémont (1250–1450)*, Part 2, 'Médecine et médecins'; J. Shatzmiller, *Médecine et justice en Provence médiévale*.

[10] P. Wolff, 'Les hostelleries toulousaines au moyen âge', in Wolff, *Regards sur le midi médiéval*; N. Coulet, *Aix-en-Provence: espace et relations d'une capitale*, p. 319.

as large-town 'marginals', were the prostitutes, often recruited from rural immigrants. In spite of the ecclesiastical condemnation of extra-marital sex (and even disapproval of sex between married couples for the sake of pleasure), there was some ambiguity in official attitudes to freelance prostitutes and to brothels. This ambiguity was well illustrated by B. Geremek in medieval Paris, where prostitution was 'one trade among others', even if not approved. Procuresses and their brothels were condemned more harshly than the prostitutes themselves, but it seems that there were indications of a recognised organisation, not a prostitutes' gild as some historians have thought, but a religious *confrérie* which enables its members to go on pilgrimages, for genuine religious purposes rather than to serve the needs of male pilgrims.[11] The ambiguity about prostitution is documented as far away from Paris as Manosque, a medium-sized town in Provence. Here, in the thirteenth century, prostitution was seen as necessarily providing for unmarried men a means of sexual release. Later, however, prostitutes were treated as vagabonds, since they were very often immigrants, without male protectors or guarantors (let alone husbands).[12] By contrast, in the later middle ages in Languedocian towns and in Perpignan in Rousillon, there were officially recognised and municipally controlled 'red light districts'.[13] Perhaps prostitutes should, in these cases, not be regarded as 'marginals', since the implication is that they were embodied into recognised urban social structures.

There is more ambiguity about any recognised social role for prostitutes in English towns. The institutionalised 'stews' of Southwark are, of course, well known and were recognised at the time. Their trade was officially prohibited during the meetings of Parliament at Westminster – not that the trade was stopped in Westminster itself, as G. Rosser has shown. Where urban records are sufficiently abundant, the presence and partial acceptance of prostitutes, satisfying the needs, especially of the clergy who could not marry, can be deduced. In York, they were even asked to act as jurors in marriage annulment cases where it was necessary to prove the impotence of the husband. In many other provincial towns –

---

[11] B. Geremek, *The Margins of Society in Late Medieval Paris*, trans. Birrell, chapter 7, 'The World of Prostitution'.
[12] Hébert, ed., *Vie privée*, chapters 1 and 2.
[13] L.L. Otis, *Prostitution in Medieval Society: the History of an Urban Institution in Languedoc*.

Winchester, Hull, Southampton, Coventry, Nottingham, Exeter, King's Lynn, and even the small town of Pershore – the presence of prostitutes and what were, in effect, brothels (some taverns and ale-houses, for instance) is recorded. Although the records usually imply official rejection, the covert recognition or acceptance of the trade by the authorities is obvious. On the other hand, the amount of prostitution must not be over-estimated. If one were to take too literally the court records of the small borough of Halesowen in the late thirteenth century, prostitution, among other things for the benefit of the canons of the local Premonstratension abbey, might seem to have been rife. But it is clear that to call a woman a prostitute (*meretrix*) was a common form of abuse, which could itself be punished, as when an abusive woman was sentenced to the pillory.[14]

These aspects of large-town life, which contrast with those of the market town, emphasise the context of different forms of sociability and of mental outlook. We must beware, however, of assuming an incompatibility with the overall structures and assumptions of feudal society. Accumulations of merchant capital, the presence of usurious moneylenders, the presence among the marginals of a large potential labour force, did not make the big cities of France and England the harbingers of industrial capitalism, even though merchant capital might eventually be invested in industrial pro-duction – usually outside those big cities.

THE ARTISANS

It might seem normal to consider first the ruling elites of the medieval towns as the key element in urban–feudal relationships, but there are also good reasons for first examining those who were the basic producers and without whom the urban economy could not exist. For whatever the function of the bigger towns and the varying composition, therefore, of the urban upper classes, there would be more homogeneity in the artisan class, especially among those providing for the local or regional market. As we have mentioned already, the most widespread unit of production in the

---

[14] J. Post, 'A Fifteenth Century Customary of the Southwark Stews'; A. G. Rosser, *Medieval Westminster 1200–1540*, pp. 143–4; P.J. Goldberg, 'Women in Fifteenth Century Town Life' in J.A.F. Thomson, ed., *Towns and Townspeople of the Fifteenth Century*; D.M. Owen, ed., *The Makings of King's Lynn*, p. 268; R.H. Hilton, *The English Peasantry in the Later Middle Ages*, p. 191; Hilton, 'Small Town Society in England before the Black Death', pp. 71–2.

medieval town was the artisan workshop. In principle, the master craftsman was the owner of the means of small-scale production and controlled the labour force of the workshop. This consisted of the family, male and female alike. The family would sometimes be the conjugal family, made up of the married couple and their offspring. It could be extended, not merely including grandparents, but also one or more siblings of man or wife, and cousins of the offspring. It no doubt fluctuated in size and composition over time. There might be one or two apprentices from outside who lived with the family, learned the craft and provided a cheap labour force; and one or two journeymen,[15] who might live in but who often had separate lodgings and were married. The resemblance between this structure of production and the peasant economy in the countryside is obvious. The emphasis which is often placed on a gulf between village and town life should be modified – the peasant immigrant would find the town to have a pattern of economic and social activity, based on the individual household, which would by no means be unfamiliar.

Peasant immigrants could swell the marginal population of the town, but the evidence of rural place-name surnames in urban tax lists demonstrates that many country people moved into established social structures. In some of the growing towns of the English West Midlands, such as Bristol and Coventry, more than a third of the tax-payers in the early fourteenth century had surnames indicating a rural origin. During this same period, most of London's growing population was supplied by immigrants rather than by natural growth, a high proportion of whom were of rural origin. This is confirmed by apprenticeship indentures between craft masters and rural families for their offspring. In the early fourteenth century, a high proportion of London apprentices (as well as other immigrants) came from the East Midlands, in such great numbers that the language spoken by Londoners became that of East Anglia rather than of the Home Counties.[16] If a rent and service-paying peasantry was an essential part of the feudal social formation, then so was the urban artisanate; its structure was similar to that of the peasantry,

---

[15] The bibliography on craft production in the medieval town is considerable. See the latest study by Heather Swanson, *Medieval Artisans*; Swanson, *Craftsmen and Industry in Late Medieval York* – a comprehensive study within a wide-ranging comparative context.

[16] Hilton, *A Medieval Society*, p. 184; E. Ekwall, *Two Early London Subsidy Rolls*.

and it was constantly reinforced by immigrants from a feudal rural background.

Rebellious peasants posed a more basic threat to the interests of the feudal landowners than any other class in medieval society. But they did not bear the seeds, either intentionally or otherwise, of another mode of production. They were not the harbingers of capitalism, whatever the role in the early modern period of the rich yeomanry. Indeed, they were rather the victims of early modern agrarian capitalism. What about the artisans? Can this class be regarded either as incompatible with feudal society or as containing tendencies which would lead to its transformation?

The conventional picture of a conservative and unchanging structure of craft production is well known. The workshop was organised hierarchically on the basis of the control of the family, the apprentices and the journeymen by the master. The hierarchy within the workshop was re-created within the gild organisation. This was ruled from on high by a group of masters who were wardens and searchers. They combined quality control with dictates on the length of the working day, on the distribution of labour between workshops and on the enforcement of a craft monopoly on the production and sale of its commodities. This was the practical expression of the 'one man, one trade' ethos. And as the phrase implies, from top to bottom, with few exceptions, all positions of power and control were in male hands.

In fact, the conventional image briefly sketched above does not correspond much with reality, and was largely based on the late medieval craft regulations, which, far from being the expression of the wishes of the craft producers, were often imposed from above by the rulers of towns, whether feudal lords, the crown or ruling mercantile elites.[17] These late medieval craft regulations, in the towns both of England and France, were often copied from those of the craft organisations in the two capital cities, London and Paris. So, the conventional image referred to owes much to these two metropolitan examples. In both cities, we find well established craft organisations by the end of the thirteenth century, which we will briefly examine before considering the evidence which seriously undermines the conventional image.

It is worth considering Paris first, because of the codification of craft regulations – the *Livre des métiers* – made during the period

---

[17] See Swanson, 'The Illusion of Economic Structure: Craft Gilds in Late Medieval English Towns'.

when Etienne Boileau was the king's provost (*prévot*) of Paris in the 1260s.[18] The codification at this period implies, of course, the previous existence of the craft organisations. They certainly existed in the middle of the twelfth century. The *marchands de l'eau*, an organisation of general merchants, originally concerned with the river trade, was given its first privileges in 1121. It eventually took over such municipal administration as was not controlled by the crown, its provost becoming almost analogous to a mayor. Furthermore, several of the crafts in the *Livre des métiers* claimed that their regulations went back to the reign of Philip Augustus (1180–1223).

Regulations of varying length were submitted by 101 crafts, although there may have been some which were omitted – the tallage of 1291 indicates the existence of 128. They covered a very wide range of occupations in the textile, leather, building, metal, retailing, victualling and various other trades. The content of the regulations indicates how early on the ideals, if not the reality, of the structure of craft production were to be found. Apprenticeship was almost universal (though not obligatory for ambitious second-hand clothes dealers!), the length of time varying from one to twelve years according to the craft, and with numbers restricted to one or two in each workshop. Journeymen's contracts with their masters indicated variable lengths of service, from a week to a year. Hours of work, holidays and rates of pay were included in the contract. Night work was only allowed in special cases. The number of journeymen allowed in each workshop was laid down for about two thirds of the crafts.

There are interesting, though often indirect, indications about the position of women in the Paris crafts. They were excluded from all positions of control within the craft organisation, even within those whose workers were mainly female and where a mistress, not a master, was the head of the workshop. Nevertheless, women's essential role in the process of production meant that they could not be marginalised into purely domestic activity. Their situation varied, of course, according to the craft, but they could have the *maîtrise* along with the husband and continue to do so when they became widows. They could take apprentices; and even when they did not

---

[18] R. Cazelles, *Nouvelle histoire de Paris*, chapter 3; P. Guth, ed., *Le siècle de St Louis*, chapter 5, by B. Mahieu; E. Coornaert, *Les corporations*, pp. 97–8 for Charles V's instructions that the Paris gilds should be a model; E.M. Saint Léon, *Histoire des corporations de métier*.

have the *maîtrise*, women were recognised in some trades as being the legitimate representatives (*chambrières*) at the market of single or widowed masters.[19]

Entry into mastership was already much easier for sons or close relatives of masters. Others, in nearly half of the crafts, had to buy their way in; in the rest they had, at least, to be accepted by the craft authorities. Certain masters, presumably the richer, eventually became jurors or wardens of their craft and as such exercised jurisdiction over the craft. More generally, regulations forbade the formation of societies or firms of several masters, so as to prevent price fixing. But the exercise of more than one craft was not forbidden. The interesting feature of craft subordination in Paris to higher authority was that it was not to a mercantile-dominated municipal government, but to territorial lords (mostly ecclesiastics), to the royal provost of the city and to other royal functionaries. The public responsibility of the crafts is emphasised by the fact that they were responsible for the watch and ward (*guet*) of the city, under the control of royal, not municipal, officials.

There is no London equivalent of the *Livre des métiers*. Craft organisations were becoming politically as well as commercially important in the second half of the thirteenth century.[20] The most important ones, as one would expect, were those with a mercantile rather than a manufacturing role, such as the drapers, mercers, vintners, goldsmiths, grocers (or pepperers) and fishmongers. Nevertheless, manufacturing crafts, especially in the leather and affiliated trades, were obtaining official recognition (not to speak of the few recorded in the twelfth century, which we will consider shortly). There was a minimum of twenty-five recognised organised crafts by 1328, and fifty-one took part in the elections to the Common Council in 1377.

The history of the London craft organisations is very complex, as they were much more involved in city politics than were those of Paris. There is also evidence of considerable strains on the traditional forms of the organisation of production due to rapid late-thirteenth-

---

[19] D. Frappier-Bigras, 'La famille dans l'artisanat parisien du XIIIe siècle.'

[20] Although much research has been done on London craft gilds, both on individual gilds and more generally, George Unwin's *Gilds and Companies of London* is still essential reading. See also E.M. Veale's 'Craftsmen and the Economy of London in the Fourteenth Century' in A.E.J. Hollaender and W. Kellaway, eds., *Studies in London History*. A good example of a history of an individual gild is A.H. Johnson, *History of the Worshipful Company of Drapers of London*, I; see also G. Williams, *Medieval London: from Commune to Capital*.

century economic growth. Nevertheless, traditional aims were embodied in regulations. The lorimers (bridle makers), whose work was mainly put out to them by the saddlers, recorded their craft ordinances in 1261. Apprentices had to pay to become such, and had to serve a ten-year term. No master was to poach another's apprentice. Night work was forbidden, as was work on Saturdays and feast days. Outsiders could not work at the trade unless entering the mistery and paying a fee, part to the city and part to the craft. Four wardens were to be elected to present offenders against the regulations before the mayor.

A later set of ordinances – that of the hatters in 1348 – has many of the same features. Six lawful men were sworn to rule the trade. Only freemen of the city were to make or sell hats. Apprentices had to serve a seven-year term. The wardens were to search when necessary and to take defective hats before the mayor and aldermen. Night work was forbidden. None of the trade were to be made free of the city or to be allowed to work unless attested by the wardens. There was to be no poaching of another hatter's servant or apprentice. No stranger was to sell hats retail, but only wholesale and to freemen.

These craft ordinances from London and Paris are cited in order to illustrate the traditional content of such regulations, and because they were much imitated in other towns. Like so much regulation, they are as much evidence of behaviour which the authorities, whether of the crafts or at higher levels, would have wished to prevent, as of the norms of conduct. It has also been pointed out that when the fifty-one organised crafts elected representatives to the London Common Council in 1377, there were at least 180 separate occupations, the majority of whom declined to form an organised craft or mistery.[21]

In fact, many medieval towns had no craft organisations and in some towns, if craft organisations did occur, it was not until the fifteenth century onwards. In Lyons, although there were occasional craft assemblies and apparently a thirteenth-century organisation of skinners (*pelletiers*), there seems to have been no structure of craft organisation of the traditional type. The same seems to have been true of Tours until the fifteenth century, similarly in Reims and Poitiers. The first craft statutes in Bordeaux date from 1453. At

---

[21] Veale, 'Craftsmen and the Economy of London in the Fourteenth Century', reprinted in R. Holt and G. Rosser, eds., *The Medieval Town: A Reader in English Urban History 1200–1540*.

Arles, in Provence, there were no craft organisations even in the fifteenth century, although some craftsmen, such as barber-surgeons formed a fraternity (*confrérie*) with ostensibly social and religious functions. This was also the case in another Provençal town, Tarascon, where there were also fraternities, but not apparently associated with specific crafts.[22]

In England, there also seem to have been some sizeable towns without organised craft gilds, and, as one would expect, small market towns did not have any craft organisations. But Canterbury seems not to have had a structured gild system before the sixteenth century. Nor apparently did Leicester, a town under the lordship of the earls of Leicester and subsequently of the dukes of Lancaster. Bury St Edmunds, which was the property of the Benedictine abbey of St Edmund, only had three, Gloucester and Coventry seem not to have had any organised crafts before the end of the fourteenth century, and Worcester not before the fifteenth century. There is little evidence of separate craft organisations at Cambridge, Shrewsbury and Bishops (later King's) Lynn, although Lynn in 1389 had forty-three social and religious gilds – more than London, if we are to believe the 1389 return.[23]

Some very early craft organisations in England present something of a puzzle. The first evidence for their existence is found in documents of the royal exchequer, beginning with the earliest Pipe Roll of 1130. There were weavers gilds in London, Winchester, Lincoln, Oxford, Huntingdon, Nottingham and York, and a fullers gild at Winchester. They paid money to the king, as the direct lord of their borough, for a monopoly of their trade, not only in the

[22] P. Pouzet in A. Kleinclausz, ed., *Histoire de Lyon*, III, chapter 4; B. Chevalier, *Tours, ville royale 1255–1520*, pp. 131–43; P. Desportes, *Reims et les Rémois*, chapter 20; R. Favreau, *La ville de Poitiers*, chapter 6; L. Stouff, *Arles à la fin du moyen âge*, chapter 4, especially pp. 291–301; M. Hébert, *Tarascon au XIVe siècle: histoire d'une communauté urbaine provençale*, chapter 2, especially pp. 74–6.

[23] A.F. Butcher, 'The Decline of Canterbury 1300–1500'; M. Bateson, *The Records of the Borough of Leicester*, especially her introduction to vol. 2; M.D. Lobel, *The Borough of Bury St Edmunds*; for Coventry, see M.D. Harris, *Life in an Old English Town*, chapter 13; C. Phythian-Adams, *The Desolation of a City: Coventry and the Urban Crisis of the Late Middle Ages*, Part 3, p. 7; C. E. W. O. Fulbrook-Legatt, *Anglo-Saxon and Medieval Gloucester*, chapter 6; the references to Worcester gilds, even in fifteenth century documents, are scanty – for example, the 1467 Worcester city ordinances in L. Toulmin Smith, ed., *English Gilds*, or the 1497 Liber Legum in V. Green, *History and Antiquities of the City and Suburbs of Worcester*; H.M. Cam on Cambridge in *The Victoria County History of Cambridgeshire*, III; Shrewsbury is not much written about, but little indication of craft gilds in H. Owen and J.B. Blakeway, *History of Shrewsbury*, I; for King's Lynn, see D. M. Owen, ed., *The Making of King's Lynn*.

borough itself but sometimes in the rural hinterland.[24] Such a monopoly seems to fit in well with the conventional image of the later craft gilds. But, in fact, by the middle of the thirteenth century, these gilds of textile craftsmen had been made toothless. Further, the exercise of their craft was considered so demeaning that they were not allowed to become freemen of their borough. The reason, however, for the brevity of their monopoly was basically economic. By the thirteenth century, these towns had become dominated, usually through the gild merchant, by merchant entrepreneurs whose aim was to monopolise cloth sales, especially for export. The textile craftsmen had to be subordinated, and were deprived of the right to sell cloth other than to the merchant entrepreneur.[25] It is interesting to note, however, that dyers, being at the end of the process of production and necessarily capable of buying expensive equipment and raw materials, assumed a mercantile role, and (as for instance at Leicester) were allowed into the gild merchant.

The textile gilds were not the only ones to appear in the twelfth century. In 1179–80 a number of so-called 'adulterine' gilds in London were fined, some quite heavily (though later pardoned) because of their presumably illegal existence. It is important to note that not all of them were craft organisations, though these existed – goldsmiths, pepperers (later to be known as grocers), clothmakers and butchers. Fourteen other gilds obviously had religious, charitable or convivial functions – five were devoted to the construction of London bridge, one was dedicated to St Lazarus, another to pilgrims. Seven were only identified by the names of their aldermen. The same Pipe Roll of 1179–80, besides recording payments by the textile gilds already referred to, also lists corvesers in Oxford, and glovers, hosiers, saddlers and curriers in York. There were also gilds whose purpose was unspecified, but declared to be without warrant, in Exeter, Barnstaple, Bodmin, Launceston, Wareham, Dorchester, Axbridge, Langport and Ilchester. These may very well have been gilds set up for social or religious purposes, not representing craft interests.[26]

The appearance of these gilds in twelfth-century England, not all

---

[24] C. Brooke and G. Keir, *London, the Shaping of a City*, p. 279, and J. Hunter, ed., *The Pipe Roll of 31 Henry I*.

[25] E. Carus-Wilson, 'The English Cloth Industry in the Twelfth and Thirteenth Centuries', in Carus-Wilson, *Medieval Merchant Venturers*.

[26] The payments by gilds in 1179–80 are reprinted from the Pipe Rolls in A.E. Bland, P.A. Brown and R.H. Tawney, eds., *English Economic History: Select Documents*, pp. 114–16.

associated with specific crafts or indeed with crafts at all, may pose a slight problem of terminology, but in all cases imply early forms of collective identity. Analogies have been suggested with the village communities of peasant society, which were very important also for collective identity, face to face with seigneurial power.[27] There were, of course, significant differences between peasant communities and urban gilds. It is generally agreed that an important element in the cohesion of the village communities was their vital economic interest in common rights to pasture, woodland and other resources. Evidently, the issue of common rights of this type was not to the forefront in urban societies (though, as we shall later see, not absent). Nevertheless, whether called 'gilds', 'fraternities', or 'fellowships', institutions expressing collective identity, whether class-based or otherwise, played an important role in the medieval town.

The term 'gild' (*ghilde*) is very old and was not necessarily in early times confined to towns. E. Coornaert has discovered the term as early as the fifth century, used for a sacrificial feast of (probably) Frankish soldiers.[28] Gilds certainly existed in Carolingian France, mainly as festive, that is, drinking, clubs, with possibly pagan associations (or so the authorities suspected); but also with more orthodox religious intentions, such as maintaining lights on altars, as well as providing mutual help. Early English examples also suggest that they were not necessarily urban or artisan in composition. The early tenth century 'frith' or 'peace gild' of London and the surrounding counties probably had mainly rural members. The eleventh-century gild of thegns in Cambridge, a spontaneous body for mutual solidarity, religious observance and charity was not necessarily urban-focussed. Thegns were well-to-do landowners. But the ninth-century gild of *cnihtas* in Canterbury and the tenth-century gild of *cnihtas* in London had a specifically urban focus. The London *cnihtengild* even had jurisdiction in a 'soke' just outside the city walls, which was eventually, in the twelfth century, handed over to the canons of the Holy Trinity. The *cnihtas* were originally probably urban retainers of great landowners, but the exact meaning of the term is still uncertain.[29]

---

[27] Guy Bois, *The Crisis of Feudalism: Economy and Society in Eastern Normandy*, p. 395.   [28] Coornaert, 'Les ghildes médiévales'.

[29] Brooke and Keir, *London*, pp. 96–9; and D. Whitelock, ed., *English Historical Documents*, I, pp. 948–9 (London), and p. 557 (Cambridge); for Canterbury, see N.P. Brooks, *The Early History of the Church of Canterbury*.

As is well known, the term 'gild' was also used in England for associations of urban merchants, who as burgesses exercised the right to trade toll-free in the borough, together with the enjoyment of other urban franchises. These gilds go back to the eleventh century, and are very well documented from the twelfth century onwards. When towns were granted elements of self-government, those who took over as the ruling elite were already members of the *gilda mercatoria*. In some towns, therefore, the merchant gild was no longer considered necessary once its leading members had assumed power as aldermen or councillors.[30]

The fact that many craft gilds in England, like the *métiers* in French towns, became organisations for the policing of craft manufacture for the urban authorities, did not result in the disappearance of other groupings for mutual solidarity among craftsmen and women. Fraternities in England and in France sometimes became – or started as – craft organisations, or were kept on as the social and religious side of a craft. But many of them were also spontaneous gatherings for both overt and covert common activity, ranging from mutual support in case of poverty, to charity and religious observance, as well as engaging in activities which the state and municipal authorities considered to be subversive. In the towns of both countries there was considerable variety in the types of fraternity, as well as of their aims and purposes and their relationship with the crafts. Differences in the time of their arrival also vary, complicated in England by the ambiguity of the term 'gild', which, as we have seen, could be used to mean a craft organisation, a fraternity independent of the crafts or a combination of both.

This ambiguity is illustrated by the returns, already mentioned, which English gilds had to make in 1389 to a government which, because of the 1381 rising, was somewhat paranoiac about subversive organisations.[31] Not all of the returns have survived. There are about 500 in all, mostly from the eastern counties. Only a minority were craft gilds which combined the religious fraternity aspect. Furthermore, in order to rid the government of suspicion about their purposes, it seems likely that the respondents laid heavy emphasis on their commitment to the cult of a saint in a particular church. Many of these gilds were in villages. The biggest concentrations were, however, in towns. There were forty in London,

---

[30] Gild merchants are considered in more detail below, pp. 92–6.

[31] These gilds are listed in H.F. Westlake, *The Parish Gilds of Medieval England*.

only nine of which were associated with a specific craft; twenty-eight in Lincoln, of which eleven had craft links; forty-three in Bishops Lynn. Six of these had occupational rather than craft links. One of them (the Trinity Gild) was the gild merchant; others were for young scholars; young merchants; and clerks. Those for shipmen and coifmakers were, of course, near to being craft organisations. Norwich had nineteen, of which seven had craft associations; Bury St Edmunds had eighteen, none with craft links. Some large towns had remarkably few – in the returns – four in Coventry, one of which was called the Gild Merchant; two in York. The returns were obviously defective. According to Tanner, there were thirty-six non-craft fraternities in Norwich, besides those in the 1389 returns.[32] Other gilds, of course, were founded after 1389, such as York's Corpus Christi gild, founded by the clergy in 1408.

Whatever the variety within France and England of fraternities, of their aims and purposes, of their relationships with the crafts and their chronology, it is striking how similar their varying manifestations were in both countries.

Some historians of French towns have assumed that the craft organisations developed from the fraternities. This is made as a generalisation for all towns by B. Chevalier, and for the towns of Maine by A. Bouton.[33] It is, however, not easy to find evidence from studies of individual towns of many fraternities earlier than the thirteenth century, especially in connection with craft organisations. There are occasional references to fraternities as early as the twelfth century – that of the St Esprit at Marseilles, for example, in 1188, created to help a newly-founded hospital. Their purposes and roles were very varied. Many of the fraternities of the St Esprit in Savoy, Provence, Forez and Auvergne became, in effect, the governing bodies of villages or small towns, especially after consulates were abolished.[34]

Smaller fraternities, often named after some locally popular patron saint, were ostensibly for purely charitable or convivial purposes. The lay and ecclesiastical authorities in the thirteenth century regarded them with suspicion as potentially subversive or heretical, but from the fourteenth century, they regained the favour

[32] N.P. Tanner, *Popular Religion in Norwich with Special Reference to the Evidence of Wills, 1370–1532*, pp. 148 ff.

[33] B. Chevalier, *Les bonnes villes de France aux XIVe et XVe siècles*, chapter 3, ii; H. Bouton, *Le Maine*, chapter 8, esp. p. 541.

[34] V.L. Bourilly, *Essai sur l'histoire politique de la Commune de Marseille*, chapter 3; P. Duparc, 'Confréries du St Esprit et communautés d'habitants au moyen âge'.

of the authorities, possibly for the opposite reasons. It has been suggested that in Normandy, from the fourteenth century, their main role was, in fact, to reinforce established hierarchical social structures. They were very numerous, especially in towns. By the fifteenth century, there were 130 of them in Rouen and its suburbs. A similar proliferation is to be found in Provence, where the devotional function was so emphasised that there was often a terminological confusion between *confratria* or fraternity and *luminaria*, an organisation for maintaining an altar light. By the fifteenth century, there were one hundred fraternities in Avignon, forty in Marseilles and about thirty in both Aix-en-Provence and Arles; fewer, of course in small towns and villages. Given the popularity of fraternities, it is not surprising that many of them should have become associated with crafts.[35]

According to A. Gouron, some urban fraternities in Languedoc, both charitable and overtly political (or heretical), did appear in the twelfth century, but were not connected with the crafts. It was not until the fourteenth century that craft fraternities became generalised, following the examples of Le Puy and Montpellier at the end of the thirteenth century.[36] It is suggested that a fraternity of smiths (*fèvres*) in 1401 at Caen, with regulations both of a religious and an economic aim, might go back to the twelfth century. A fraternity of smiths with St Eloi as patron was founded in Béthune in 1188. There were thirteenth-century fraternities in Lyons and in Metz, the latter being unofficial craft organisations, which had to be sanctioned after 1336 by the municipal authorities. The religious role of fraternities associated with crafts is illustrated at Chartres and Le Mans in the thirteenth century. In both towns, decorated glass windows in their cathedrals were donated by the fraternities acting on behalf of the crafts. But in many towns, fraternities, as we have seen, were of later date. Craft fraternities in Breton towns are dated to the fourteenth century; at Reims, to the fourteenth and fifteenth centuries; at Arles, to the fifteenth century. At the end of the fifteenth century at Aurillac, reflecting perhaps the general late-

---

[35] C. Vincent, 'La confrérie comme structure d'intégration: l'exemple de la Normandie'; J. Chippoleau, 'Entre le religieux et la politique: les confréries de St Esprit en Provence et Comtat-Venaisson à la fin du moyen âge'; N. Coulet, 'Le mouvement confraternel en Provence et dans le Comtat-Venaisson au moyen âge'. All these articles are in Ecole Française de Rome, *Le mouvement confraternel au moyen âge: France, Italie, Suisse.*

[36] A. Gouron, *La règlementation des métiers en Languedoc au moyen âge*, pp. 338 ff., 348–52.

medieval tendency for craft amalgamations, about thirty-five crafts were grouped within eleven fraternities, similar to the grouping of twenty-one crafts at St Flour in the mid-sixteenth century.[37]

What must we conclude from these differing chronologies and associations between craft organisations and religious fraternities? The argument concerning the emergence of craft organisations from fraternities is perhaps irrelevant. If we accept that people working together develop a collective identity, it may seem unnecessary to seek priority for one form of such identity against another, especially since the real aims of various groups might not be overtly expressed. The suspicion of ecclesiastical and lay authorities about religious fraternities in the thirteenth century has already been mentioned. But even when fraternities or gilds became acceptable again in the fourteenth century, there were some which were still regarded as subversive. As is well known from the history of both French and English towns, the possibility for journeymen, even long after the term of their apprenticeship was finished, of becoming masters in charge of their own workshop, was becoming more and more restricted. They therefore began to organise in order to maintain reasonable wages and hours of work. In London, they began by meeting in taverns and were denounced for setting up 'covins'. Eventually, as also in Paris, they began to organise as fraternities, devoted to a patron saint and located in a particular parish church. At this period, and especially after the Black Death, organisations of rebellious journeymen were suspected by their employers and by the municipal authorities.[38] In 1441, the mayor and aldermen of London declared that there were too many fraternities meeting under the pretence of piety for scandalous purposes. This was echoed at Norwich in 1443 where the city authorities complained to the bishop of Norwich and to the earl of Suffolk about too many brotherhoods. It may be that in earlier centuries, municipal authorities had similar attitudes towards associations of master craftsmen.[39]

[37] M. de Bouard, 'De la confrérie pieuse au métier organisé: la fraternité des fères de Caen (fin du XIIe siècle)'; P. Leguay, *Un réseau urbain au moyen âge*, p. 34; P. Desportes, *Reims et les Rémois*, Part 3, chapter 26; L. Stouff, *Arles à la fin du moyen âge*, chapter 4, p. 300; A. Rigaudière, *St Flour. Ville d'Auvergne au bas moyen âge: étude d'histoire administrative et financière*, I, chapter 2, pp. 180 ff.
[38] See below for further detail, pp. 145–9.
[39] See Unwin, *Gilds*, chapter 9. Also W. Hudson and J.C. Tingey, *Records of the City of Norwich*, I, p. 114. This is to be seen in the context of the 'Gladman Insurrection' and the suspension of the city's liberties.

It has been suggested that the early craft organisations were independent of municipal authority. Lipson's traditional account of medieval English gilds states that they were voluntary organisations before being subject to municipal control. Platt thinks that the relationship between borough government and craft gilds was co-operative, not coercive. Chevalier, believing that the craft corporations emerged from the fraternities, assumes that they sought the approval of the state rather than having it imposed upon them. De Bouard suggests that it was the relative weakness of the mercantile *haute bourgeoisie* in Caen which allowed autonomous craft organisations to develop in the twelfth century.[40] But as we have seen, craft organisations in most towns did not develop before the fourteenth century, so that the craftsmen who eventually became members must have been controlled directly by the municipal powers, whether royal, feudal or mercantile – unless we make the unlikely assumption that they were entirely free to organise themselves.

Gouron's broad study of the regulation of the crafts in the towns of Languedoc, confirmed by the more detailed local studies of Wolff, makes clear that the urban crafts were subject, first to seigneurial, then to consular, control before they developed any corporate identity. Even then, regulations were imposed from above, by royal officials in the fourteenth century following the previous examples of the consular governments and the feudal lords. By the fifteenth century, the masters of the crafts were performing a policing function for the authorities.[41] And whatever peculiarities there might be about the towns of Languedoc, the craft corporation as a subordinated organ for municipal control, whether effective or not, is to be found in towns of varying sizes and functions all over France, from the small Norman cloth-manufacturing town of Montivilliers to the episcopal city of Metz in Lorraine. The same is true of most English towns. When, as in most royal boroughs, the gild merchant became, in effect, the governing body of the town, mercantile interests inevitably predominated. Merchants had a special interest in controlling the craftsmen, their interest being as consumers when the craftsmen were producing for the local market,

---

[40] E. Lipson, *Economic History of England*, I, p. 384; C. Platt, *The English Medieval Town*, p. 87; Chevalier, *Bonnes villes*, chapter 3, ii, p. 82?; de Bouard, 'De la confrérie'.

[41] Gouron, *La règlementation*; P. Wolff, *Commerce et marchands de Toulouse 1350–1450*, p. 21; Wolff, *Regards sur le midi médiéval*.

and as entrepreneurs if they were producing for a long-distance market (textiles, for instance) when the merchants would be the middlemen.

In the towns with a structured system of craft organisations – often wrongly assumed to be typical – as well as in those which were less well structured or entirely lacking in such organisations, the artisan and shopkeeper population was closely controlled by the municipal authorities. Such authority could be seigneurial or royal. It could also be mercantile, exercised through such ruling institutions as communes or consulates in France, and councils emerging from the gilds merchant in England. In the twelfth and thirteenth centuries in both countries, relatively autonomous rule by councils with predominantly mercantile interests became more and more common. But there were interesting differences, in spite of so many similarities between French and English towns, even before the domination of French town governments by royal officials which we see beginning in the late fourteenth century. The earlier differences have much to do with the relative scarcity of towns under private feudal lordship in England, where the great majority of towns were royal boroughs and where the king's authority was delegated to the mercantile borough councils. It was these councils, therefore, which controlled the craft organisations. Analogous controls were certainly not lacking in French towns, but the authority of individual lords over ,craft organisations, quite scarce in England, was fairly well spread.

As we have already seen, in Paris a number of crafts were enfeoffed to territorial lords, such as the abbeys of St Germain, St Victor, and so on; to the royal provost; and to various officials of the royal household, such as the *panetier*, the chamberlain, the constable, and the marshal. These masters of the crafts profited from entrance fees and jurisdictional fines. At Metz, in the twelfth century, some ten crafts paid dues to the bishop and his officials. In the thirteenth century, when they became *francs métiers*, they were put under the direction of a master, an episcopal fief-holder, who was usually drawn from the patrician elite. At Amiens, five crafts at the end of the twelfth century were paying dues to the bishop. At Toul, masters of most of the crafts were appointed by the bishop or the cathedral chapter. At Besançon, the archbishop drew feudal dues, such as sales taxes, from a number of crafts, some of which he sub-enfeoffed to the abbeys of St Paul and St Vincent. The count of Maine enfeoffed crafts to various lords, such as the cutlers and other metal workers to the lord of La Fresnie in Le Mans. The mercers of Chartres paid 50 livres a year to their count.[42]

It was not, however, simply the existence of feudal jurisdictions within towns and suburbs; nor the occasional enfeoffment of crafts to lords; nor even the total control of towns by dukes, counts, bishops or abbot, which oblige us to accept the medieval town as part of feudal society rather than as an antagonistic element within it. Within the monarchies, where the public authority was feudal, towns without feudal lords, whether or not we accept the concept of their being *seigneuries collectives*, were nevertheless entirely parts of the feudal social formation.[43] Urban social, economic and political structures in which the household unit of production was subordinated to elites, whether 'patrician' or mercantile – or both – were closely linked with the feudal monarchies and landed aristocracies. The hierarchical structures of town and country, even though not identical, were part of a single system.

We must not retain too simplified an image of artisan production in the medieval towns. It seems likely that many artisan households were multi-occupational rather than obeying the 'one man, one trade' ethos, as we have seen in the case of Berre. This is not so much a question of the well-known possession by artisans of small cultivated plots or vineyards, as of the widespread involvement of artisan households in the victualling trades. York artisan families were involved in the retail fish trade; in most English towns, brewing and the retail selling of ale was an important activity additional to the other crafts,[44] as was wine-making and its sale in those French towns which were in wine-producing regions, such as Provence, Languedoc, the Bordelais, Alsace, the Ile de France and southern Brittany. The evidence for ale-brewing comes mainly from prosecutions of those accused of breaking the Assize of Ale by overcharging; using incorrect measures; or selling a sub-standard product. So many brewers or brewstresses were prosecuted without the precise nature of the offence being specified that the fine they paid seems, in practice, to have been simply a licence fee. When

---

[42] J. Schneider, *La ville de Metz aux XIIIe et XIVe siècles* (craft organisations); Schneider, 'Note sur l'organisation des métiers à Toul au moyen âge'; R. Fiétier, *La cité de Besançon*, part 2, chapter 1, a; Bouton, *Le Maine*, chapter 8, pp. 537 ff.; A. Chédeville, *Chartres et ses campagnes XIe–XIIIe siècles*, Part 3, chapter 2.

[43] See Petit-Dutaillis' critique of Luchaire in *Les communes françaises*, p. 114 ff.

[44] Swanson, 'The Illusion of Economic Structure'; Hilton, 'Pain et cervoise dans les villes anglaises au moyen âge' in *L'approvisionnement des villes*.

names are given, it might be possible to link the brewer with an artisan household whose primary occupation might be deducible from other evidence. This evidence is by no means always available. All we know, therefore, is that brewing was a very widespread secondary occupation.

Brewing and wine-making as secondary occupations lead us to consider another important question. In large and medium-sized towns there must have been a high demand for foodstuffs, whether processed or not. It is assumed that the provision of grain, vegetables, poultry, dairy produce and so on, must have come through various channels of supply. There were certainly peasants who brought their products to small-town – and perhaps even larger-town – markets, most frequently, perhaps, the women of the family. However, it seems that most of the provisioning of urban markets was done by intermediaries, such as cornmongers, who brought the product either direct from the producer, or from village or small-town markets before bringing it to the bigger towns.[45] There were also retail traders in victuals in towns who performed an important distributory function. These, too, may very well have been female members of households which had other occupations, and who frequently acted illegally in by-passing the official market. They illustrate again that artisan households were multi-occupational. If we examine the urban court records where such traders in victuals were presented, the numerical importance of these victuallers is striking. The records also confirm that there must have been a very considerable quantity of victuals going for sale. Unfortunately, the fact that so much of the evidence comes from court prosecutions makes quantification impossible, and the family background of the offenders hardly ever traceable.

It is not surprising that urban rulers were so concerned to control the (mainly) retail trade in foodstuffs. High food prices would not only provoke lower-class discontent, but, in the long run, increase the cost of labour and of craft-produced commodities. Consequently, the presentment and punishment of 'forestallers', that is, people who bought from those coming from outside before they got to the market, and of 'regrators', that is, people who sold retail outside official markets, is not only much to the fore in the court records, but punishments were very severe.

[45] Hilton, *The English Peasantry*, chapter 5; for peasant women at the markets see Hilton, 'Women Traders in Medieval England' in *Class Conflict and the Crisis of Feudalism*.

In London, as one would expect, forestallers and regrators were numerous, given the vast demand for foodstuffs. They were therefore frequently prosecuted. For example, in 1306, a woman was found guilty of forestalling hens and capons at Southwark, outside the city. She was first imprisoned and then fined 40d. In the same year, eleven named persons referred to as poulterers were arrested by the sheriff for forestalling pigeons, hens, capons, pullets, eggs and cheeses in their own lodgings, as well as meeting outsiders on their way to the city. They were imprisoned. Presentments of this sort were repeated. In 1338, two female hucksters and six men, one a cornmonger, were accused of forestalling the corn market. All except one of the women were imprisoned until paying a fine. In 1372, a man acknowledged forestalling 3,000 eggs in order to raise the price; they were forfeited and sold officially for a lower price. In 1422, in Queenehythe ward, a number of persons were presented for buying up fish, cheese, chickens and other victuals from boats, secretly, in the evening, not only causing shortage but keeping the fish until it stank. These are some examples of frequent London presentments, which included regular prosecutions of brewers for selling by illicit measures and above the fixed price, not to speak of bakers for breaking the Assize of Bread.[46]

The late-fourteenth-century leet presentments at Norwich are full of prosecutions against forestallers buying grain and other victuals, such as fish and poultry, before they came to the official market. Apart from pushing up prices, the forestallers were also charged with depriving the city bailiffs of toll revenue.[47] The same preoccupation with the price of victuals appears in the court records of that other major cloth producing town, Coventry. The Justices of the Peace for Coventry in the 1370s, in addition to applying the laws against high wages, were also punishing fish and poultry retailers and innkeepers who sold grain at excessive prices; in fact, much the same sort of offences which were being dealt with in the city court leet later on. For example, in 1428, hucksters were not allowed to buy victuals for re-sale until 11 a.m., that is, after the market was open to local purchasers. In 1431, bakers were forbidden to sell

---

[46] A.H. Thomas, ed., *Calendar of Early Mayor's Court Rolls of the City of London, 1298–1307*, pp. 234, 242; Thomas, ed., *Calendar of Plea and Memoranda Rolls of the City of London, 1323–1364*, p. 166; *ibid., 1364–1381*, p. 139; *ibid., 1413–1437*, pp. 115 ff.

[47] Hudson, ed., *Leet Jurisdiction in the City of Norwich*, Leet Roll of 16 Edward I (1287–8).

bread to hucksters who would then re-sell retail. In 1448, instructions were given to poulterers that they should only sell in a restricted (and presumably supervised) place near the Priory gate. In 1473, prices were fixed for horse-bread.[48]

The courts of smaller towns were also much concerned with any activity which would put up food prices and deprive the town authorities of toll revenue. At Colchester in the fourteenth century, the court records are almost dominated by prosecutions against – often female – members of local households forestalling corn, poultry, cheese and fish, thus pushing up prices, as well as selling ale and wine above legal price levels. The preoccupation with the evasion of the market, where prices were controlled, is very widespread. Even in the small town of Henley-on-Thames, an order was made in 1472 that no one was to receive any grain on market day unless it was first placed on the market. This order was subsequently repeated and may well have been issued previously, before the records begin.[49] All these prosecutions of victuallers provide further evidence of, at least, dual occupations in individual households – not to speak of emphasising the importance of the trade in foodstuffs.

There was, of course, a considerable preoccupation with the trade in foodstuffs in French towns. A feature there which was less important in English towns was the direct supply from cultivated areas immediately outside the town walls. This was especially the case with wine. Although at Toulouse, in 1405, twenty-six per cent of the municipal income came from the tax on retail sales of wine, mostly that supplied to taverns from such relatively distant areas as the Tarn valley, much of what was consumed came from the citizens' own vineyards. The area under vines in the Toulouse *banlieue* had diminished somewhat by the early fifteenth century, but in 1335, vines occupied sixty per cent of the area.[50] Vineyards also predominated around Arles in Provence, mainly exploited by the town's inhabitants for their own use. Many families owned land in

---

[48] E.G. Kimball, ed., *Rolls of the Warwickshire and Coventry Sessions of the Peace, 1377–1397*; M.D. Harris, ed., *The Coventry Leet Book*, pp. 115, 139, 233, 385.

[49] W.G. Benham and I.H. Jeayes, eds., *Court Rolls of the Borough of Colchester, I, 1310–1352*; P.M. Briers, ed., *Henley Borough Records: Assembly Books I–IV, 1395–1543*.

[50] Wolff, 'L'approvisionnement des villes en France au moyen âge' in *L'approvisionnement des villes*, p. 23, note 79; Wolff, *Commerce et marchands de Toulouse 1350–1450*, p. 190.

the urban periphery, and eighty per cent of the urban families' properties which were recorded included vineyards.[51] The considerable number of vineyards around Aix-en-Provence were simply producing wine for the households who owned them.[52] Wine consumption at Tours was about 170 litres a head per annum and was mainly produced by urban vineyard owners, many of whom (especially the bigger proprietors) sold retail as well as drinking their own product. Périgueux was another town surrounded by small vineyards, many of which were owned by artisans who considered wine to be an essential part of their diet. As far north as Brittany, urban vineyards supplied the inhabitants of the towns. These people were big drinkers (*gros buveurs*) – 120 litres a head per annum in late medieval Nantes. Nantes was not unique. Rennes, Guérande, Vannes, Quimper and Redon also had vineyards in their immediate vicinity – all well away from the Loire valley.[53]

Even though small vineyards on the outskirts of French towns, often owned by artisans as well as by richer townspeople, seem to have dominated the extra-mural cultivated areas, there were also small vegetable gardens. These again provided direct access to foodstuffs for their owners, even though surpluses might have been sold, as in the case of wine. Leeks, beans, cabbage and other vegetables were grown in gardens in the suburbs of Périgueux. Suburban gardens at Aix-en-Provence produced cabbage, onions, garlic, spinach and so on, primarily for home supply, but to some extent for retail sale. Around Arles, there were vegetable gardens and many small proprietors concentrated on fruit, both cultivated mainly for household consumption, though there was some gardening for local sales, including by women.[54]

French urban authorities were as much concerned as their English counterparts with the victualling of their towns and had to control imports of grain, for instance, which was not grown in important quantities on suburban arable plots. The processes of control would, of course, be reflected in the proceedings of the urban courts, which seem not to have survived as well as those of English borough courts. Regulations, especially concerning grain imports, have been

---

[51] Stouff, *Arles*, p. 390.   [52] Coulet, 'Le mouvement', pp. 153–60.

[53] Chevalier, *Tours*, pp. 159–60; Higounet-Nadal, *Périgueux*, p. 100; J.P. Leguay, 'Le rôle de la zone péri-urbaine dans l'approvisionnement des villes armoricaines au moyen âge', p. 195.

[54] Higounet-Nadal, *Périgueux*, pp. 94–9; Coulet, 'Le mouvement', pp. 124 ff.; Stouff, *Arles*, chapter 6.

summarised by P. Wolff. More detail is given for individual towns, such as Amiens; Tarascon, where ninety-six per cent of regulations concerning imports and exports between 1370 and 1400 were concerned with victuals; Marseilles, where, from the mid-thirteenth century onwards, the city authorities used various methods for keeping down grain prices.[55] And, as one would expect, apart from controlling grain prices, elaborate regulations concerning the baking and selling of bread matched those of England under The Assize of Bread. This is well illustrated in F. Desportes' study of bread in a number of Norman towns at the end of the middle ages.[56]

There was a noticeable difference in the supply of victuals to French and to English towns. Although English urban artisans certainly owned small garden plots both within and outside the towns, there seems to have been a much higher proportion of vegetables and wine acquired direct by French urban households without going through the market. However, the evidence quoted concerning the provision of foodstuffs in the towns of both countries emphasises an important aspect of the multi-occupational character of artisan households. It also demonstrates how important was the supply of victuals as an aspect of the urban economies. Might it not be argued that the role of the craftsman's wife as a 'huckster' of essential victuals was as important as, although different from, the work of the craftsman?

Other evidence exists which undermines the 'one man, one trade' image. Quarrels in the fourteenth century between closely allied crafts, and the amalgamation of craft organisations in the fifteenth century suggest that the production of different commodities for which the tools and equipment were similar would be undertaken in the same workshop. In London, in the fourteenth century, potters made spurs and candlesticks as well as brass pots. The fifteenth-century integration of glovers, pursers, whittawyers and pouch-makers with the leather seller suggests that there had previously been a considerable overlap of the manufacturing artisans. Prohibitions against craftsmen combining weaving and fulling, or cordwainers engaging in currying in late-medieval Colchester, suggest that (as so often in the case of prohibitions) this was in fact happening. In York, fullers sheared as well as fulled lower-quality cloth,

---

[55] *Flaran 5*; E. Maugis, *Recherches*, p. 440 ff.; Hébert, *Tarascon au XIVe et XVe siècle*, pp. 161 ff.; Zarb, *Histoire d'une autonomie communale*, chapter 6.

[56] F. Desportes, 'Le pain en Normandie à la fin du moyen âge'.

cordwainers tanned, potters were also bellfounders and braziers. Spinning, like brewing, was a well known additional occupation in a variety of artisan households.[57]

The fluidity of craft production, and the probability that gilds and gild regulations were neither so effective nor so widespread as was once thought, need not alter our perception of the urban household unit of production as being entirely compatible with the feudal social formation. There was, however, a late medieval development which might call into question this suggested compatibility, namely the mobilisation of artisan production on a large scale in order to produce a big volume of goods for a wide market. To what extent did this transform medieval urban economic and social structures?

The principal commodities produced for an international market were textiles, especially high quality woollens, so we will take the cloth trade as an example of large-scale production. George Unwin demonstrated many years ago that the 'domestic' or 'putting out' system, which is often associated with rural industry, was, in fact, already to be found in fourteenth- and fifteenth-century towns.[58] It not only involved the merchant providing the raw material for the artisan workshop and selling the finished product – a well-known phenomenon in Flemish and Italian cloth-producing terms – but a curious transformation of the organisation of artisan labour. In London, especially, the journeymen were used as piece workers (paid by the piece rather than by the day or week) and eventually did much of the work in their own homes rather than in the master's workshop. Eventually, poor masters and journeymen became indistinguishable.

Many English and French towns specialised in cloth production and made large quantities far beyond local or regional needs. This was already well under way in the late twelfth or thirteenth centuries in England, in Beverley, Lincoln, Stamford, Northampton, York, Winchester and Leicester. By the end of the fourteenth century, there was a much greater volume of production in towns such as Coventry, Salisbury, Bristol and London. Much of this cloth was

---

[57] Unwin, *Gilds*, pp. 166–8; Veale, 'Craftsmen and the Economy of London in the Fourteenth Century' in Hollaender and Kellaway, eds., *Studies in London History*; R.H. Britnell, *Growth and Decline of Colchester 1300–1525*, chapter 20; Swanson, *Craftsmen and Industry*, pp. 37, 55 ff., 96–100, 159 ff., 190–1, 471 ff.

[58] Unwin, *Industrial Organisations in the Sixteenth and Seventeenth Centuries*, Parts 1 and 2 – a surprisingly neglected book, considering its insights in the introductory chapters on the fourteenth and fifteenth centuries. See also F. Consitt, *The London Weavers' Company. I. Twelfth to Close of Sixteenth Century*.

exported overseas, some 40–50,000 pieces from a dozen ports.[59] Leaving French Flanders on one side, French cloth production may have seemed less geared for export, but we must bear in mind, not only that much was exported, but also that France was three times the size of England, thus providing a considerable 'home' demand. Chartres, which at the end of the thirteenth century was producing mainly for a regional market, with some sales at the big fairs, made about 3,600 woollen and 2,900 linen cloths a year. Provins, the Champagne fair town, was at the same period producing up to 50,000 cloths a year and Troyes, another fair town, made 48,000 linens a year. Reims, also a major linen-producing town in the twelfth century, was, by the thirteenth century, exporting its linens to the Levant, England and Scandinavia. Norman towns, such as Rouen, Louviers and Montivilliers were selling their cloths in the big French fairs, in Languedoc and in Italy. Languedoc itself was an urban cloth-producing area, though mainly of lower-quality stuffs. As well as in the bigger towns, such as Toulouse, Carcassonne, Béziers and Montpellier, cloth was being produced in the seventy or so smaller centres to which we have already referred. Much of this cloth was sold all over southern France and Provence, and also in Spain and other Mediterranean countries.[60]

The manufacture of large quantities of marketable textiles was done in the family-based artisan workshops. What impact did the manufacture for export have on an industrial structure which seems to have been so well integrated with the overall structures of the feudal social formation? Eventually, there were important developments, manifested in the proto-industrialisation of the early modern period, most marked in England and outside the old manufacturing centres. But the putting out system, in which the master craftsmen neither bought his own raw materials nor sold the finished product to the consumer, was also inevitable in the medieval towns producing for a wide market. Nevertheless, this process does not seem to have had any significant impact on the basic industrial structure.

There were very many different channels used by merchants for

---

[59] A.R. Bridbury, *Medieval Clothmaking: an Economic Survey*; Carus-Wilson and O. Coleman, *England's Export Trade 1275–1547* (especially cloth export figures, pp. 75 ff.).

[60] Chédeville, *Chartres*, Part 3, chapter 2; E. Chapin, *Les villes de foire de Champagne des origines au début du XIVe siècle*, chapter 4; Desportes, *Reims*, pp. 93–103; M. Mollat, 'La draperie normande, moyen âge–XIVe siècle'; Wolff, see note 18, chapter 2, above.

the disposal of the product for far-off markets, ranging from the placing of the commodities at intermediate fairs and markets to the highly organised shipping direct to the final destination. This is, of course, an important aspect of economic history which is not my concern. What has been important for our examination of the place of the town in feudal society is whether the nature of the urban ruling class was in any way transformed by involvement in the placing of craft-manufactured commodities on an international market. It would seem that there would, as yet, be no move by mercantile urban elites to become industrial capitalists, just as there was no transformation of the household unit of craft production into anything approaching a factory system.

4. *Urban rulers*

The social composition of the urban ruling classes in England and France and their relationship with the feudal landowning interest is a fundamental issue. The answer, or rather answers, to this problem are by no means simple but of great importance, if we are to consider, not only the origins, but also the later history of the urban patriciate.

Our consideration of the place of urban craft production within feudalism has tended to stress the mercantile interest in controlling it. In so far as the manufacturing crafts were producing for so wide a market that they did not have contact with the ultimate consumer, the role of the merchant middleman would be crucial economically and would (ideally, from the point of view of the merchant) best be enforceable in political terms by a mercantile ruling group. Ruling elites which were primarily mercantile emerged in some towns, especially with the development of international trade in luxury or long-distance commodities from the twelfth century. But in fact, the social composition of urban ruling elites, or 'patricians' was never homogeneous and often changed over time.

As we have seen, in the early middle ages, the towns which best survived the post-Roman chaos tended to be administrative centres rather than focal points for what was left of long-distance trade, though they had an urban function as local market centres. The first survivals were episcopal cities, soon becoming centres also of lay powers representing (theoretically, at any rate) the royal or imperial rulers. These were earls and royal reeves in Anglo-Saxon England, and counts in Carolingian and post-Carolingian France. By the tenth century, most English cathedral cities were under royal control, though the bishops and cathedral chapters had property, independence and (probably) some jurisdictional powers. In France, before the appearance of any consular or communal institutions representing the townspeople, urban affairs seem to have been dominated by bishops and their cathedral chapters, sometimes by wealthy monasteries, sometimes by feudal lay powers.

For the most part, the lay powers in France were not subordinated to the Capetian monarchy. In Languedoc, the most powerful lay lords were the counts of Toulouse, or the viscounts under their lordship. Albi was first under the direct control of the counts until the tenth century and then under their vassals, the Trencavel viscounts, who, until the early thirteenth century, shared the market profits and the urban jurisdiction with the bishop. Cahors was another episcopal city, where the bishops and the counts of Toulouse shared power until, in 1213, the bishop was made count of Cahors and lord of the city. Going north from Languedoc, at Limoges, the episcopal city and the people of the castle of Puy St Martial were at odds from the twelfth century onwards. The lord of the castle was the viscount of Limousin until he sold it in 1162 to the abbot of Cluny. Here, as one might expect, feudal politics became complicated by the Capetian–Plantagenet conflict, as they were at Saintes, another episcopal city at the junction of the Plantagenet and Capetian domains. At Vienne, in the Rhone valley, where the overlord was the Holy Roman Emperor, the bishop and the cathedral chapter were given the county and all regalian rights in the city and the castle of Pipet, in 1023. In 1155, the emperor, Frederick Barbarossa, gave the county to the Dauphin of the Viennois, even though the Dauphin was the archbishop's vassal. Nevertheless, the archbishops continued to be very powerful lords in the city in the twelfth and thirteenth centuries.[1]

Our knowledge of the early history of French towns tends to be dominated by the concerns of the feudal nobility, lay and ecclesiastical. This may be due to a bias of the documentation. When, then, does an urban patriciate emerge which can be described in terms of its social origins and functions?

It is an established truism that a special feature of the early consulates in southern France was that they were composed in part, perhaps the larger part, of an urban knightly class whose fortunes were largely in landed property, rural as well as urban, and who were often officials (*ministeriales*) of the counts, viscounts, archbishops and bishops. According to Timbal, consulates were as if collective

[1] F. Lot, *Recherches sur la population et la superficie des cités remontant à la période gallo-romaine*, Part 1 (Vienne), Part 2 (Albi, Cahors, Limoges, Saintes).

vassals of feudal lords; before the twelfth century, the consuls were aristocratic. Only in the thirteenth century were merchants making their entry, and they too were landowners as well as traders. This description is confirmed by Sautel and by Poly. Mundy's description of the twelfth-century Toulouse emphasises that the city had a mainly landowning patriciate. P. Wolff also emphasises the landed property economic base of the early Toulouse ruling group. He insists on the importance of the urban and rural real property element in their fortunes as late as the fourteenth century, together with money lending.[2]

This pattern was fairly general throughout Languedoc and seems to have been much the same in Provence. At Arles in the middle of the twelfth century, the consuls were chosen by the archbishop from a group of about a dozen knightly families, though here again the thirteenth century saw the entry of a mercantile element – who also owned much urban property as well as some rural land. Similarly, at Tarascon, the twelfth-century consulate was composed of knights, though by the thirteenth century, nobles and the mercantile bourgeoisie shared equally. The merchants nevertheless had rural property, principally arable, contrasting with the nobles who tended to concentrate on woodland and meadow.[3]

The feudal and landowning character of the early southern patriciates was not peculiar to the south of France. The old thesis that merchants, as the initiators of the eleventh to twelfth-centuries urban revival, dominated the urban scene was undermined, as we have mentioned, by, among others, Lestocquoy. He showed that Arras' twelfth-century patricians were landowners drawn from the entourages of counts of Flanders and of the abbey of St Vaast, moving later into money lending and trade. The bourgeois patrician families of Metz in the twelfth century were mainly real property owners and episcopal officials. The Reims upper bourgeoisie in the twelfth century were real property owners as well as engaged in trade and finance. They were organised in lineages and coexisted with the knights of the episcopal *cité*, who, in the thirteenth century, began to move into the countryside. The bourgeois of Mâcon in the twelfth century were mainly comital officials – and money lenders. The real

---

[2] P.-C. Timbal, 'Les villes de consulat dans le midi de la France'; J.P. Poly, *La Provence et la société féodale 870–1166*, Part 2, chapter 3; G. Sautel, 'Les villes du midi méditerrannéen au moyen âge'; J.H. Mundy, *Liberty and Political Power in Toulouse*, pp. 10–12, 44, 67–8; P. Wolff, *Histoire de Toulouse*, pp. 70 ff., 102, 132. However, for one important exception, Montpellier, see pp. 96–7.

[3] L. Stouff, *Arles*, Part 2, chapter 2, pp. 156–63; M. Hébert, *Tarascon*, pp. 125–31.

power in Chartres was held by the count and by ecclesiastics in their enclaves. The bourgeoisie appeared mainly as officials of the count, then the king, and of the bishop. Their wealth was mainly in real property.[4]

This emphasis on the ministerial function and real property interests of the early bourgeoisie, which we see from studies of individual towns, is generally confirmed for northern and western towns by Chédeville in the *Histoire de la France urbaine*.[5] But there were, as mentioned, a few towns in which a commercial bourgeoisie developed early. Montpellier, in Languedoc, was, as we shall see, an example unique in the region and very early. There were others further north, especially in, and near to, French Flanders. At Amiens, the bourgeoisie very early got a monopoly of the trade in woad, granted by Philip Augustus to the mayor and commune in 1185. The oligarchic families who were ruling Lille by the thirteenth century traded in any commodities – wool, cloth, grain and wine – as well as being money lenders. The burgesses of St Omer, formed under the aegis of the abbey of St Bertin, seem already to have had a *gilda mercatoria* by the end of the eleventh century, with its own *gildhalla*.[6]

The landed interests of the early patricians are very well documented, and are to be expected in a group which had close ties, as agents, retainers and officials, to the great feudal landowners, especially the episcopal and monastic, who were so powerful in the older cities. It seems to be agreed that they did, in fact, take up commercial activities from the thirteenth century onwards, and may have had some links with lesser merchants engaged in local and regional trade. It is also to be noticed that the early bourgeoisie were money lenders too. This may have been encouraged by their close links with the landed aristocracy, whose mode of existence led them into debt. Also, one of the most important tasks of agents of the greater feudal powers in their cities was to act as mint masters and, consequently, as money changers, activities closely linked with

---

[4] J. Lestocquoy, *Les dynasties*, chapter 1; J. Schneider, *La ville de Metz*, section 2; P. Desportes, *Reims*, pp. 73–91, 149–54; G. Duby, *La société aux XIe et XIIIe siècles dans la région mâconnaise*, pp. 468–9; A. Chédeville, *Chartres*, Part 2, chapter 3.   [5] Duby, ed., *Histoire de la France urbaine*, II, pp. 134–9.

[6] E. Maugis, *Recherches sur la transformation du régime politique et social de la ville d'Amiens des origines de la commune à la fin du XVIe siècle*, pp. 15–16; L. Trénard, ed., *Histoire d'une métropole: Lille, Roubaix, Tourcoing*, pp. 111–24; G. Espinas, *Les origines du capitalisme III: deux fondations de villes dans l'Artois et la Flandre française. St Omer, Lannoy du Nord*, pp. 60 ff.

money lending. This led to an additional route to landownership, namely, the acquisition of landed property which had been used as security for loans and which fell into the hands of the lender when the debtor was unable to repay his or her debts.

It might well be asked, if the early urban bourgeoisie consisted of a narrow group of ruling families whose interests were mainly in landed property and money lending, where were most of the merchants? Of course they existed, but they were not yet politically prominent in most French towns outside Flanders until the thirteenth century. This was when urban expansion, with the growth of regional and long-distance trade, not only increased mercantile wealth but also produced a social fusion between the earlier patricians and the rich merchants.

Studies of English towns suggest a somewhat different social composition of the early ruling elites compared with many French towns. In particular, although the early English bourgeoisie often had interests in real property, and might be agents of feudal landowners, they seem to have had more mercantile interests than their French opposite numbers. This should not, however, be taken as a general rule. The small ruling group in London before the end of the twelfth century was composed of families mainly with landed interests, though moving into commerce by the end of the century, especially the provisioning of the royal household with wine. They were also in royal service and were often money lenders. F. W. Maitland, in *Township and Borough*, suggested that the early urban patriciates might, as ward aldermen, have been of military origin, like 'lawmen' in Danelaw towns. Although he questioned whether these patricians were arable landowners, a landed interest seems likely. Furthermore, Maitland was drawing conclusions from a study mainly of Cambridge, and H. M. Cam later confirmed the strong rural property interests of the burgesses.[7]

In Lincoln, the 'lawmen', that is, the late eleventh-century urban elite, were urban and rural landowners and money lenders. But mercantile interests soon predominated. What, in fact, we see in the English towns is a varying interest by a primarily mercantile ruling class in real property investment, without this predominating over

---

[7] S. Reynolds, 'The Rulers of London in the Twelfth Century'; C. Brooke and G. Keir, *London*, pp. 282–4; G. Williams, *Medieval London*, pp. 63, 65; F.W. Maitland, *Township and Borough*, pp. 49–50; H.M. Cam, 'The Early Burgesses of Cambridge in Relation to the Surrounding Countryside' in Cam, *Liberties and Communities in Medieval England*.

their trading concerns. There were occasional exceptions. It has been suggested that as late as the early fourteenth century, landowners and clerics were more important than merchants in the government of Colchester. The urban elite of Durham was drawn from families in lay and clerical administration, linked especially with the cathedral chapter. York's ruling class, as late as the mid-fourteenth century, was primarily a landowning patriciate. But in most towns, the merchants held power from the twelfth century onwards.[8]

The explanation for this merchant power may be political as much as economic. Owing to the fact that most of the bigger English towns were under the direct rule of the crown rather than of feudal lay or ecclesiastical lords, the 'private' feudal interests, though certainly not absent, were not so widely privileged in urban government as in France. The king's government – and it must be said, one or two feudal lords – granted (or sold) charters of privilege to towns in which an existing, though unofficial, gild merchant was recognised – or one was created by the charter.[9]

The essence of belonging to the gild merchant, for its members, was the right to buy and sell in the borough market without paying any toll or custom. It was a privilege which could also be held, should there happen to be no gild merchant, by those with burgess status, or as it was also called, 'the freedom of the borough'. It was restricted to those who bought the freedom or who achieved it by other means, such as being admitted into a recognised craft organisation, which could be even more costly. Consequently, big towns had populations most of whose members were not 'free' – two thirds, for example in late-thirteenth-century London, a half in Oxford and more than three quarters in Exeter.[10] The gild merchant was, however, more than an aggregate of those possessing the freedom of the borough for trading purposes. As the term 'gild' implies, it was an organisation representing a sectional interest – the interest of the mercantile elite. When urban franchises included a measure of self-government, the distinction between the ruling body

[8] J.W.F. Hill, *Medieval Lincoln*, pp. 39–40; R.H. Britnell, *Growth and Decline of Colchester 1300–1525*, chapter 13; R.B. Dobson, 'Cathedral Chapters and Cathedral Cities'; E. Miller, 'Medieval York'.

[9] The most useful source of information on the gild merchant is still C. Gross, *The Gild Merchant*.

[10] A.H. Thomas, ed., *Calendar of Plea and Memoranda Rolls of the City of London 1323–1437*, Introduction to vol. II. H.E. Salter, *Medieval Oxford*; M. Kowaleski, 'The Commercial Dominance of a Provincial Oligarchy: Exeter in the Late Fourteenth Century'.

specified in the grant and the ruling body of the gild merchant was often obscure, and sometimes the gild merchant specifically became the governing body.

The well-known model charter of 1200 granted to the borough of Ipswich included, early in the listing of the various privileges, that the burgesses should have their gild merchant. When the undefined 'common council' of the town chose the governing officials – two reeves, four coroners and twelve chief 'portmen' – it also chose the alderman or head of the gild merchant, together with four advisers. The alderman chosen was, of course, one of the portmen, as were three of his four associates, the other being one of the coroners. All freemen of the borough were instructed to place themselves in the gild merchant.[11]

The identity of borough and gild merchant was even more obvious in Gloucester's royal charter granted in the same year. It contained a standard set of borough franchises, ranging from the right to plead only in the borough court (with certain traditional exceptions) to freedom from toll throughout the kingdom. But the charter refers in almost every clause not simply to 'our burgesses of Gloucester', but to 'our burgesses of Gloucester of the gild merchant'. The gild merchant was obviously in existence before the borough got its liberties and its elected officials. The borough seal attached to the charter must have been in existence before the grant of the charter. Its inscription was: 'The seal of the burgesses of the gild merchant of Gloucester'.[12]

Gild assemblies were often called 'morning speeches', as at Leicester, and could operate parallel with the borough court, the personnel being virtually identical. In some boroughs it would appear that the gild's 'morning speech' became, in practice, the governing body, as at Andover, a small cloth-making town in Hampshire. The same was true of the much larger port-town of Southampton, probably before the middle of the thirteenth century.[13]

The emphasis has been placed on the role of the royal government in setting the pattern for limited urban autonomy, and in granting or confirming a gild merchant. Most of the bigger towns were royal boroughs. For example, out of the fifteen provincial towns highest

[11] Gross, *The Gild Merchant*, II, pp. 115–123.   [12] *Ibid.*

[13] M. Bateson, *The Records of the Borough of Leicester*, I; Gross, *The Gild Merchant*, pp. 3–11; C. Platt, *Medieval Southampton: the Port and Trading Community, AD 1000–1600*, p. 20.

assessed for the Lay Subsidy of 1334, fourteen were royal and one was seigneurial (Beverley). All of them had gilds merchant by 1500 except for Boston (1545). But it is also worth noting that fourteen royal boroughs out of thirty-five paying aids to the king during the reign of Henry II had no gilds merchant during the middle ages. It could be, therefore, that towns whose merchants had all the advantages attached to the freedom of the borough, or to burgess tenurial status, did not feel the need to set up a gild merchant. Their control of borough government was perhaps complete without it. It seems likely that in the bigger towns the gild merchant had been set up to protect mercantile interests, as at Gloucester, when the town was ruled by royal or feudal officials. It was legitimated by the eventual grant of franchise and self-government, and was accepted by the lord of the town either as the new governing body or as part of it.

It is clear that feudal lords, as well as the king, were prepared to legitimise the gild merchant. Indeed, the earliest known example of a charter which does so is not royal, but that of Robert fitz Hamon (d. 1107) confirmed by William, earl of Gloucester (d. 1173), granted to his men of Burford in Oxfordshire. One can also find confirmation here that the grant of a charter did not necessarily precede the formation of a gild merchant. What the men of Burford got was stated in their charter to be the same gild and customs which the burgesses of Oxford had in their *gilda mercatorum*. The earliest known Oxford charter to mention a gild merchant was a confirmation to the citizens by Henry II of a grant by Henry I. The Oxford gild may than have been unofficially in existence before Henry I's grant.

A charter of 1199 to Oxford allowed the town to pay to the king's exchequer an annual lump sum (*firma burgi*). Before then, the two port reeves had collected the profits of the market, of the mill, the urban rents and so on, which they had to hand over to the royal sheriff. They now presided over the borough court, the portmoot or Husteng, to which only freemen of the borough owed suit – they became freemen by being members of the gild merchant.[14]

Burford was only a small market town, so an early grant of a gild merchant might have been somewhat of an aberration. The town's historian, R. H. Gretton, was convinced that these early privileges were imposed by the lord rather than demanded by the inhabitants.

[14] R.H. Gretton, *Burford Records*; Gross, *The Gild Merchant*, pp. 28–9, 386–7; Salter, *Medieval Oxford*.

This seems likely, given the town's size. The lord may simply have hoped to encourage its development as a market centre, and as such, profitable to him.

There was a much bigger seigneurialised town which acquired recognition of its gild merchant at about the same time. By then, Leicester belonged to the earl of Meulan (between 1107 and 1118) and was to remain a seigneurial borough until the duke of Lancaster became king of England in 1399. Meulan conceded by charter that his merchants of Leicester should have their gild merchant and all the customs as they had held them since the days of William the Conqueror. Another sizeable seigneurial borough was that of Beverley, which was granted its gild merchant (also called the 'hanshus'), by the lord of the town, the archbishop of York, Thurstan (1119–40), a grant which was confirmed by Henry I and specified as being based on the existing privileges of York.[15]

The earl of Chester (1190–1211) recognised the gild merchant of Chester, indicating its previous existence, in his charter, as having been held in the time of his ancestors. The existence of the Bury St Edmunds gild merchant was indirectly acknowledged in the description of an internal dispute between the abbey's cellarer and its sacristan in the 1190s, as reported by the chronicler, Jocelin of Brakelond. A much smaller seigneurial borough, Petersfield (Hampshire) had its gild merchant recognised by its lady, Hawisia, countess of Gloucester, the charter being a confirmation of a grant by her late husband, Earl William (d. 1173).[16]

The gild merchant is, then, found quite early, in seigneurial as well as in royal boroughs, though it is worth noting that only six gilds in seigneurial boroughs were of eleventh- or twelfth-century date, as compared with twenty-three gilds merchant in existence in royal boroughs by 1200. Most of the latter were sizeable towns, such as York and Bristol at the top end of the scale, down to Nottingham and Derby. Some, such as Andover, Helston, Wallingford, Wilton and Bath were quite small. Henry II's charter to Wallingford is worth noting, for it suggests that the privileges, including the gild merchant, went back to the time of Edward the Confessor.[17]

The gild merchant was not an English peculiarity. As we have seen, there was a merchant gild at St Omer in the eleventh century and, as Coornaert has observed, there were others just as early on

[15] Bateson, *The Records*, I, p. 1; Gross, *The Gild Merchant*, pp. 21–3.
[16] *Ibid.*, pp. 40, 29–30, 387; L.C. Jane, trans., *The Chronicle of Jocelin of Brakelond*, p. 159.   [17] Gross, *The Gild Merchant*, p. 244.

trade routes in Flanders, the Low countries and northern Germany. Elsewhere in France they hardly existed, though we should remember the early twelfth-century recognition of the *Marchands de l'eau* in Paris, in effect a merchant gild which came to exercise considerable authority alongside the royal *prévôt*.

The appearance of merchant gilds from the eleventh century onwards in both Flanders and England has led to discussion as to priority. Many English historians are inclined to accept continental (basically Flemish) influence in the formation of the English gilds merchant, with an often unexpressed assumption that this must have been the consequence of French influence following the Norman Conquest. But there were no merchant gilds in Norman towns, and just as it is now suggested that the customs of Breteuil could as well have been influenced from England as vice versa, one might also give priority to English urban merchant gilds. Such speculations are not very helpful. Similar causes, that is, involvement in the Rhineland–Frisian–Scandinavian long-distance trade, may well have produced similar institutions at the early date. What is special about the English situation is the early spread of merchant gilds, and the recognition of their political as well as socio-economic role, as charters of urban autonomy were issued by the Anglo-Norman and Plantagenet kings.

To conclude, we must expect to find an earlier mercantile presence in urban ruling elites in a greater proportion of English as compared with French towns. As we have seen, for example in Arras, the patriciate up to the end of the twelfth century was dominated by feudal landowning elements, very often *ministeriales* of local feudal magnates who were often also overlords of all or part of the town. It was not until the thirteenth century that mercantile interests became important, both because the old landowning lineages moved into commerce and money ending, and because the richer merchant families acquired political prestige.

In many French towns by the thirteenth century, the mercantile interests penetrated, and in some places dominated, the ruling patriciate. One town, in particular, already mentioned, should be further described, even if its mercantile ruling bourgeoisie, from early times, was hardly representative of French towns in general. Montpellier had a population at the beginning of the fourteenth century of about 40,000. It was mostly under the lordship of the kings of Aragon (later of Majorca), with a smaller part (Montpellieret) under the lordship of the bishops of Maguelone. Its position on one of the pilgrim routes to Compostella, and its proximity to the Mediterranean, led to its early development as a commercial centre. It received a charter in 1204 from Peter II, king of Aragon, which established a consulate of unique character, chosen by the mercantile and manual crafts, a development of their previous role in the manning and maintenance of the walls and gates. As one would expect, the consulate was dominated by money changers and merchants, such as drapers, spicers, furriers and grain dealers. But some manual crafts had a voice in the choice of a consul, such as tanners and masons. Even the many peasants (*laboureurs*) who lived in the town were able to choose a consul. There was no provision for consuls chosen by lawyers or clergy. This must be the explanation for the emergence in the early fourteenth century of a faction of well-to-do self-styled *populares* – lawyers and some merchants excluded from the consulate – who used the urban lower classes to support a campaign against taxation ordered by the consulate.[18]

In general, however, the trajectory of ruling urban oligarchies – as far as their social composition was concerned – took different directions in France and England, especially from the middle of the fourteenth century onwards. This is illustrated by the history of the capital cities, Paris and London.

We have briefly indicated above that although the narrow landowning oligarchy of twelfth-century London was still politically dominant in the early thirteenth century, wealthy merchants such as vintners and mercers were emerging, with an important market for their wines and expensive textiles in royal and aristocratic households. By the middle of the thirteenth century, London politics was becoming dominated by gilds which, though sometimes appearing to represent manufacturing interests, were, in fact, controlled by merchants whose main connection with manufacture was in putting out work to subordinated craftsmen. Merchant saddlers put out work to lorimers, painters and joiners; burillers (later drapers) to weavers; skinners to tawyers; and cutlers to sheathers and blademakers.[19]

By the beginning of the fourteenth century, the richest gilds were those of the drapers, the mercers, the grocers, the fishmongers, the skinners and the goldsmiths, all of whom became involved in

---

[18] L.J. Thomas, *Montpellier, ville marchande*; J. Rogozinski, *Power, Caste and Law: Social Conflict in Fourteenth Century Montpellier*.

[19] As demonstrated many years ago by George Unwin in *Gilds and Companies of London*.

lucrative long-distance trade in grain, wool, textiles and so on, whatever the supposedly specialised interests of their gilds. In the second half of the fourteenth century, the illusory nature of apparently specialised craft interests is revealed when we look at the realities behind the pretended opposition between the 'victualling' and 'manufacturing' interests. In fact, drapers and fishmongers and others (such as grocers) were equally involved in wool exports. The support for the draper, John of Northampton (mayor in 1381), by artisan elements was not a genuine class alliance. It was clearly an exploitation by Northampton's party of a fear of high food prices, for which victualling interests might seem responsible, in a political battle between rival merchant capitalist interests.[20]

Rich merchants dominated London politics through their control of the organs of city government in the fifteenth as well as the fourteenth century. This did not mean, of course, that they were indifferent to the acquisition of rural property or even to some social gentrification, but their mercantile interests came first. Studies of two individuals illustrate this theme. Gilbert Maghfeld, a rich ironmonger, in the late fourteenth century dealt in many other commodities than those implied by his gild affiliation. He was involved, among other things, in the export of wool and grain. He also acquired rural property. A more important Londoner, Richard Whittington, came from a Gloucestershire gentry family. He became a wealthy mercer, occupied posts in city government (1384–1419), including that of mayor, exported wool, and not only sold goods to the royal household but also lent money to the king.[21]

In spite of occasional concessions to lesser (and still mercantile) interests in the Common Council, the mayor and aldermen, a narrow elite of the richest merchants, remained firmly in control. As Sylvia Thrupp insists, there was little change in the social basis of city government between the mid-thirteenth century and the end of the fifteenth century – 'The city government had been controlled throughout by a mercantile elite with the acquiescence and assistance of the rank and file of the wholesale merchants.'[22]

Paris was, by the twelfth century, the capital city of the Capetian kings of France, even though only of that France entered from the

[20] See Ruth Bird, *The Turbulent London of Richard II*, an important re-evaluation of Unwin's interpretation; and P. Nightingale, 'Capitalists, Crafts and Constitutional Change in Late Fourteenth-Century London'.

[21] S. L. Thrupp, *The Merchant Class*, pp. 118 ff.; M.K. James, 'Gilbert Maghfeld, a London Merchant of the Fourteenth Century'; C.M. Barron, 'Richard Whittington: the Man and the Myth'.   [22] Thrupp, *The Merchant Class*.

south-west at Orléans.[23] By the mid-thirteenth century, it had become one or Europe's largest cities, with a population of over 60,000, to be more than doubled, as a result of immigration, in the next three quarters of a century. Although it was at a distance from the routes from Italy, by the Rhine, to Flanders and Scandinavia, it was nevertheless on other important trade routes along the Seine and its tributaries, and eastwards towards the Champagne fairs. Until the middle of the fourteenth century, it had an important exporting textile industry, and, even more important, supplied a local market with both luxury and everyday commodities.

The components of the market which made the fortunes of the Parisian merchants were as numerous and complex as those of London – perhaps more so. In the first place, there was the apparatus of royal government, finally settled down there by the mid-thirteenth century, ranging from the royal household (*hôtel du roi*), through the law courts (especially the *parlement*) to such financial offices as the *chambres des comptes*. There were other royal households in Paris, such as that of the queen, with their retainers. Official representatives of provincial and foreign interests should be added, and all this officialdom constituted a considerable demand for commodities. Although there was virtually no Parisian lay nobility, there was an enormous ecclesiastical seigneurial presence. This included the bishop of Paris and the cathedral chapter on the Ile de la Cité, other colleges of secular canons, and a large number of wealthy monastic houses on both the right and left banks of the Seine. All had private jurisdictions and considerable administrative apparatuses – *haute justice* covering the inhabitants of nearly six hundred of the streets of Paris. Furthermore, in addition to the clergy of the thirty-four parishes, the chantry chaplains and the clergy serving the many hospitals, there was a large number of university students, possibly 40,000 by the beginning of the fourteenth century.

It is not surprising that the elite of wealthy mercantile families should emerge in the thirteenth century, members, as we have seen, of the *hanse* of the *marchands de l'eau*, and quite distinct from the manufacturing crafts. They were dealing in luxury commodities such as wine and furs, but also in wool, grain, timber and other essentials. As one would expect, they included money changers and money lenders, lending especially to the crown and aristocracy. The money

---

[23] The volumes in the *Nouvelle histoire de Paris* have superseded many good older works (such as M. Poëte's *Une vie de cité. Paris*). For the following remarks, see Cazelles, *Paris*, and J. Favier, *Paris au XVe siècle*, pp. 372–83.

changers played a particularly important role in the fourteenth century, with the frequent currency changes imposed by the royal government. But this bourgeoisie also early on became much involved with the royal government as farmers of office, of revenues and of mints. They penetrated the royal administration, holding offices in various branches of government, including the treasury, *parlement* and the royal household.

Reform movements attempted to check the bourgeois speculators who profited from their government positions. In the mid-fourteenth century, the reformers were associated with the draper and *prévot des marchands*, Etienne Marcel, assassinated in 1358, a fate which might have been due to the hostility he had aroused among elements of the bourgeoisie. By the early fifteenth century, the Parisian haute bourgeoisie was becoming a class of royal officials rather than of merchants. About eighty per cent of the tax paid by the bourgeoisie in 1421 came from officials of *parlement* and government offices. Money changers paid sixteen per cent, and the drapers most of the rest of the bourgeois contribution. Investment was in urban and rural real property rather than in trade.[24]

The examples of London and Paris are useful in illustrating the contrast between the ruling elites of the two capitals in the late middle ages – entirely mercantile in London, primarily drawn from state officials in Paris. To what extent did this pattern of development occur in the provincial towns?

English provincial towns were governed by narrow oligarchies, usually not elected, but self-renewing by co-option. Constitutions varied, but in addition to the mayor and his co-officials there was usually a council of twelve, from whom the mayor and the leading officials had been and would be chosen. Some towns had additional common councils of twenty-four, usually purely advisory.[25] The social composition of the ruling elites was almost invariably mercantile, though, as we have seen, some cities' older landowning elites lasted rather longer than in others. York's landowning patriciate predominated until the early 1360s, but afterwards the city government was dominated by drapers and mercers, with interests in cloth export, as was also the case at Beverley. At Colchester, the clerics and landowners who predominated in the town's government until the middle of the fourteenth century, were then replaced by

---

[24] Favier, *Paris*, pp. 496 ff.
[25] These constitutional developments are described by James Tait, *The Medieval English Borough*.

merchants interested in overseas trade in cloth and wine – an oligarchy of merchant clothiers (equivalent to drapers), mercers and occasionally a landowner.

Given the growth in the late middle ages of the English cloth export trade, it is understandable that drapers and mercers should predominate in many of the bigger towns, even though much cloth production was rural. Late medieval Shrewsbury's urban rulers were mainly drapers, wool mongers and grain merchants. Leicester's oligarchy was predominantly of wool and cloth merchants. Norwich was dominated by the mercers. The rich oligarchs of Gloucester were drapers, mercers, spicers and vintners, though a few lawyers became active in town politics. Bristol's wool and cloth merchants took over, from the fourteenth century onwards, from the old oligarchy of wine importers, and in the fifteenth century, the mayoralty was entirely controlled by merchants. Exeter's ruling elite, mayor, stewards, common councillors and holders of profitable royal offices were all merchants much involved in cloth export. As one would expect, the government of the cloth-manufacturing town of Coventry was dominated by drapers, mercers and clothiers. The same pattern is found in many smaller towns, such as Stamford in Lincolnshire, whose wealthy elite were mainly drapers and merchants.[26]

It should be mentioned that although there was some investment by urban merchants in rural property, and even some late fifteenth- and sixteenth-century gentrification, this should not be exaggerated. Even urban real property contributed relatively little to the incomes of leading townsmen, which came mainly from their mercantile activities.[27]

As we shall see, this continuing predominance of mercantile interests in the late medieval English towns is not found, for the most part, in French towns. The mercantile character of the urban ruling classes in England necessarily implied the subordination of the manufacturing craftsmen through the regulations imposed on the craft gilds (where they existed). The attempted imposition of the 'one man, one trade' ethos was a generalised expression of merchant domination. In particular, the merchants involved in the sale for

---

[26] See references above for works on towns referred to here. For Chester, R.H. Morris, *Chester*, see above; for Stamford, A. Rogers, 'Medieval Stamford' in Rogers, ed., *The Making of Stamford*; not outdated is H. Owen and J.B. Blakeway, *History of Shrewsbury*, I.

[27] R.H. Hilton, 'Some Problems of Urban Real Property in the Middle Ages'.

export of craft manufactured commodities, especially textiles, feared any situation in which a chain of operations, from the acquisition of the raw material to the marketing of the final product, could be undertaken by the craftsmen themselves. Weavers must be kept separate from fullers and dyers, and so on. Selling was a craft or trade in itself, only to be undertaken by merchants. Not that regulations succeeded – they are, after all, evidence for the existence of what was prohibited, not for the success of the prohibition. Fullers, dyers and even weavers could and did from time to time act as sellers of the final product. But more important than the question of how successful were the merchants in subordinating craft production is, as we have suggested, the extent to which merchants invested the capital acquired by buying and selling in industrial production itself. Did merchant capital become industrial capital? Can the urban putting out system be recognised as a means by which merchant capital would be transformed into industrial capital if it did not transform the industrial base, that is, the fragmented production based on the small workshop? Was not the devolution of quality control and such matters as the length of the working day to the searchers of individual crafts a demonstration of the distance between the merchant capitalists who dominated urban governments and the craftsmen producers – a distance comparable to that between lords and peasants?

If one looks at the evidence from the major cloth-producing towns of late-medieval England where, if anywhere, one might expect to find investment of merchant capital in the production of textiles for export, the general impression is that the merchants who ruled the towns entirely failed to transform the industrial structure, and that urban craft production for the wider market went into decline as the rural textile industry took over the export trade. This is as true of the old established cloth centres such as York, Salisbury or Lincoln as it is of relatively recent manufacturing centres at Coventry and Norwich. The social distance between merchants and craftsmen was maintained, as at Norwich, where, if a craftsman became rich enough to quality for being a mayor, he had to renounce his craft; and where even entry to the common council was denied to a shoemaker because of his trade.[28]

It now seems accepted as a truism, summarised by Bernard

[28] Hudson and Tingey, *Records of the City of Norwich*, I, no. 226 (1463); II, Introduction, pp. xlviii ff.

Chevalier in *Les bonnes villes de France*, that a largely mercantile elite by the fifteenth century was being replaced in most big towns in France by a ruling group of royal officials, lawyers and clerics. This is attributed to the wars of the fourteenth and fifteenth centuries, which obliged urban populations to cut themselves off from the countryside, to build walls, pull down suburbs, and concern themselves with a political and military rather than a commercial role. Whatever the feudal factionalism at the centre of royal government, that government insisted on the town as a fortress and located its agents within, most of them lawyers. In Tours, although rich merchants who served the royal court in the fifteenth century still had a role, the number of *élus* in the municipal government who were lawyers increased from twenty-six per cent in the late fourteenth century to forty-seven per cent in the mid-fifteenth century. A. Bouton, the historian of Maine, states that at this time the main ambition of the bourgeoisie of Le Mans was to enter royal or seigneurial service.[29]

Some of the bourgeois of late-medieval Lille were moving into a *noblesse de robe*. Others were abandoning mercantile activity and turning to banking. Lawyers and officials became predominant among the bourgeois of Poitiers by the fifteenth century. Two thirds of the sixty-seven mayors of the city after 1414 were royal officials; very few were merchants; all of the lieutenants-general of the *sénéchaussé* – royal officials *par excellence* – became mayors in the fifteenth century. Inevitably, the mercantile and money lending bourgeoisie tried to move upwards into the elite of lawyers and royal officials. They also sought tax-free noble status. In Rouen, from the fourteenth century, the patriciate lived off rents and the profits of office, rather than commerce, and by the fifteenth century were penetrated by lawyers and officials – apparently a phenomenon found in most Norman towns. At Reims and at Metz, the leading bourgeois were financiers, lending money to the local nobility and themselves investing in real property; as were the top bourgeois families of Bordeaux, though they at any rate kept some interest in the wine trade. Even at Lyons, when it was developing its role as a centre of international trade (rather dominated by Italians), its old consular mercantile class was merging into the new class of officials. Between 1430 and 1450, 54 out of a total of 184 consuls were

---

[29] Chevalier, *Les bonnes villes*, chapter 3, i; Chevalier, *Tours*, pp. 182 ff.; Bouton, *Le Maine*, p. 470.

lawyers. Amiens, according to E. Maugis, was dominated by lawyers by the end of the fifteenth century.[30]

The ruling oligarchies in the larger French and English towns in the later middle ages were in no sense antagonistic, economically, socially, or politically, to the feudal order. Nevertheless, our comparison of the towns in these two countries has brought out an interesting contrast. The English urban oligarchs were still, for the most part, merchant capitalists, especially in London. In the French towns, the ruling bourgeoisie was becoming more and more attracted into royal officialdom. Sons were diverted from the counting house to the lawyers' studios. Legal qualifications were regarded as appropriate for posts in royal administration and, as we have seen, lawyers and officials came to dominate French urban governments. Although the English mercantile bourgeoisie invested in rural landed property – some even merging with the landed gentry – and although, in the fifteenth century, there were many families living in English provincial towns who were regarded (and who regarded themselves) as gentry, mercantile interests predominated.[31] So, even though we may not locate the forces which would lead from feudalism to capitalism in the medieval town, it may be that the relative precocity of England, as compared with France, in the transition to capitalism may have something to do with the survival of an urban mercantile elite in the English towns, as opposed to the 'trahison de la bourgeoisie' (B. Chevalier) in France, with their flight into officialdom.

[30] For Lille, see Trénard, ed., *Histoire d'une métropole*, p. 142; Favreau, *La ville de Poitiers*, p. 496 ff.; Desportes, *Reims*, chapter 26; Schneider, *La ville de Metz*, in his chapter on bourgeois expansion shows that these trends were already to be found at Metz in the early fourteenth century; C. Higounet, ed., *Histoire de Bordeaux*, II, Part 3, chapter 5 also shows these developments in the early fourteenth century; Kleinclausz, ed., *Histoire de Lyon*, I, pp. 314–19; Maugis, *Recherches*, pp. 101 ff.

[31] R.E. Horrox, 'The Urban Gentry in the Fifteenth Century'.

5. *How urban society was imagined*

The social classes of medieval towns – or representative individuals from them – appear in the imaginative and moralising literature of the period, though not as prominently as the clergy, the knights and the peasants. The theme of social 'orders' or 'estates', which is frequently found in the literature, is mainly focussed on the three major classes of medieval agrarian society, especially those who prayed and those who fought, with a lesser role for those who toiled on the land to provide for the prayers and the fighters – who were also their landlords.

The analysis of urban structures which we have presented is based on documentary evidence generated by the economic, social and political activity of the inhabitants of the towns and the cities, just as historical research into landlords and their tenants is based on analogous evidence. But there were also images of towns and their inhabitants in imaginative and moralising writings which must be taken into account as sources for the understanding of towns in feudal society. The relevant imaginative literature, especially that of the twelfth century, consists mainly of chivalric epics and romances whose aim was the exaltation of knightly virtues, frequently within the theme of courtly love. What might be interpreted as certain 'feudal' attitudes to towns, to merchants and to artisans appear briefly in some of the romances, though others altogether ignore the existence of towns and their inhabitants. Otherwise their attitude is somewhat ambivalent, in that as warriors they appreciate the strength of collective urban military mobilisation, but, on the whole they are contemptuous of the 'bourgeois' and the 'merchant'. Whether the expressed attitude of the knightly class should be accepted as typical of 'feudal' attitudes in general is, however, uncertain.

From the middle of the twelfth century in France, somewhat later in England, there was a social differentiation within the free landowners, those who later would be regarded as 'gentry'. Many of them, as baronial vassals or even as professional warriors, had performed a military function without any special social prestige. The division developed between the majority of these lesser landowners and an upper stratum, who could afford increasingly expensive military equipment, and who formed a – ceremonially – separate knightly class. They derived prestige from the participation by some of them in the crusades, and from ecclesiastical approval of their role. This was the group which was particularly exalted by the writers of romance. They and their literary admirers might well be expected at this time to emphasise their separation, not merely from the peasantry and the lesser landowners, but from the bourgeoisie to whom they were often in debt.[1]

A knightly hero of a romance proudly dismisses any idea that he might appeal for financial aid from bourgeois or merchant (*Girart de Vienne*). A daughter successfully reproves her father for acting like a bourgeois because he had not arranged a suitable marriage for her (*Raoul de Cambrai*). When the hero Gawain avoids a tournament because of more important duties, a lady contemptuously dismisses him as a merchant, who is bringing his horses, not to join in the tournament, but to sell them. Another lady speculates that he must be a money changer. In a description of a communal uprising of townspeople, who had been led to believe that Gawain's lady love had offered herself in marriage to her father's assassin, the townspeople are described as 'villeins' and the heroine denounces them as 'a rabble, mad dogs, vile serfs' (*Perceval*).

The attitude of the romance writers to the town as an entity was not invariably hostile, as Jacques le Goff has well demonstrated – in spite of the normally lofty contempt for merchants and artisans. He illustrates from the adventures of William of Orange in *Le charroi de Nîmes* and *La prise d'Orange* how the cities were the essential landmarks in these courtly narratives. Nîmes appears as a much admired urban stereotype, with its walls, its gates and its towers, high and pointed. It is not surprising that the city as fortification should appeal to these knightly heroes, but Nîmes was also admired for its network of streets and open places, its churches and palaces

---

[1] See G. Duby, *The Chivalrous Society*, trans. C. Postan, especially no. 6, and also R.H. Hilton, *A Medieval Society*, pp. 51 ff.

– and its market. Le Goff even suggests that the knights saw the city as the image of 'woman', to be admired as well as feared, and, of course, to be captured. Nevertheless, the attitude of writers of romance, such as Chrétien de Troyes, was very ambiguous. His heroes, as we have seen, despised the bourgeoisie and artisans, but the town, as *chastel*, provided them with a refuge. Furthermore, Jean Renart, in *L'Escoufle*, recognises the attraction for nobles and knights of the comforts and luxury commodities found in towns, not to speak of the processions and feastings in which they, the nobles, played a leading role.[2]

By the fourteenth century, especially in England, even the so-called 'courtly' literature projects a much more positive image of urban life. Even though the social background of the most important of these writers, Geoffrey Chaucer, may seem to suggest ambiguity, it may rather be typical. He came from a family of London vintners, but in early manhood was closely associated with aristocratic households and the royal court, representing the king abroad and holding many important official posts. The English royal court was metropolitan based, so there would have been no obvious gap between court and urban life. Chaucer's positive depictions of merchants and master craftsmen, as in the *Canterbury Tales*, cannot simply be taken as stereotypes, but as genuine reflections of reality, acceptable, no doubt, to the contemporary 'feudal' outlook, as well as to this poet from a mercantile background.[3]

Chaucer's presentation of the typical urban classes – merchants and craftsmen – implies a favourable attitude towards towns without mentioning them as such. But as V. J. Scattergood has demonstrated in considerable detail, fifteenth-century poetry continued the traditional condemnation of the money-loving greed of merchants, which appears so strongly in William Langland's *Piers Plowman*. Yet Langland's condemnation of Lady Meed and of the merchants large and small who enjoy the exploitation of the poor, for money's sake, does not necessarily imply, as D. Pearsall hesitantly suggests,

[2] J. Le Goff, 'Guerriers et bourgeois conquérants. L'image de la ville dans la littérature française du XIIe siècle', in Le Goff, *L'imaginaire médiéval*; see also his contribution to C.M. Cipolla, ed., *The Fontana Economic History of Europe: the Middle Ages*, London, 1972, chapter 2, 'The Town as an Agent of Civilisation 1200–1500'; J.-G. Gouttebroze, 'L'image de la ville dans l'œuvre romanesque de Chrétien de Troyes', and J. Lermat, 'La ville dans *l'Escoufle* de Jean Renart'; and P.S. Noble, '*Knights and Burgesses in the Feudal Epic*'.
[3] M. Crow and C. Olson, eds., *Chaucer Life Records*.

that the sweeping away of Lady Meed means 'in practical terms, to abolish urban society and return to an idealised agrarian feudalism'. Money-making merchants may be condemned by Langland, but there is not the same pejorative use of the term 'burgess', the characteristic townsman. Most striking, perhaps, is the insistence that Christ was born in no cottage or caitiff's house but 'in a burgess house, the best of the town'.[4]

A slightly later positive reference to the city in French literature is worth mentioning. It is that of the feminist writer, Christine de Pisan. Apart from her passionate defence of the rights of women, she could be said to have impeccably 'feudal' attitudes. Born in Italy, she had been brought up in the court of Charles V, where her father was an astrologer. She became the official biographer of Charles V, and wrote many works in verse and prose in the early years of the fifteenth century. These included a treatise on arms and chivalry – a manual of instruction for knights. There was also the *Corps de policie*, a discussion on the orders of society. The point here, however, is that one of her most trenchant feminist writings was the *Livre des cités des dames*, in which Christine imagines herself building 'the city' as the ideal place for women persecuted by men to retreat to. There is not much detail about Christine's city. It is mostly about its ladies, but it does somewhat contradict Frantisek Graus' insistence that the medieval Utopia is always a village, never a town.[5]

THE IDEOLOGY OF THE ORDERS

The moralising and 'estate' literature which has influenced historical interpretation, perhaps more than the imaginative literature, is of a somewhat different nature. It can be interpreted as a fleshing out of symbolic imagery by illustrations derived from perceptions of contemporary reality. But it also constitutes an ideology, not a reflection of real life but a project for acting upon it – to quote G. Duby, a 'projet d'agir sur le vécu', not a 'reflet du vécu'.[6]

---

[4] V.J. Scattergood, *Politics and Poetry in the Fifteenth century*, p. 332 ff.; D. Pearsall, ed., *Piers Plowman by William Langland: an Edition of the C Text*, p. 14. See also David Aers, *Chaucer, Langland and the Creative Imagination*, London, 1980, for a perceptive discussion of the problems of Langland and Chaucer with regard to ideology and reality in the fourteenth century; and see also Jill Mann, *Chaucer and Medieval Estates Satire*, Cambridge, 1973.

[5] Christine de Pisan's *Livre des cités des Dames* is available in English translation, *The Book of the City of Ladies*; F. Graus, 'Social Utopias in the Middle Ages'.

[6] Duby, *Les trois ordres*, p. 20.

The idea of a tripartite social order is much older than the middle ages. In writing about the three Germanic gods named by Julius Caesar, Sol, Vulcan and Luna, G. Dumézil demonstrated that these were connected with an even more ancient Indo-European tripartite division of social functions – magicians, warriors and herdsmen-farmers.[7] This tripartite image comes and goes. It appears in King Alfred of Wessex's translation of Boethius in the late ninth century, and explicitly in the writings of Aelfric of Eynsham in the late tenth century. Aelfric wrote that every throne stood on three props, those who pray (*oratores*), those who toil (*laboratores*) and those who fight (*bellatores*). The connection between royalty and three orders was repeated again in the eleventh century by Adalbero, bishop of Laon, with an emphasis on the servile condition of the *laboratores*. For Adalbero, 'This triple assemblage is as one, and so the law may triumph and the world enjoy peace.'[8]

The theme persists through the middle ages, though the image is varied, sometimes to stress a twofold division between the rulers (including the clergy) and the ruled – peasants, artisans and labourers. Other classes are sometimes included as separate orders, such as merchants and urban artisans.

Another image emphasising the interdependence of high- and low-status groups was that of the human body, well known through John of Salisbury's *Policraticus* (late twelfth century), though certainly not originated by him. Various parts of the body represented social classes. The soul represented the clergy; the head, the prince; the heart, the senate (an anachronistic classical echo); the eyes, ears and tongue were judges and provincial governors; the hands, officials and soldiers; the sides, the prince's entourage; the belly and intestines, the treasurers and keepers of the privy chest; and the feet, the tillers of the soil. Changes in social structures were reflected by later writers in different attributions of bodily parts. Thomas Brinton, bishop of Rochester (1373–89) used the bodily image: 'Many are members of the mystic body'. He compares the head to kings, princes and prelates; the eyes to judges and wise and true councillors; the ears to the religious; the tongue to good and learned men; the right hand to the knights, ready to defend; the left

---

[7] G. Dumézil, *Mythes et dieux des Germains*, chapter 1.

[8] D. Whitelock, ed., *English Historical Documents*, I, pp. 845–6, 853–4; Duby, *Les trois ordres*, pp. 127–40, has an interesting discussion on the contributions of these Anglo-Saxon writers to the 'three estate' theory. For Adalbero of Laon's remarks, see also Hilton, *Bond Men Made Free*, p. 54.

hand to merchants and faithful artisans; the heart, placed as if in the middle, to citizens and burgesses; and the feet to cultivators and labourers, firmly supporting the whole body.[9]

The image of the body was less frequently used than that of the three estates, but it could be used with the same ideological intent. In 1267, Henry III of England justified a ban on unauthorised meetings, parliaments, conventicles or congregations in London by saying that 'all citizens, rich and poor, are as one body and one man... faithfully observing the king's peace'.[10]

Whatever the variations between these different images, one theme persists. The separate orders have their special and divinely ordained functions. There should be no movement between the orders. In particular, no person of the lower orders who engaged in manual labour should aspire to enter the higher orders. The ideological function of the theories or images is clear. It was to justify a social morality which would sustain the existing class structure. Social critics recognised typical faults within each order. Princes might fail to give justice; knights might engage in rapine; merchants and craftsmen might cheat and commit theft and perjury; burgesses might be usurious; and peasants might be envious and thieving, for instance, by not paying tithes. But these faults would be controlled by preaching and by ordering penance from the sinners; and as far as the lower orders were concerned, if necessary, by the exercise of force. In no way, however, could the faults of individuals justify any disturbance of the social order. To avoid this, no preacher should condemn the faults of the lords and the rich in sermons delivered to an audience of poor and low-status persons.

URBAN SOCIETY WITHIN THE SYSTEM OF ORDERS

The power of the three order (or estate) image was very strong and persisted beyond the end of the middle ages.[11] But social changes had to be recognised. In a society ruled by lay and ecclesiastical

---

[9] For the relevant portion of John of Salisbury's *Policraticus*, see Ewart Lewis, ed., *Medieval Political Ideas*, I, p. 225; see also M.A. Devlin, ed., *The Sermons of Thomas Brinton, Bishop of Rochester 1373–1389*.

[10] 'Cronica Maiorum et Vicecomitum Londoniarum' in *Liber de Antiquis Legibus*, ed. Thomas Stapleton, Camden Society, London, 1846, p. 98.

[11] R. Mousnier, *Les hiérarchies sociales de 1450 à nos jours*.

landlords, and in which peasant rebellion was endemic, the traditional division between noble warriors, clergy and peasants was only slowly adjusted. But the growth of towns and the emergence of urban merchants and craftsmen could not be ignored. For some clerical ideologues money was rotten. The city was another Babylon. But the existence of merchants had to be admitted. There was even a tendency in the later middle ages to make the third estate respectable by confining it to merchants, leading to the towns choosing the representatives of the Third Estate in the French General Assemblies, and, with the gentry, in the English House of Commons. The traditional component of the third estate, the manual workers of town and country, were relegated as a fourth and marginal, even though necessary, element in the social order.

French moralising literature from the twelfth to the fourteenth centuries, like so much of its kind throughout Europe, presented both the duties and the characteristic sins of all social orders, including princes, high ecclesiastics and knights, as well as merchants, peasants and labourers.[12] In spite of the persistence of the three-estate image, which tended to ignore the urban classes, moralists as early as the late twelfth century brought merchants into their scheme. Etienne de Fougères (d. 1178), bishop of Rennes and chaplain to Henry II Plantagenet, wrote a *Livre des manières*. There is much about merchants and the bourgeois with an emphasis on such faults as price fiddling, selling goods dear which might be bought cheap, and usurious money lending. But it is interesting that tricks of the borrowers (typically people from the landed classes) are condemned as well as those of the lenders.

An early-thirteenth-century writer, the recluse of Molliens, stuck to the three estate image in his *Miserere* – the clergy to pray, the knights to defend and give justice, and the peasants to provide bread for the rest – but added that merchants, suffering heat and cold in their occupation, also deserved sustenance. The early-fourteenth-century anonymous author of the *Contrefait de Renard*, a former cleric who became an *épicier* (apothecary or grocer) in Troyes, listed many social groups for criticism. He even suggested that the oppression of the people by the nobility should lead to rebellion. Nevertheless, he condemned labourers for not working a full day for

[12] Twelve moralising treatises are presented in C.-V. Langlois, *La vie en France au moyen âge. II, de la fin du XIIe au milieu du XIVe siècle d'après les moralistes du temps*. Those quoted below are from this collection.

their wages, and craft journeymen for haunting taverns. Not surprisingly, merchants appear in a favourable light, though he condemns usurious money changers, and drapers and goldsmiths who sold faulty goods at the wrong price. A writer of the 1350s, Gilles de Musis, abbot of St Martin of Tournai, condemns most classes, whether clerics, princes or labourers. But he praises merchants, indispensable intermediaries, who have to travel by land and sea, go to feasts and fairs, and keep track of the changing value of currencies. This author excuses himself for not enumerating the 'estates' of society. In fact, the three- or four-order framework is stressed by only a minority of the moralists.

An interesting presentation of the three-estate ideology, again with necessary additions, is by the late-fourteenth-century English author, John Gower, a Kentish landowner and poet. He did this in French in his *Mirour de l'homme*, but more revealingly in Latin in the *Vox clamantis*.[13] This includes an account of a dream about the rising of 1381 in which, characteristic of many writings about the third estate, the peasants are represented as beasts who fail to fulfil their proper role – asses refuse to carry sacks to the city, oxen refuse to be yoked to the plough. After his story of the dream and a section on theology, Gower begins book III as follows: 'We know that there are three estates [*status*] within which everyone in the world lives as is customary.' There follow descriptions of the clergy (together with monks, canons, nuns and friars), the knighthood and peasants.

But having stated at the beginning of this part of his disquisition that the three estates are clerics, knights and peasants, whose duties are respectively to teach, fight and till the soil, he adds to his statement about peasants – who have to bear Adam's punishment for his sins by their everlasting toil – a sequence describing other groups not covered by the traditional three-estate model. First, there are labourers, wage workers who insist on working and being paid by the day, not by the year or even by the month, and demand good food and drink instead of water. Only terror will rule them. Then come the merchants, who are treated very well by Gower. They are necessary for the distribution of goods. As citizens, they have both honour and obligation (*onus*). Citizens are of two degrees, merchants and artisans, the greater and the lesser, who must agree for all to go well. Gower does not pretend that all *is* well in urban mercantile society. Fraud is possible in the provision of all

[13]   E.W. Stockton, ed., *The Major Latin Works of John Gower*.

commodities, from wool, jewellery and gold and silver work to poultry and cooked meats. Usury, too, is dealt with at this point. It enables city houses to be built and country houses to be destroyed, the city man is enriched, and the knight is robbed of his land and gold.

The reference by Gower to the need for harmony between city merchants and artisans suggests that an ideology which for centuries had emphasised the need for each person to keep to his or her estate – from nobles down to peasants – could very well have its reflection within the town or city. Specifically urban models of the state ideology are, however, rather rare. One such is contained within Christine de Pisan's *Corps de policie*. She gives a description of society as a whole, based on the analogy of the human body, as in John of Salisbury's *Policraticus*. She first addresses the prince, the head of the body, then the knights and nobles – the arms and hands. But the third estate, the 'Universal People', is, in effect, presented as a tripartite division of urban society (with Paris in mind) – clergy; bourgeoisie and merchants; and the *commun*, that is, craftsmen and labourers.[14] There is, however, evidence other than literary which emphasises an image of the harmonious co-existence of status groups rather than one of competing classes with incompatible economic interests.

URBAN PERCEPTIONS OF THE SYSTEM OF ORDERS

As we have observed, in most medieval English and French towns, the main classes were merchants; city knights in some, and especially southern, French towns; master craftsmen and retail shopkeepers; journeymen; and a marginal, though often numerous, population of unskilled labourers, rural immigrants, criminals, prostitutes and so on. Members of urban classes are often referred to in various town documents by their actual occupations. But when their role in urban politics is described, a set of designations indicating status rather than occupation is used. It is interesting that, from town to town, in both France and England, the terminology is much the same.

Perhaps more significantly, the urban status designations seem carefully to avoid any reference to wealth, any suggestion that those

[14] See *The Middle English Translation of Christine de Pisan's Livre du Corps de policie*, ed. Diane Bornstein.

enjoying high status do so because they are rich. In view of the frequent emphasis in moralising literature on the corrupting influence of money, this is perhaps not surprising. It is also possible that even in the later middle ages, the denigration of the poor would be considered inappropriate in view of earlier theologians' emphasis on the holiness of poverty. One of the few overall designations of the class rather than the status composition of an urban population was made by the clergy of the cathedral city of Reims, who classified the laity according to their income.[15] It was, as so often, a tripartite division. In the top grade there were knights and grand rich bourgeois; next were merchants dealing in leather, cloth, spices, furs, and innkeepers; last were the craftsmen, such as masons, carpenters and roofers (*couvreurs*).

A tripartite division by status is more frequently indicated, either explicitly or implicitly. Explicitly in England, we can quote a reference to a royal inquiry in 1275 into the misdeeds of a ruling clique in Lincoln. Three juries were to help the inquiry, no doubt designated as such in Lincoln itself for the royal inquisitors, the *magni*, the *secondarii* and the *minores*. Also at Lincoln, in 1390, a conflict was described as being between the mayor, bailiffs and 'high and mighty' persons on the one hand, and the 'middling subjects' on the other, the implication being that there was still a group of *minores* at the bottom of the social heap.[16] At Toulouse, from 1256 onwards, half of the consuls were to be chosen from the *maiores*, half from the *medii*, implying a third group of *inferiores*. In 1311, when a council was chosen to rule the small town of Saintes Maries de la Mer on the Mediterranean coast, it was supposed to represent the 'middling' and 'poor' people as well as the rich (a rare reference to wealth), and to be approved by the *major et sanior pars* of the population, a choice selection, no doubt, from the rich.[17]

More often than the tripartite status image, we find a dual division. In 1315, there was a conflict at Rouen between the *petit commun* and the *gros bourgeois*. The Reims tax payers in the early fourteenth century were divided, not between the rich and the poor, but between the *gros* and the *menus*. At Aix-en-Provence and at

[15] P. Desportes, *Reims*, p. 672.
[16] *Rotuli Hundredorum*, ed. W. Illingworth, pp. 309–28; J. W. F. Hill, *Medieval Lincoln*, pp. 259–61.
[17] J.P. Buffelan, *La noblesse des capitouls de Toulouse*, p. 68. He follows Dognon (*Institutions politiques et administratives du pays de Languedoc*) in saying that this was general in Languedocian towns; P. Amargier, 'Autour de la création du conseil de communauté aux Saintes Maries de la Mer, 1307'.

Arles in the thirteenth century, there was a dual division among the governing elite between the knights and the *prud'hommes*. At St Flour, in the fourteenth and fifteenth centuries, the status division of the town's population was between the *magna communitas* of bourgeois and citizens, and the *parva communitas* (or *basse commune*) of craftsmen and those below. In 1278, at Condom in Gascony, the status division was described as being between *borgues* and *pobles*, that is, between the bourgeois and the 'people'. Similar duality is found in English towns. In Shrewsbury, before the Black Death, the 'lesser' people listened respectfully to the 'greater' who governed them. Canterbury in the thirteenth century had its *major et sanior pars* and its *minor parts et infirmior*. At Beverley, the Corpus Christi procession was supposed to contribute to 'the peaceful union of the worthier and lesser commons of the town'.[18]

Even more revealing of the emphasis on status than these examples of dual or tripartite divisions of the towns' inhabitants, are the specific designations, particularly of those whom in practice we can identify as the well-to-do ruling groups of merchants. The most frequent designation used is that of *prud'hommes* or *probi homines*, the 'worthy men'. We find them at Southampton, Norwich, London, Winchester, Louviers (in Normandy), Toulouse, Agde, Besançon, Tarascon, Aix-en-Provence, Arles, Marseille, Tours and Montbrison (Forez).

Where the actual term *prud'homme* is not used, there are other terms which are meant to be analogous. Most of them seek to assert the moral superiority of the richer townsmen. The ruling elite of the Staffordshire town of Newcastle-under-Lyme, the 'twenty-four', shared power with the 'best' of the citizens. It was twenty-four of the 'more worthy' citizens of Lincoln who, in 1422, aided the mayor and his twelve peers to make ordinances for the 'common good'. Access to the freedom of the borough at Hereford was allowed by a meeting of 'the better sort' of the community. Norwich's officials were chosen by the *bons gentz*. The urban elite of twelfth-century Winchester was described as composed of the 'more worthy citizens' ('digniores cives'). Leicester's narrow oligarchy of the mayor and

---

[18] A. Salournay in M. Mollat, ed., *Histoire de Rouen*, Part 4; Desportes, *Reims*, pp. 103–5; N. Coulet, *Aix-en-Provence: espace et relations d'une capitale,* p. 44; L. Stouff, *Arles*, p. 196; A. Rigaudière, *St Flour*, pp. 110 ff.; R. Moussot-Goulard, 'Les bourgeois de Condom, décimateurs au XIIIe siècle'; H. Owen and J. B. Blakeway, *History of Shrewsbury*, chapter 3; M. James, 'Ritual, Drama and the Social Body in the Late Medieval English Town'.

twenty-four was aided in the making of ordinances by the 'honest' and 'discreet' from whom they would have been chosen.[19]

The moral tone in the description of the leading burgesses of French towns is very similar. The patricians of Lyons were the 'greater and the better' ('majores et meliores'), also described as 'honourable and provident' ('honorabiles et providi viri'). Merchants and officials in late-medieval Tours were also described as 'honourable men'. The *probi homines* of Avignon were described as truly honourable bourgeois accustomed to enjoy the lifestyle of knights ('burgenses vero honorabiles qui ut milites vivere consueverunt'). These leading personalities, or their scribes, no doubt formulated these moralistic synonyms which, in fact, indicated their wealth and their power. Expressions of disdain for the craftsmen and labourers are less frequent, perhaps hardly necessary for the documents. The lower classes are normally referred to in French towns as the *menu commun* or the *menu peuple*, though the term *probi homines* was occasionally applied to leading masters of the crafts, as in Languedoc. At the lowest end of the social scale, the marginals, including not only the idle and the criminal, but also essential, though unskilled, labourers, were thought of in Paris as 'useless' ('inutile au monde'). Even that phrase does not match the words that were used at Shrewsbury, when the rich people fled from the borough to the countryside at the time of the Black Death, leaving the borough in the hands of their inferiors, whom they described as 'animales viles'.[20]

Class was disguised as status, and the proper behaviour of each status group was preached from the parish pulpit, the *hôtels de ville* and the town halls, not to speak of the lessons of the moralising writers of whom we have given French examples. In England, it went further. As I have mentioned, the monarchy was very sensitive – long before 1381 – to any signs of social subversion. The monarchy and the ruling class in Parliament sought to emphasise status

[19] T. Pape, *Medieval Newcastle-under-Lyme*, pp. 133–7; Hill, *Medieval Lincoln*, p. 276; A.G. Rosser, 'Conflict and Community in English Medieval Towns: Disputes and their Resolution in Hereford 1200–1500'; W. Hudson and J. C. Tingey, *Records*, I, Introduction, p. 14; M. Biddle, ed., *Winchester*, p. 480; M. Bateson, *Records*, II, Introduction, pp. xliii ff.

[20] Francoise Censier, 'Le patriciat lyonnais au début du XIVe siècle'; G. de Valous, *Le patriciat lyonnais aux XIIIe et XIVe siècles*, pp. 89–90; B. Chevalier, *Tours*, III, chapter 3; G. Sautel, 'Les villes du midi meditérranéan'; Gouron, *La règlementation*, p. 201; B. Geremek, *Margins*, pp. 270–5; Owen and Blakeway, *History of Shrewsbury*, p. 167.

distinctions even in the clothing and food consumption allowed to the various social groups. The English sumptuary laws, much more strongly emphasised than those in France, covered the social hierarchies of both town and country.[21] Some of the early regulations are contained in the famous (and ineffective) statute of 1363, which attempted to impose a 'one man, one trade' law. The sumptuary regulations contained within the statute may well have been equally ineffective, but they reveal the ruling class preoccupation with status symbols. Servants, whether of lords or of master craftsmen, were not to eat meat or fish more than once a day, and other victuals, such as milk or cheeses 'according to their estate'; their clothes were to be made only of the cheapest cloth. Silk or embroidered cloth was forbidden. Their wives and daughters could only wear veils below a certain price. Craft journeymen were allowed to wear a slightly more expensive cloth, but not silk, silver cloth, girdles, knives, garters, brooches and so on. Their wives and daughters should not wear veils of silk, but only of native fabric. It is interesting, however, that merchants and master craftsmen, provided they had chattels worth £500 or more (a very high sum), were allowed to wear the same apparel as gentry who had incomes of £100 a year; if they had £1,000 worth of chattels, they could dress like esquires with £200 a year.[22]

A later law (1464) shows that attitudes had not changed. This was more detailed and comprehensive than that of 1363, and again suggested social equivalences between classes of town and country. The lord mayor of London could wear furs of sable and ermine, as did lords and knights and high state officials; London aldermen, together with the mayors, recorders, sheriffs, aldermen and bailiffs of other cities and boroughs, could dress like esquires and gentlemen worth £40 a year, and so on down the social scale to the servants of craftsmen who, like servants in husbandry and common labourers could wear only the cheapest cloths and hose, and no silvered girdles.[23]

CIVIC CEREMONY

The hierarchical concepts which reflected the structures of feudal society were not only voiced in cities and towns from the pulpit, in

[21] F. Piponnier, *Costume et vie sociale: la cour d'Anjou, XIVe–XVe siècles*, pp. 24, 195. [22] *Statutes of the Realm*, I, pp. 379 f.
[23] *Rotuli Parliamentorum*, I, pp. 504–5.

mandates from on high and in moralising literature. They were also emphasised in various forms of civic ceremony. As we have suggested, gilds and fraternities in England and France were, for the most part, originally spontaneous creations for mutual solidarity and for religious and social purposes. They were usually placed under the patronage of a saint, in whose name the gild or fraternity would keep a light (*luminaire*) burning on a church altar. They were open to women as well as to men and had very simple aims – mutual aid, charity and convivial feasting. These features continued in the late medieval period when many fraternities were linked with, or indeed transformed into, officially recognised craft organisations. We must recognise, therefore, that civic ceremony was not simply imposed from above. It embodied and extended the gild and fraternity conviviality and solidarity, which must have meant a good deal to urban populations of artisans, whose working day normally began at dawn and ended at dusk. Doubts only began to arise in the minds of these artisans in the late fifteenth century when the gilds had to bear the costs of the ceremonies.

Many feasts in French towns had to be organised, and paid for, by the civic authorities. This was especially when kings and queens made their so-called 'joyous entry' into cities and the people were given free food and, above all, drink. When Isabeau of Bavaria made her entry into Paris, in 1389, the fountains flowed with wine instead of water. When dukes and other nobles ceremonially entered Breton towns, minstrels were hired and the people participated, a relief, as J. P. Leguay puts it, from an otherwise difficult existence.[24]

The 'joyous entries' of kings, dukes and other lords into French towns were not so regular as the Corpus Christi processions, which, as we shall see, developed in some English towns in the fourteenth and fifteenth centuries. Nevertheless, they fulfilled the same function in emphasising hierarchy, while at the same time providing amusement and diversion for the hard-working population.

The emphasis on social harmony is shown in Georges Duby's account of a chronicler's description of one of the earliest of the royal entries into Paris, that of Philip Augustus after his victory at the battle of Bouvines in 1214 over the excommunicated German emperor, Otto of Brunswick, who was supported by John, king of England. According to the chronicler, Guillaume le Breton, Philip

---

[24] J. Heers, *Fêtes, jeux et joutes dans les sociétés d'occident à la fin du moyen âge*, and, more useful, Heers, 'Les métiers et les fêtes médiévales en France du Nord et en Angleterre'; J.P. Leguay, *Un réseau urbain*, chapter 19.

Augustus and his troops, together with their prisoners, entered Paris to universal jubilation; the three 'orders' were reconciled, and this harmony ended the conflict between classes. The knights had fulfilled their role and were received by the clergy and the craftsmen, that is, in the language of the 'orders', the 'Church' and the 'Poor'. There was singing and dancing, with everybody, of course, keeping their proper place.[25]

The most spectacular of the later 'joyous entries', as one would expect, followed the crownings of the kings of France at Reims. An early description is from the thirteenth century, when Louis VIII came from Reims (1223) with his queen and entered Paris to be greeted by the bourgeois of the city with gifts of luxury cloths, jewels and gold ornaments. The amount of splendour varied, very little in the case of Louis IX (1226), but developing in the late thirteenth and fourteenth centuries, especially under the Valois. Paris was not the only town to enjoy the 'joyous entries' on the way from Reims. In 1350, Jean II passed through various towns, including Laon, Soissons and Senlis, before arriving on the outskirts of Paris at St Denis, traditional burial place of kings and queens. He and his queen then entered Paris, and feasting lasted a whole week. The streets were clad in fine cloths; the craftsmen, in distinct costume according to their gild, went in front of the royal cortège, with the bourgeois in their particular uniforms. Among others, the Lombard inhabitants of Paris presented themselves in rich silken robes and high hats. On foot and on horse, all preceded the king and queen to the cathedral of Notre Dame, where the king was met by the clergy and promised to observe their canonical privileges.[26]

A very detailed description of the 'joyous entry' of Louis XI in 1461 has been preserved. It was the first entry of a legitimate French king after the end of the English occupation. It was also different in character from other 'joyous entries' in that the procession seems to have been entirely dominated by innumerable nobles and their followers, all mounted and clad in elaborate armour or clothing. The nobles included the duke of Burgundy, the count of Charolais, and the duke Jean de Clèves, to mention only a few. The streets were crowded with spectators as the procession made its way along the traditional route from St Denis to Notre Dame. There are few references to the bourgeois, and none to the crafts, unless they are included in the *menu peuple* who followed the procession of the

---

[25] Duby, *Le dimanche de Bouvines*, pp. 176–80.   [26] Heers, 'Les métiers'.

nobility. When the king arrived at the front of the cathedral of Notre Dame, as customary, he received the homage of the university; then, after having promised to observe the rights and privileges of the church of Paris, he entered the cathedral.

This splendid 'joyous entry' was supposed to affirm the role of Paris as the capital of France, symbolised on the route to Notre Dame by various theatrical displays representing the city. But it was different from the traditional 'entries', such as that of Jean II. The absence of the craft gilds from the ceremony, and the exceptional predominance of the elaborately clad nobles provided, as Paris' historian, Marcel Poëte, describes it, an occasion for vanity, for showing off ('foire aux vanités') and for the promotion of self-interest ('foire aux intérêts'). The real object of these nobles, ecclesiastics and bourgeois was not so much to celebrate as to acquire public office[27] – a sign of the times?

Feasting and ceremony were not confined to the celebrations of royal or seigneurial 'joyous entries'. The drinking and entertainment accompanying these entries was, no doubt, intended to encourage and reward loyalty to authority. There were, however, elements in some urban festivals which, in their early manifestations, might seem to threaten the social order. This was particularly marked at the time of Carnival, the feasting on the eve of Lent. In many places, there is evidence from the thirteenth century of images of 'the world turned upside down'. Feasts of the fools (*fêtes des fous*) were organised by groups of minor clergy and choirboys,who mocked the bishops and higher clergy and even satirised holy rituals such as the mass. Alongside them, and normally apart from them, would be set up *abbayes de jeunesse*, that is, young men who were bachelors. They chose a 'king' to guide them in drunken and derisory acts of misrule – a total takeover of the town for the whole of Shrove Tuesday (*Mardi Gras*). The bigger the town, the more there were of these abbeys or fraternities, usually based on an urban quarter. They had many different titles, the *Conards* at Rouen and Evreux, the *Mère folle* at Dijon, and most expressive of all, the *Malgouverne* at Macon, meaning precisely 'misrule'.[28]

These *abbayes de jeunesse*, celebrating feasts which might have a pre-Christian origin, were to be found in villages as well as in towns,

[27] Marcel Poëte, *Une vie de cité. Paris, de sa naissance à nos jours*, II, pp. 5–12.
[28] M. Grinberg, 'Carnaval et société urbaine, XIVe–XVIe siècles: le royaume dans la ville'; N.Z. Davies, 'The Reasons of Misrule: Youth Groups and Charivari in Sixteenth Century France'.

but clearly would not have had as much impact there as in a densely populated urban centre. How did the urban authorities, the merchant-dominated *échevinage* and the (often ecclesiastical) lords of towns, cope with these self-confident and anti-authoritarian actions of those who were, above all, expected to be obedient and submissive – unbeneficed clergy, apprentices and journeymen? It seems that by the later middle ages, the secular authorities were coping very well, the ecclesiastics perhaps less so. They recognised that this 'letting off steam', provided it was kept under control and limited in time, could be beneficial to the over-all exercise of authority. The 'abbeys' began to include young men higher up the social scale than the artisans and labourers, and soon reflected conceptions of hierarchy. This was all the more inevitable because, in the town, Carnival and other feasts where there was, above all, a lot of drinking, became very expensive. The urban authorities, from the late fourteenth century, took over the feasts, which were becoming so expensive that the authorities at Lille, for example, had to beg a substantial sum, in 1426, to help to pay for the feast from the duke of Burgundy.[29] The processions themselves, now often including the officially recognised craft organisations, moved to the *hôtel de ville*, then to the cathedral (or other principal church) and then to the market hall, thus recognising the symbols of authority on the ground.

From town to town, in both countries, the details of the symbolic processions naturally varied, though there were many common features. In fourteenth-century London, after the election of the mayor by the aldermen and the 'discreeter and richer citizens', there was a series of processions and ceremonies. The new mayor, followed by those of his own livery and representatives of various craft gilds, went from the Gild hall, through the city streets, to the exchequer in Westminster, to swear by oath to keep the peace in the city and supervise the price of victuals. On return, and after lunch, he proceeded to the church of St Thomas Acon and then to St Paul's cathedral – visits to other churches being repeated on various subsequent feast days.[30] At Bristol, after the mayor had been chosen on 15 September, the masters of the various recognised craft organisations were also elected, as part of a series of ceremonies and processions through the city, lasting four days. But ceremony

---

[29] Grinberg, 'Carnaval et société urbaine', p. 226.
[30] H.T. Riley, ed., *Munimenta Gildhallae Londoniensis, I, Liber Albus*, chapters 6–8.

persisted on and off from September to Christmas. How much drinking took place is not stated, but an ordinance of 1450, which attempted to regulate the distribution by the mayor and the sheriff, laid down that ninety-nine gallons of wine were to be distributed among the twenty-one craft gilds for drinking on the nights of St John and St Peter.[31] In Coventry, according to Phythian-Adams, rituals were not only played out on such feast days as May Day, Hock Tuesday and Midsummer Day, but the whole year can be seen as divided between a religious and ritual half from Christmas until Midsummer, and a secular half from Midsummer to Christmas.[32]

Coventry was one of a number of English towns whose authorities organised an impressive demonstration of hierarchy, combined with social consensus. By the fifteenth century, this was expressed in the celebrations of the relatively recent feast of Corpus Christi, created by the pope in 1264 and published in England in 1317. According to M. James, Corpus Christi celebrations, with thoughts focussed on the body of Christ, could be used to emphasise the 'social wholeness' of a divided society. Processions were made up of the recognised craft gilds. The order of the crafts in the Corpus Christi procession, and in the watch on Midsummer Eve, was written down in the Coventry Leet Book, a record of the proceedings of the municipal government, in 1445. The procession was ordered so that the least important crafts came first and the two most powerful, last – beginning with fishmongers and cooks, and ending with drapers and mercers.[33]

Norwich also had organised Corpus Christi processions through the city, in which the craftsmen carried their banners, the humbler crafts in the lead. The drapers, grocers and mercers came last, followed by the city officials and the mayor. As at Coventry, the crafts were also responsible for 'pageants', representing the biblical themes characteristic of mystery plays. The mercers, grocers and haberdashers presented 'The Creation of the World'; 'Hell' was acted out by glaziers, carpenters and seven other crafts; 'The Resurrection' by butchers, fishmongers and watermen; and nine other themes by four dozen other groups of craftsmen. The evidence

---

[31] L. Toulmin-Smith, *The Maire of Bristowe is Kalendar by Robert Ricard*, pp. 69 ff.; E.W.W. Veale, ed., *The Great Red Book of Bristol*, I, p. 125.

[32] C. Phythian-Adams, 'Ceremony and the Citizen: the Communal Year at Coventry 1450–1550'.

[33] James, *Ritual*; M.D. Harris, ed., *The Coventry Leet Book: or Mayor's Register*, p. 220.

for these processions and pageants comes from the late forties and fifties of the fifteenth century, a period of considerable social and political tension within the city.[34]

'GLADMAN'S INSURRECTION'

These tensions may have been worsened by the usual division between a narrow mercantile elite and the craftsmen and petty traders, which was expressed institutionally as well as socially. The domination of the mercantile elite is shown by the fact that in the first half of the fifteenth century, all mayors were mercers, as were a majority of the exclusive governing group of twenty-four aldermen. It is clear, however, that there were factional divisions within the elite. John Wetherby, a mercer, who was mayor in 1433, was the leader of one faction and was supported by county magnates, such as the duke of Norfolk and the earl of Suffolk. The undiminished presence in and near the city of the powerful ecclesiastical lords, whom we have already mentioned, such as the cathedral priory, the abbey of St Benet's Hulme, the nunnery of Carrow and so on, made things worse. The priory's continued control over city fairs and the various private feudal jurisdictions within the city caused considerable resentment. The Wetherby faction within the mercantile elite tended to side with the ecclesiastical landlords and were supported by the local magnates. The mercantile elite's Gild of St George, an organisation of which local magnates and gentry were members, and which in 1451 became, in effect, part of the governing body of the city, excluded craftsmen, who evidently resented the way in which they were treated.

It is against this background that we may see a ceremonial demonstration of civic disharmony, the so-called 'Gladman's Insurrection' of 1443.[35] It occurred shortly after the period when conflicts between most of the citizens, the cathedral priory and other ecclesiastics were at their height, at first about jurisdictional claims and control of the fairs. Then, the abbey of St Benet's Hulme complained about the city's mills which, they claimed, interfered with their boats on the river Wensum. The earl of Suffolk, appointed as an arbitrator on the recommendation of the former mayor,

---

[34] Hudson and Tingey, *Records of the City of Norwich*, II, pp. 230, 312.
[35] *Ibid.*, pp. 340 ff.; R.L. Storey, *The End of the House of Lancaster*, Appendix 3.

Thomas Wetherby, tried to make the citizens enter into a bond of £100 with the abbey; they refused; there was a dispute about the sealing of the bond, followed by a riot on 23 January. A jury of inquisition was set up to inquire into 'various treasons'. It consisted not of men from Norwich, but from the county of Norfolk, who were very likely influenced by the landowning supporters of the St George's Gild or Wetherby faction. They did not sit in Norwich, but in Thetford, a small town of the county. This jury presented a version of events favourable to the feudal lords and the oligarchs. It stated that the then mayor and the commonalty, who belonged to a faction hostile to the Wetherby group and who had the support of the artisans, were plotting an insurrection against the bishop, the cathedral priory and the abbey of St Benet's.

The supposed insurrection took the form of a procession led by John Gladman (described as a merchant, possibly originally a smith). Gladman pretended to be a king, riding his horse with a crown, a sword and a sceptre carried before him by a group of twenty-four craftsmen, the most prominent of whom were identified – a shoemaker, an 'osteler' and a cutler. They wore a crown as a badge on their sleeves, and were armed as if they were yeomen of the crown (*valetti corone*). They were followed by a hundred other persons on horse and on foot. Bells were rung in the steeple, and the mayor and the commonalty threatened to attack the priory. Documents were taken from the priory, and the prior was forced to abandon some of his jurisdiction. The city gates were closed, and the duke of Norfolk, the earl of Oxford and other royal officers were excluded from the city.

The city's reply presented an alternative version of the events. It was interpreted as a celebration of Shrove Tuesday ('Fastyngong' Tuesday). John Gladman made 'disport' with his neighbours. His horse was 'trapped' with tinsel, and Gladman, also disguised, was crowned as 'king of Christmas', in token that all mirth should end with the twelve months of the year. He was preceded by men disguised to represent the seasons of the year. He who represented Lent was clad in white, with red herring skins and his horse 'trapped' with oyster shells in token of sadness and absence of mirth. They rode about the various streets of the city with other people, also disguised, making 'mirth and disport and plays'.

The two interpretations of Gladman's procession by those representing the rival factions are not altogether incompatible, except that the one presented by the Wetherby faction is linked with the attack, said to have followed it, by the then mayor and the commonalty against the priory. Otherwise, the chief differences between the two descriptions are, first, that whereas the Thetford jury linked the procession with the January riots, the other faction stated that it took place on Shrove Tuesday (5 March in 1443) – what would be Carnival Day in France and Italy. The other difference is that the Thetford jurors stressed the support for Gladman by low-class artisans. It could also be said that this version emphasises Gladman's appropriation of the symbols of royalty – attendants carrying his sword, crown and sceptre before him, and those attending him pretending to be *valetti corone*.

There is no doubt that the Thetford version heavily stresses what they would, no doubt, consider to be Gladman's 'royal' pretensions. But the other version also presents Gladman as a 'king' – the 'king of Christmas'. 'King' was, of course, frequently used as a medieval image for a leader. So one must not read too much into the presentation of Gladman as a 'king', even in the version hostile to him. On the other hand, when compared to the solemn ritual processions on Corpus Christi day, when all recognised ranks of the urban social order kept their proper place, any such procession, whether it was on 25 January – the feast of the conversion of St Paul – or on Shrove Tuesday, would seem subversive, especially if the leading figures in the twenty-four 'yeomen of the crown' were drawn from the sort of occupations rejected as unfit even for membership of the Common Council.

One of the interesting aspects of the so-called 'Gladman Insurrection' is that, although it would seem to have been appropriately 'Carnivalesque' as well as being subversive, the term 'Carnival' does not appear in any of the descriptions of the events. The fact is that although Shrove Tuesday has traditionally been associated with pre-Lent feasting and jollity, in England the term 'Carnival' as such is virtually absent from descriptions of popular ceremonial. And yet, even though the word is absent, what could this be but another example of Carnival as subversion?

Coventry and Norwich were not the only places where the crafts presented 'pageants'. Ceremonial processions and celebrations were enhanced by the performance of plays in the open air by the various crafts of other towns. Eight English towns are known to have put on play cycles representing stages in sacred world history, from the Creation to the Last Judgement. Eighteen other towns presented rather less elaborate performances. Since these plays would each take some time to perform, they would not necessarily be part of the procession, but would nevertheless be part of the whole civic ceremony. Not only would the urban population be present, but also people from villages outside the town – and from time to time, visiting nobles and members of the royal family.[36]

All these processions, ceremonies and drinkings have been summed up by J. Heers as collective manifestations of popular culture, his emphasis being on the establishment of social links, not only between different urban classes but also between town and country, when peasants came from surrounding villages to enjoy the spectacles and the feasting. As we have seen, in some places there were elements of satire and burlesque, of the world turned upside down, which could be dangerous to the established order in times of conflict, but the urban authorities attempted to project on to rituals, whether of religious or secular origin, a structure emphasising not only the existence of hierarchy, but also its legitimation as part of the natural order. In describing the cycle of ceremony at Coventry, Phythian-Adams states that this had the function of binding the urban community together, stressing functional interdependence rather than class divisions – 'a structurally integrative commensality'. A similar interpretation of a supposed religious and cultural consensus in French towns of the later middle ages is given by B. Chevalier – 'urbanism...was an attribute shared by a collectivity strictly delimited by the town walls, so that no division of class or quarter could basically disturb this cultural unanimity, this system of values, of undisputed obligations and of infallible consensus'.[37]

Chevalier does admit that urban life was in no way short of violence, but attributes this to the irrational and emotional hatred of the rich by the poor. He also admits the absence of the *menu peuple* from much of the ceremony of so-called popular religion. Conclusions of this sort faithfully reflect the official ideology of the ruling groups of medieval urban society. They ignore, or distort, the reality of social conflict. If these conflicts are simply dismissed as irrational, any serious analysis of the economic, social and political conflicts between the various urban classes will be by-passed.

[36] Alan H. Nelson, *The Medieval English Stage: Corpus Christi Pageants and Plays*.
[37] Phythian-Adams, 'Ceremony'; Chevalier, *Bonnes villes*, p. 287.

6. *Urban communities and conflict*

As we have seen, the concept that towns were an essential component of the feudal social formation does not imply the existence of a social harmony such as was preached by the exponents of the theory of the three orders. Class conflict was as much present in feudal as in capitalist society. Our concern here is to examine these conflicts which were specific to the towns. These may be summarised as those between urban communities and the various representatives of feudal interests; those between the crafts and their allies against the mercantile oligarchies; and those within the crafts between the masters and the journeymen. These categories of social conflict no doubt appear somewhat simplified here, so we have to take into account also the involvement of other social strata, such as the unskilled workers outside the craft structure, and the marginals, not to speak of splits within the main classes – that at Norwich in the mid-fifteenth century, for example, which we have just described in another context.

COMMUNES AND BOROUGH FRANCHISES

Early medieval urban communities, or rather the merchants who spoke for them, asked for the privileges which would give them freedom for mercantile activity. These privileges were very much the same in the French communes, in the *villes de franchise* and the *villes de consulat* as well as in the English free boroughs. The urban bourgeoisie had specific class interests in the achievement of privileges, which not only enabled it to control its mercantile activities, but also to subordinate the artisans, to organise municipal finance, and to use the crucial instrument of power in feudal society, jurisdiction, over the town's inhabitants.

Urban privileges, granted by a charter from the lord of a town, whether king, count or bishop, naturally varied according to different factors. These included the size and status of the town, the power of the lord, the lord's financial needs, the character and influence of the urban bourgeoisie and, of course, the historical and regional context. There were, nevertheless, considerable similarities, especially between the privileges of English towns and those of northern and central France. Most of them have been mentioned above, but it would be useful to give a brief summary at this point of those most frequently included in the charters. They are as follows:

1 Legal security for the burgesses, personally, against arbitrary feudal jurisdiction. This was implied by the personal freedom conveyed by burgess statutes and by there being no obligation to attend (with few exceptions) courts outside the town.

2 Simplified legal processes in urban courts. Decision by duel and ordeal, if not entirely abolished, was limited. There were reduced and fixed penalties.

3 Tenure of urban real property was a form of free tenure. It was expressed as 'burgage tenure' in Normandy and England. Rents were normally paid only in money.

4 Burgesses were exempt from seigneurial impositions such as tolls, *banalités*, *gîte* and tallage.

5 Property was secured against arbitrary seizure, though measures against debtors from outside could include the right of distraint on the debtor's goods, and even on goods of fellow townsmen of the debtor.

6 There was a varying degree of financial autonomy, usually by giving the townsmen the right to collect various dues previously collected by royal and seigneurial officials, and to pay an annual lump sum to the king or the lord (*firma burgi* in England).

7 There were varying degrees of political or administrative autonomy, usually involving the government of the town by a number of elected officials, such as mayor, *échevins*, consuls and so on. The smaller the town, the less likely was self-government – the urban court would be presided over by the lord's steward.

As we have seen, in England these privileges were often associated with the grant or legitimation of a gild merchant.

The acquisition of these privileges was by no means easy, and often involved conflict between the lords of towns and the townspeople, usually represented by the merchants. The movement for the establishment of urban communes, mainly in France but to a much lesser extent in England, has been thought of as a form of bourgeois self-assertion against feudal lords, arising from an incompatibility of outlook and interests. There is no doubt that great hostility to communes was expressed by spokesmen for feudal (especially ecclesiastical) interests. An example from France in the mid-twelfth century is given in the chronicle of Hugues of Poitiers, monk and chronicler of the abbey of Vézelay, which was lord of the town of Vézelay in Burgundy. No doubt expressing the views of the abbot and his fellow monks, Hugues described those demanding a commune in 1152–5 as impious, faithless and sacrilegious traitors. He states that the bourgeois of the town were conspirators, and their execrable commune was a league of evil plotters against the virtuous rule of the abbey.[1]

Hostility to communes in England was also expressed by the chronicler, Richard of Devizes, a monk of Winchester, towards the end of the twelfth century. Commenting with hostility on the grant of a commune to the city of London in 1191, he quoted a supposed saying, 'Communia est tumor plebis, timor regni, tepor sacerdoti'.[2] An aspect of the commune which horrified this monk was similar to that which shocked Hugues of Poitiers; that it had evidently emerged from a *conjuratio*, that is, a mutual oath between those requesting the formation of a commune. This is the aspect of the French communal movement stressed by C. Petit-Dutaillis – who also pointed out that the privileges of a *ville de franchise*, where there was no mutual oath among the burgesses, could be as wide ranging, or even greater, than those of many communes.[3] The hostility – where it existed – of the authorities in feudal society to such mutual oaths is understandable. They were regarded as subversive of the essentially hierarchical concept within the feudal order, in which oaths of loyalty should be sworn, not among equals, but from the lower to the higher, from vassals to their lords.

In fact, the history of the urban communal movements hardly bears out at all the interpretation of it as bourgeois anti-feudalism.

[1] Yves Sassier, 'Une condamnation de la révolte au XIIe siècle. Hugues de Poitier et la commune de Vézelay'.

[2] C. Brooke and G. Keir, *London*, p. 45, and W. Stubbs, *Select Charters and other Illustrations of English Constitutional History*, p. 245.

[3] C. Petit-Dutaillis, *Les Communes*, pp. 37–61.

If some individual communal movements are taken out of context, there might seem to be some justification for such an interpretation. But considered as a whole, there is little confirmation from the evidence.

Many of the urban franchises listed above were granted to English towns by the crown with little need for agitation. The farm of the borough was a much more convenient financial device for the royal exchequer than collection by royal officials. In any case, the (usually two) bailiffs chosen by the burgesses to collect the moneys which constituted the income for the farm payment were regarded as crown officials, as contrasted with the mayor (when such an official emerged) who was considered to represent the burgesses. The 'commune' was hardly needed as an instrument of burgess privilege.

Two English communes are mentioned in the exchequer Pipe Rolls of 1170 and 1176, those of Gloucester and York, but only because fines were imposed for their creation on individuals, presumably suspected as leaders.[4] Little more is known of them, and the punishment may simply have been for too eager anticipation of chartered franchises, rather than because of any serious fear of communal agitation. The 1191 commune of London, accepted by the Regent, Prince John, the king's brother, and other magnates, in the absence of Richard I, was clearly not in any way regarded as dangerous by the crown. It simply perpetuated an existing oligarchy, hence the popular uprising against it in the middle 1190s. It acquired the new – and long-lasting – office of mayor.

The English feudal monarchy may have found it convenient to grant franchises to the mercantile communities of the royal boroughs. It did not go out of its way to support discontented townspeople against other feudal magnates. The example of Bury St Edmunds is worth quoting. This town, which was becoming a leading centre of cloth production in the fourteenth century, was owned by the rich Benedictine abbey of St Edmund, the abbey's sacristan being the immediate lord of the town. Bury had acquired, from various abbots, during the course of the twelfth century, a number of elementary urban privileges, including the right to have a gild merchant, headed by an alderman. But although some of the abbots were reasonably conciliatory towards the burgesses, the sacristan, the cellarer and the monks were less so. After 1180 especially, they were increasingly concerned to extract the maximum

[4] J. Tait, *The Medieval English Borough*, pp. 176–7.

profit from this flourishing town, including an increase in the farm of the borough. The burgesses were not allowed to collect their own tallage, which was done by the monks.

It would seem that relations between abbey and town continued to deteriorate during the thirteenth century. In 1264, during the upheaval of the barons' wars, a movement for independence developed, not among the rich burgesses of the gild merchant, but among a, presumably, lower urban stratum. They were referred to as the *bachilarii*. They set up a *gilda iuvenum* with its own alderman and bailiffs, intended to replace the existing borough court (portmanmoot) and gild. An alliance between the leading burgesses of the gild merchant and the abbey succeeded in suppressing what was, in effect, an attempted commune. Nevertheless the town was fined 200 marks by the crown for supporting Simon de Montfort.

Further conflicts after 1264 gave the impression of a more united burgess front at Bury St Edmunds. Claims for municipal self-government were made in 1290, 1304 and 1327 under the leadership of the old gild merchant and its aldermen. According to the version given by hostile monastic chroniclers, there were violent acts against the sacristan's officials. But, as the final charter of 1327, forced on the abbey by the burgesses with local support from knights and Franciscan friars, shows, what was being demanded was no more radical than the privileges already granted by the crown to many towns, such as Ipswich. The king had given half-hearted support to some of the minor claims of the townspeople in 1292, but failed to confirm their twelfth-century privileges. He supported the abolition of the gild merchant in 1305. His successor abolished the new charter of 1327 and annulled all previous (though minor) privileges ever granted to the town.[5]

Does this contradictory attitude of a feudal monarchy, which granted extensive liberties elsewhere, suggest an underlying incompatibility of feudal and mercantile interests? This seems unlikely. Royal hostility to some urban communities remained at this period because of their support for the new baronial movement in the 1260s. But alignment with Simon de Montfort and the barons would hardly be an anti-feudal gesture. It would seem that royal support for what was clearly a very oppressive feudal lord at Bury St Edmunds was an aspect of something approaching a phobia about

[5] H.W.C. Davies, 'The Liberties of Bury St Edmunds' and 'The Commune of Bury St Edmunds 1264'; M.D. Lobel, *The Borough of Bury St Edmunds*; R.S. Gottfried, *Bury St Edmunds and the Urban Crisis 1290–1539*.

any suspected conspiracy to undermine any sort of established authority, also manifested in hostility to self-expression by social groups as far down the social scale as urban craft journeymen.

The history of the more widespread communal movements in France in no way supports the concept of a clash between the interests of the mercantile bourgeoisie and those of the feudal order. We have a rather bizarre event in 1193 when the seneschal of Normandy, acting on behalf of Richard Plantagenet, ordered the bourgeoisie of Evreux to set up a sworn commune, with special responsibility for the town's fortification against the Capetian monarchy.[6] Both the Capetian and Plantagenet kings were quite willing to back communal movements for political purposes, whether against each other, as in the case of Evreux, or, as Petit-Dutaillis noted in the case of the Capetians, so as to establish a royal urban foothold at the expense of a lord of the town. Other lords also used communes as pawns in conflict with their feudal rivals. In fact, towns which came into conflict with their lords, over privileges and jurisdiction, over *banalités*, or over the profits of fairs and markets, could be regarded more as rivals in the game of feudal politics than as standard-bearers of bourgeois class demands – even though their demands were clearly linked with the needs of a commercial, not a landowning, entity.

The complex involvement of a commune with feudal politics is illustrated by an early case – Le Mans, a sworn commune which, in the end, came to nothing for lack of a rich bourgeoisie to maintain it. The people who swore to create a commune were more of a petty bourgeoisie of small traders and craftsmen. They came together as a *conspiratio* after William, duke of Normandy, had annexed the county of Maine, but who, by 1066, was preoccupied with conquering England. They invited an Italian marquis, Azzo, son-in-law of the displaced count of Maine, to replace Duke William. Azzo soon retreated, living his wife and son, Hugues, in charge. But they provoked popular discontent by heavy taxation, and the people were supported by local nobles and clerics, some of whom had begun by supporting Azzo and his son. The townsmen even switched to supporting the Norman appointed bishop of Le Mans, when he pronounced an interdict against Hugues.[7]

This example of the mixture of communal aspirations and feudal

---

[6] A. and S. Plaisse, *La vie municipale à Evreux pendant la guerre de cent ans*, chapter 2.   [7] R. Latouche, 'La commune du Mans, 1070'.

politics might seem of little importance, considering the short life of the commune, but it would appear that this sort of mixture was not uncommon. Vézelay, mentioned above, provides an example. The bourgeois of the town had been seeking communal privileges well before the events of 1152–5, without success; but at that point they found an ally in the count of Nevers, one of whose aims as consolidator of his comital authority was to assert his jurisdictional superiority over the abbey. He was prepared to support the burgesses.[8] Petit-Dutaillis cites half a dozen late-eleventh-century examples of communes being created or supported by bishops or abbots as an ally against local nobles, sometimes with the encouragement of the king. He also cites about a dozen other examples, where communes were encouraged and supported either by the king or by local counts, to counter the violence of the lesser nobility. Even the commune of Laon, which had begun with an insurrection in 1112, was recognised in 1128 as an *institutio pacis* by the bishop, whose predecessor had been killed during the revolt.[9]

The willing grants of urban privileges in England by the Norman and Angevin kings have been noticed. They were matched in Normandy well before the creation, under orders, of the commune of Evreux. The *Etablissements* of Rouen were granted between 1160 and 1170. The town had already gained some of the basic privileges of an urban community in 1149–50. These were considerably extended in the *Etablissements* on the basis of a sworn commune. A typically narrow oligarchy of a mayor, twelve *échevins* and twelve councillors was chosen from a hundred peers, with extensive powers of jurisdiction, except for *haute justice* which (as in other communes) remained in the hands of the king–duke. Rouen citizens could only be judged in their own court; the commune collected and handed over the ducal revenues, and was responsible for military service.[10]

The communal movements and the analogous creation of consulates in Languedoc and Provence varied greatly from one town to another. There was very little insurrectional violence in the consular movement in the south. Boulet-Sautel insists on the revolutionary character of the communal movements in central France, but nevertheless admits that there were several cases (Auxerre, Vézelay, Sens, Dijon) where one feudal lord would be

---

[8] Sassier, 'Une condamnation'.
[9] Petit-Dutaillis, *Les Communes*, pp. 83–99.
[10] L. Musset in M. Mollat, ed., *Histoire de Rouen*, pp. 61–3.

found siding with the commune against a rival. This situation was illustrated too at Chartres in the early thirteenth century, where the townsmen opposed the cathedral chapter and were supported by the count.[11] But whether towns were communes or consulates, the ruling elites were very narrowly based, representing the interests of rich merchants and sometimes provoking popular agitation for the abolition of the commune, as at Provins. It is possible that the communal movement, as against the widespread granting of urban franchises, has been over-estimated. According to Chédeville, by the end of the twelfth century, there were only about twenty between the Loire and the Rhine.[12] It may be that in playing down the importance of the communes, Chédeville is himself exaggerating. The point, however, is that this scattered and fragmented movement cannot be regarded as an expression of bourgeois antagonism to the feudal order.

REVOLTS AGAINST TAXATION

If we may compare conflicts between feudal lords and urban communities with those between rival feudal lords, is there any analogy between the conflicts internal to urban communities with those between lords and peasants? Forms of exploitation in the towns were not so overt as in the agrarian economy. Nevertheless, the potential antagonism of the crafts against the mercantile oligarchies is evident, even though the forms of expropriation were more hidden. And although we cannot speak of a proletarianisation of the hired labour force, the issue of wage levels and of hours of work was present. The mass of poor, unskilled and casual labourers was clearly affected by the price of food, clothing and lodging.

Urban historians are unable to overlook discontent, often leading to violence. Some of them seem anxious to deny class conflict as being at the root of these disturbances. Susan Reynolds, while recognising the oppression of the poor by the rich, is sceptical about class content in the troubles which followed. Lestocquoy attributes anti-patrician movements in the towns of French Flanders to the work of ambitious agitators. P. Wolff rejects a class explanation of social struggles in Languedoc on the grounds that there were rich

---

[11] M. Boulet-Sautel, 'Les villes du centre de la France'; A. Chédeville, *Chartres*, II, pp. 493–504.

[12] Chédeville in *Histoire de la France urbaine*, II, pp. 164–75.

and poor in every social group, thus making for ease of compromise! Rossiaud interprets urban revolts as irrational violence, devoid of ideas and subject to manipulation from above. Chevalier's interpretation is similar; popular violence is due to the emotions of the poor, there is no class conflict, and the poor have no ideas other than that the rich fail to protect them against such evils as unjust taxation. Such generalised contempt for the urban lower classes does not help us to understand revolt in towns. To do so, we need to examine particular cases.[13]

The first point that should be made is that the broad distinction between rich and poor in medieval towns is by no means devoid of class content. When we look at movements which are sometimes designated as protests of the poor against the rich, we often find a political as well as a social content. The rich are the narrow group of mercantile families which control urban governments, and which specifically and overtly aim to exclude working craftsmen and anybody lower down the social scale from effective participation in any decisions concerning the government of the town. There might seem to be exceptions, as at Montpellier, where some of the consuls were chosen by manual craft gilds. But, in practice, the Montpellier consulate as a whole was dominated by money changers and merchants involved in long-distance trade. When we look at the motives behind urban rebellions, it is not difficult to see that the appropriation of the money or possessions of the mass of the population by the oligarchs was not perceived as a result of the merchants' ability to control the terms of trade with the artisan producers (especially with the development of the putting-out system). It was because they were seen as manipulators of taxation, whether of state or municipal origin. Most of the rebellions, from the thirteenth to the fifteenth century, occurred because of the popular perception that the towns' rulers were using the taxation system to spare themselves, and to place the burden on the mass of the people. And, given the assumptions made about the lack of ideas among urban rebels, it is worth mentioning that they showed an awareness of the difference between regressive and progressive taxation which is still not appreciated by many people today.

---

[13] S. Reynolds, *An Introduction to the History of Medieval English Towns*, pp. 76, 80, 136; J. Lestocquoy, *Les villes de Flandre et d'Italie*, pp. 79–85; P. Wolff, 'Les luttes sociales dans le midi français'; J. Rossiaud in G. Duby, ed., *Histoire de la France urbaine*, II, pp, 518–24; B. Chevalier, *Bonnes villes*, pp. 299–302.

One of the earliest urban rebellions in England against taxation was in London at the end of the twelfth century. It occurred in 1196, shortly after the grant in 1191, by the Regent John, of the privileges of a commune to London. The commune, as we have already mentioned, was ruled by a narrow merchant oligarchy. There is little detail about the revolt, but as described by the chronicler Roger Howden, it seems to have been provoked by characteristic upper-class tax fiddling. Owing to the captivity of King Richard I and to various other problems, heavy taxes were frequently imposed by the royal government (*auxilia* or aids, according to Howden). The rich, in order to spare their own purses, passed the burden of tax on to the poor. As was not infrequently the case, the ordinary people found an ally from a higher class, William Fitzosbert, skilled in the law according to Howden. He argued that rich and poor should pay proportionately to their resources. He was hanged, with nine other rebels.[14]

We do not know the social composition of the rebels against the tax avoidance by the rich, but it was probably the artisans and the lesser merchants. Similar complaints against the richer and more powerful citizens of London were made before the royal commissioners who were compiling the Hundred Rolls of 1274–5. The complainants named persons who were evading tallage when the poor commons (*pauper communa*) of the city had to pay, even though one rich tax evader would make more as a merchant than a hundred of his poorer fellow citizens; rich widows involved in wool trade were buying tax exemptions; and one of the sheriffs was levying a tallage in order to get money to pay the fines of dealers illegally exporting wool.[15]

By the middle of the thirteenth century, in provincial English towns, the ordinary townspeople, again probably for the most part the craftsmen, were complaining about taxation. The 'lesser commons' of Oxford, in 1257, accused the ruling elite of excessive tallage. The rulers of Lincoln in 1264 were accused of misappropriating various market profits (tronage and stallage), but more seriously of not contributing to the £1,000 fine imposed on the city for its support of the de Montfort party in the recent baronial wars. In 1290, they were again accused of forcing the poor to pay fines due by the city to the crown, as well as unfairly assessing the tallage. The

---

[14] Brooke and Keir, *London*, pp. 48–9, 247; W. Stubbs, ed., *Chronica Magistri Rogeri de Hovedon*, IV, pp. 5–6.   [15] *Rotuli Hundredorum*, I, pp. 403–7.

commons of Gloucester in the same year complained that the *potentiores villae* were excessively taxing them and presumably not paying their share.[16]

An enquiry by a royal commission in 1305 into similar accusations of taxation manipulation at York gives an interesting insight into the details. It appeared that a confraternity, which purported to have as one of its aims the support of a hospital, a *maison dieu*, was used as a cover for a group of rich citizens, one of whom was the mayor of the city. It was, in effect, a secret caucus within the oligarchy. They swore never to pursue each other at law and to protect each other, even against members of their own family. They arranged that members of the confraternity would constitute a majority, at any time, of the tax assessors, so that they would either be exempt or at least have their tax reduced. Still further, they arranged for there to be a perpetual tax on the weekly earnings of carpenters, smiths and other artisans at a rate of 1d. for every 2s. After the inquiry, the confraternity was dissolved and they were temporarily deprived of citizenship. But after a year they were re-admitted. One of them became a city bailiff and another, the mayor – within four years.[17]

The York case was unusual in that action against the urban oligarchs by the crown went as far as it did, even though forgiveness came very quickly. More frequently, there was complicity between royal judges and the urban elites. At Bristol, between 1312 and 1316, there was overt conflict between a narrow oligarchy, allied to the constable of the royal castle, and a popular party. Customs dues and a tallage triggered off the dispute. The crown backed the oligarchs. The popular mayor chosen by the commons was imprisoned in the Tower of London, and a royal commission of inquiry into the rebellion was set up. It was headed by Bristol's major ʻfeudal opponent, Lord Thomas of Berkeley and the jury was chosen from (presumably compliant) men from the county of Gloucester.[18]

The more abundant evidence from French towns confirms this picture of unjust taxation as one of the main triggers of rebellion. This is not surprising in view of the wars fought on French soil,

[16] *Calendar of Inquisitions Miscellaneous*, I, 1219–1307, p. 79; J.W.F. Hill, *Medieval Lincoln*, pp. 200–14; *Rotuli Parliamentorum*, I, p. 47.
[17] G.O. Sayles, ʻDissolution of a Gild in York'.
[18] E.A. Fuller, ʻThe Tallage of 6 Edward II and the Bristol Rebellion'. Sayles in the article cited in note 17 quotes a report of the Bristol community in 1312 in a *Coram Rege Roll* (no. 287, m. 86).

especially the Anglo-French wars in the fourteenth and fifteenth centuries. A heavy burden was imposed on town and country alike, quite apart from the depredations of the invading armies. Troops had to be mobilised and towns had to be fortified. This last burden was particularly significant for the urban tax-payer.

Already in the thirteenth century, revolts against the urban elites were caused by tax impositions. They were already beginning (and would continue) at Arras from 1253. Risings against taxation at Rouen in 1281 and 1292 resulted in the abolition of the commune by Philip IV. In 1315, not long after the restoration of the commune, there were several risings of the *petit commun* against the *gros bourgeois*, again because of financial corruption. Heavy taxation and corrupt practices caused further uprisings in 1345 and 1351, so serious in 1351 that eighty-three textile workers were hanged. At Provins in 1281, the mayor was killed in an artisan rising which was part of a generalised protest by the *menu peuple* against fiscal pressure. This eventually led to a demand in 1324 by an overwhelming majority of the population for the suppression of the commune and its transfer to the lordship of the crown, because of the fiscal oppression by the mayor and the *échevins*.[19]

In Languedoc as well as in northern and central France, anti-tax protests are to be found. In Montpellier, as we have mentioned, the self-styled *populares* faction got lower-class backing and organised an anti-tax demonstration in 1325. The people of the cathedral city of Agde, on the Mediterranean coast, protested in 1332 against the king's demand for an aid for knighting his son and marrying off his daughter. The protest was not only because this was another case of the rich exploiting the poor, but because half of the property in the city would not be taxed because it belonged to the church and was therefore exempt. This was just a beginning – between the 1350s and the 1380s, there were at least ten more anti-tax revolts in Languedocian towns. More interesting, as P. Wolff points out, there was, in Languedoc in the thirteenth and fourteenth centuries, a clear opinion expressed by the poorer members of the population. As elsewhere, they accepted the inevitability of the tax, but insisted that it should be assessed as a proportion of a person's wealth, not a poll tax and not an indirect tax on consumables. These last two forms of tax were, as would be expected, those preferred by the

---

[19] Lestocquoy, *Les dynasties bourgeoises d'Arras*, chapter 8; A. Sadournay in Mollat, ed., *Histoire de Rouen*, chapters 4 and 5; E. Chapin, *Les villes de foire*, chapter 4.

wealthy. By the time of generalised lower-class discontent throughout Europe, 1379–82, there were risings in twenty-seven French towns because of the ways in which the tax burden had been shifted on to the common people.[20]

The anti-tax risings of 1382 were provoked, after the long period of exactions during the fourteenth century, by disappointment at the failure of the government of Charles VI to fulfil his father's deathbed promise to abolish various forms of tax. Details concerning the events in many towns are unknown. Evreux, one of the many Norman towns where there was a rising, was punished by having to pay 3,000 l.t., only exceeded (in Normandy) by similar exactions from Rouen, Caen and Bayeux. Virtually nothing is known, apart from the broad outlines, of the forms of resistance attributed to most of the towns – the exclusion of officials from the shops so that they could not levy the indirect tax on consumables at the point of sale, and, of course, street riots of varying intensity. Rather more is known about the *Harelle* (riot) at Rouen. It began with street demonstrations, then pillaging of the houses of the rich (especially the mayor and former mayors), attacks on priests, money lenders and Jews. The urban bourgeoisie, some of whom supported the movement at the beginning, used this opportunity to remove jurisdictional and other rights from the cathedral chapter and the abbey of St Ouen. In the end, the king took over the city. There was the usual hanging of ring-leaders. The assembly of the Estates of Normandy then granted a series of taxes, including indirect taxes on consumables.[21]

Paris, of course, was not exempt. The 'lesser' people there too revolted against the levying of indirect taxes on consumables, after important elements among the bourgeoisie had already made their protest – partly out of fear of popular rioting. The rebels were composed of marginals, peasant immigrants, journeymen and some craftsmen. They reacted to the collection of the taxes by royal officials at the markets (the *Halles*), and armed themselves with hammers (*maillets*), which had been stored as weapons of defence in the *hôtel de ville* – hence the term used to describe the rebels:

---

[20] A. Castaldo, *Le consulat médiéval d'Agde, XIIIe–XIVe siècles*, pp. 416–24, and Part 3, chapter 1; Wolff, 'Les luttes sociales'; L. Mirot, *Les insurrections urbaines au début du règne de Charles VI, 1380–1383*.

[21] A. and S. Plaisse, *La vie municipale*, p. 210; Sadourney, in Mollat, ed., *Histoire de Rouen*, pp. 116 ff.

'maillotins'. There was no identity here, either between any bourgeois political faction or the organised crafts, and the rebels. Most of the rebels were the poor, alienated from the recognised structures of Parisian society and condemned then, and by later historians, as emotional and irrational. Scores of them were executed.[22]

The fiscal demands of the French monarchy became no less oppressive in the fifteenth century. It is not surprising that rebellions against taxation continued. A striking example is the *rebeyne* at Lyons in 1436. This was a city by no means exempt from internal conflict in earlier periods, ranging from the bourgeois-led movements against the city's feudal lord, the archbishop (1206 and 1268), to the encouragement by the archbishop, after the French monarchy had taken over the city, of attacks by clerks, journeymen and beggars against the seal of royal jurisdiction (1371–5). The anti-tax movements of the 1380s had little resonance in Lyons. But in 1436, in a period of bread shortage and unemployment, a combination of heavy tallage, a forced loan to the crown and indirect taxes on consumables triggered off a rebellion which embraced marginals, journeymen, craftsmen, petty traders and city-based agricultural workers, supported by some local lawyers, especially the notary, Jean de Condeyssie. Royal officials and bourgeois tax evaders were among those hated by the rebels. There were riotous assemblies, and some of the houses of the rich were pillaged, but otherwise there was little violence. There was even a temporary acceptance by the consular government of ten people's representatives. Demands for the rich to pay tax arrears were unsuccessful, and the rebellion collapsed. The ruling consuls abolished the ten people's representatives but were prepared to issue pardons. Then the king arrived, leaders were imprisoned, three persons were executed, a hundred and twenty exiled – and the commune was suppressed.[23]

The appropriation of tax by the urban oligarchies from the mass of the population was similar to the appropriation of rent from the peasantry by the feudal landowner, even though it was disguised, especially if it was originally a crown imposition, as a payment for public service and protection. What was opposed by the artisans and those below them was the deliberate inequality, and also the evident misappropriation, of the tax, for example by tax farmers. This

---

[22] J. Favier, *Paris*, Part 2, chapter 1; B. Geremek, *The Margins*, pp. 290–3.
[23] J. Déniau in Kleinclausz, ed., *Histoire de Lyon*, Book 4, chapter 4; R. Fédou, 'Une révolte populaire à Lyon du XVe siècle: la Rébeyne de 1436'.

shifting of the tax burden away from the well-to-do is well illustrated by the accounts of the Auvergne town of St Flour. These have been calculated in detail by A. Rigaudière. Between 1378 and 1466, fifty per cent of the total income, most of which was spent on defence, was derived from indirect taxes on consumables. Only thirty per cent was derived from tallage. The tallage was a direct tax on property, but it was not levied without discrimination. The increasing numbers of bourgeois who managed to get themselves ennobled paid nothing, for that reason; nor did officials or clergy. There was a fifty per cent abatement for urban dwellings, gardens and mills, but artisans' workshops paid one hundred per cent – a clear fiscal privilege for rich property owners and merchants, as the author points out. There were also deductions from the valuations of taxable property. These deductions consisted of the capital value of pious foundations, pensions for relatives and clergy, and alms. On the whole, these were confined to the rich, some of whom, therefore, had to pay no tax at all.[24]

ARTISAN PROTEST AND POLITICAL FACTION

Although most of the protests and revolts against taxation, and especially against its corrupt manipulation by urban authorities, were unambiguous expressions of discontent against this form of appropriation, the protesters, from time to time, became involved, or were used, in political factions within ruling groups. The conflicts in mid-fourteenth-century Paris seemed to contemporaries, and to modern historians, to be between reformers and those bourgeois who manipulated their financial connections with the royal household and government. This conflict led to demands for the summoning of assemblies of the three estates (clergy, nobles and towns) to discuss taxation. Etienne Marcel, the draper who dissociated himself from the corrupt financiers, some of whom were his relatives, became *prévot des marchands* in 1354, supported the reformers, and represented the towns in the estate assemblies. He was seen to represent Paris against noble factions, indeed against the nobles as a class. He established his power in the city by an alliance with the people and the crafts in 1357 – an alliance based on their shared hostility to monetary manipulation, used by the Regent as an alternative device to taxation for raising money. His basic aim was the domination by Paris of the third estate in the assembly, which

[24] A. Rigaudière, *St Flour*, Book 3, chapter 2; see also p. 911, diagram 3.

represented all the kingdom's towns. But he lost the support of his popular allies, who disliked his acceptance of English troops. The so-called Paris revolution ended with his assassination at the end of July 1358.[25]

If the rising of the maillotins in Paris in 1382 had little or no connection with bourgeois political factions, the affair of the 'Cabochiens' was so involved. It took place against a background of popular discontent. The atmosphere is well conveyed in the diary of the Bourgeois de Paris (possibly a cathedral canon).[26] He shows that the lesser people of Paris (the *menu commun*), including the marginals, were well aware that, in addition to taxation, it was shortages due to the pillaging of rival armies which brought them starvation. Hence their desire for peace, expressed in 1413, before the provocative activities of the Armagnacs moved the people to support their massacre in 1418.

Popular fears in Paris seem to have been generated originally by rumours that taxation would be imposed at a meeting of an assembly of the three estates. But this was in the context of the national political rivalries between Armagnacs and Burgundians, which were reflected in Parisian factions. The bourgeoisie tended to support the duke of Burgundy against the Armagnac supporters of the king and the dauphin. These bourgeois, allied with the university, represented a continuing tradition in favour of moderate administrative reform. But the powerful, rich, but much disdained, Paris butchers (the Cabochiens) wanted the total destruction of the Armagnacs and were supported by the mass of the people. After 1413, power swung between the parties and, in the end, the Armagnacs were defeated in 1418.[27]

The widespread urban discontent of the early 1380s affected England, even before the rising of May–June 1381. Here too we find examples of an overlapping of craft protest with internal factional struggles within the ruling mercantile oligarchies. At York, the next biggest city after London, in November 1380, an unpopular mayor, John of Gisburne, was deposed, mainly by a body of 'commoners', but among whom were some merchants – a mercer and three drapers. The successor chosen as mayor was a rival of Gisburne within the elite, but evidently acceptable to the commons. He

[25] Apart from Jacques d'Avout, *31 juillet 1358: le meurtre d'Etienne Marcel*, the best assessment is by R. Cazelles, *Paris*, Part 2, chapter 5.

[26] A. Tuetey, ed., *Journal d'un bourgeois de Paris*.

[27] A. Coville, *Les Cabochiens et l'ordonnance de 1413*; Favier, *Paris*, pp. 150 ff.

survived the suppression of the general rebellion later in 1381 and continued as mayor. It would seem that the artisans' hostility to the ruling group under Gisburne, and their resentment at their exclusion from any part in city government, rather than any economic grievances, such as arising from taxation, provoked their action. Their attack at this time on various religious houses may well have reflected an anti-authoritarian feeling.

But at Beverley, a large Yorkshire town, tenth in ranking order of population after London in 1377, fiscal oppression seems to have provoked the craftsmen. In May 1381, they actually took over the town's government from a narrow oligarchy of merchants, who operated under the lordship of the archbishop of York. Here again the craftsmen ruled under the leadership of the town's alderman, who was a draper. The royal government supported the oligarchy, of course. After the suppression of the rising, Beverley was fined even more than York – £1,000 as against 1,000 marks.[28]

COMMON RIGHTS

A cause of contention in late medieval towns which may have been somewhat neglected by historians – perhaps through shortage of evidence – was, in a sense, an inevitable consequence of the agrarian context of urban settlement.[29] Many medieval towns still had fields and woodland as well as rivers and lakes, in which the townspeople claimed certain common rights, especially for pasture, but also for timber and fish. The disputes are perhaps more prominent in late medieval English towns, because of the enclosure of pasture resulting from the development of wool production for the home and Flemish textile industries, but they also occurred in French towns.

Householders in French towns, like their English counterparts, would have one or two domestic animals. In late medieval Evreux, up to 2,000 pigs were pastured each year in the woods around the town, their owners paying pannage to the revenue farmers. The citizens of Besançon claimed rights in nearby forests, and were in dispute with the local nobility on this issue. One of the best examples of conflict over common rights, partly because of the town's location but also because of the survival of good documentary evidence, is from the city of Agde. As early as 1260, the settlement of a conflict

---

[28] R.B. Dobson, 'The Risings in York, Beverley and Scarborough 1380–1381'.
[29] The issue was at the forefront of F.W. Maitland's *Township and Borough*, but has not been a major concern of English urban historians since then.

between the *universitas* of the city and the bishop as overlord included the concession by the bishop to the citizens of pasture and fishing rights within the extra-mural territory. Disputes continued well into the fourteenth century, especially because of the over-zealous insistence on the bishop's rights by his officials. In 1338, an arbitration favourable to the citizens revealed not only that their access to the fisheries of local small lakes and the river Hérault, and to common pasture on fallow land, had been hindered, but also that common land and fishing rights had been sold off to individuals, thus reducing citizens' access.[30]

In England, towards the end of the fourteenth century and in the fifteenth century, similar grievances of the middling elements of the population, not only against feudal lords but also against the oligarchs, appear. These concerned the erosion of common rights, mainly of pasture, in the fields around the town. This resulted from the enclosure of meadowland and pasture by landowning urban institutions and wealthy merchants. In 1381, in Cambridge, one of the reasons why the middling elements supported the peasants' revolt was because of the enclosure of the commons by rich bourgeois and landowning ecclesiastical bodies. There were similar disputes at York and Durham in the 1430s and 1480s, and anti-enclosure riots against the landowning cathedral chapters, whose canons were normally members of the ruling urban families. But the most famous case was that of Coventry, where rich landowning merchants and the cathedral priory either overcrowded the common pastures with their flocks or fenced them off. It culminated in a popular movement in the 1490s, led by a member of the leading craft family, Laurence Saunders. The people went into the fields and pulled down the fences. A poem was pinned on the door of the priory church expounding the grievances of the popular party:

> This cyte is bound that shuld be fre / the right is holden fro the commonalte / our comons that at Lammas open should be cast / They be closed and hedged full fast ... / Be it knowen and understand / this cite shulde be free and now is bonde / Dame Good Eve made hit free.

Saunders was imprisoned in 1496. A repeat of the same protests

---

[30] A. and S. Plaisse, *La vie municipale*, chapter 4; R. Fiétier, *La cité de Besançon*, Book 1, part 2, chapter 1, and Book 2, part 1, chapter 1; Castaldo, *Le consulat médiéval*, pp. 107, 180–91.

took place again in 1525, now under the leadership of a craftsman mayor, the capper, Nicholas Heynes. He was deposed by a royal agent, the marquess of Dorset, and sent to London for questioning.[31]

The grievances at Coventry focussed most on the deprivation of common pasture, the right to put one or two domestic animals on to them being destroyed by the merchants and others with grazier interests. The leadership of the protests was by the crafts, and there were also specific craft grievances. They also protested against the imposition by the ruling elite of high apprenticeship fees, together with municipal control of apprentices. In addition, the textile craftsmen object to the restriction of cloth sales to the supervised cloth hall (drapery), and to the tolls levied on the sale of wool. All craftsmen objected to restrictions on the free sale of their products. But on the whole, in the English towns, craft grievances were not as prominent in social disturbances as were the movements against taxation and the engrossment of the commons. The same seems to be true in France, though the towns of the north-east were, as one would expect, affected by the *guerre des métiers* of the Flemish towns at the turn of the fourteenth century. As is well known, these were involved with the Franco-Flemish war of the early fourteenth century. In Lille, there were craft assemblies which denounced the ruling bourgeoisie as *leliaerts*, that is, supporters of the king of France against the count of Flanders, who sought the support of the crafts.[32]

MASTERS AND JOURNEYMEN

Apart from these conflicts, specific to Flanders, the principal disturbances which affected craft production were those involving masters and their journeymen. Craft masters were prepared to take the lead against the mercantile oligarchies on matters of unjust taxation, especially since, as a class, they were usually excluded from those bodies which decided on essential matters of urban government. But they relied on the oligarchs for the enforcement, in particular, of regulations which controlled their journeymen and, in certain trades, the poorer masters, whose conditions differed very little from those of the journeymen.

[31] M.D. Harris, *Life in an Old English Town*, p. 250; Harris, *The Coventry Leet Book*, pp. 577–8; C. Phythian-Adams, *The Desolation of a City*, pp. 254–6.
[32] L. Trénard, ed., *Histoire d'une métropole*, pp. 125–6.

The medieval workshop has been regarded as a domestic unit of production, with the assumption of harmonious relationships between its members. Although the apprentice, after the end of his period of training, might expect to spend some time as a journeyman, in theory he could also expect soon to become a workshop master himself. Whether, and for how long, this ideal state of affairs existed is difficult to prove, for most of the evidence comes from the period – late thirteenth century onwards – when things were changing. The constant replenishment of urban populations by rural immigrants was reflected in recruitment to the workshops of young people from villages in the region. In the fourteenth century, it is clear that the upward movement of journeymen into the position of masters was much slowed down. In France, as Coornaert has emphasised, masters were succeeded by sons and sons-in-law; few journeymen had the capital to set up for themselves; and the gilds insisted that aspirant masters should provide prohibitively costly *chefs d'oeuvre*, entry fees and contributions to entrance feasts. There were special exemptions for the sons of existing masters.[33] In conditions such as these, it was inevitable that journeymen, who were often married and did not live in the master's household, should be much concerned with wages and hours of work.

The court records of London, especially those of the mayor's court and those of the mayor and sheriffs' court,[34] only yield evidence from the late thirteenth century onwards. They are full of records of clashes between masters and journeymen, almost always concerning wages. Also recorded are attempts by journeymen to set up organisations to promote their interests – 'conspiracies' in the eyes of the authorities.

Several accusations of conspiracy were made before the mayor's court. In two cases in 1299 – one concerning carpenters, the other concerning smiths – the accused conspirators were said to have referred to their illegal associations as 'parliaments'. The most detailed of these early descriptions of conspiracies concerned a number of journeymen spurriers in 1300. They were said to have made an ordinance which they swore upon the Gospels to observe. Among the provisions of the ordinance were that no-one should work between sunset and sunrise; that apprenticeship should last for

[33]   E. Coornaert, *Les corporations*, pp. 194–7, 243–5.
[34]   A.H. Thomas, ed., *Calendar of Early Mayor's Court Rolls of the City of London, 1298–1307*; and Thomas, ed., *Calendar of Plea and Memoranda Rolls of the City of London, 1323–1437*.

at least ten years; and that injuries to any spurrier would be dealt with by the spurriers themselves, not by any king's servant. The case came to court because the journeymen spurriers brought one of their number before an ecclesiastical court for not observing their sworn oath, where he was punished by excommunication. The case petered out, perhaps because of a compromise between the journeymen and the master spurrier who had brought the case against them. What is interesting, however, is that in April 1381 (*before* the rising) another group of journeymen spurriers was presented for having maintained an illegal fraternity for nine years, one of whose purposes was to prevent journeymen spurriers from outside London competing for jobs. These conspirators were also accused of summoning rebellious members of the fraternity for perjury before an ecclesiastical court, in fact, the bishop of London's consistory court.[35]

In 1339, five carpenters were charged with making a confederacy among men of their trade, to prevent working carpenters who came from outside London from taking less than 6d. and an after dinner drink as a day's wage. In 1349, the master cordwainers accused their employees of conspiracy, because sixty of them had agreed to work only by the day and on their own terms. No doubt many of these confederacies met in taverns. But by 1380 they were beginning to meet in churches, like a group of journeymen saddlers who met in the church of St Mary atte Bowe without their masters' consent, as in the case of the spurriers, already quoted.[36]

Other 'covins' or 'conspiracies' were presented before the mayor and sheriffs' court during the fourteenth century, usually journeymen who wanted to improve wages and keep out competitors from outside London. They included carpenters, cordwainers, brewers, tawyers, Flemish weavers, skinners and saddlers. The alleged conspirators, though usually journeymen, sometimes involved masters. Some master fullers and journeymen were accused of conspiracy in 1366. As in the case of illegal journeymen's gatherings, they met in various churches in the city and in Southwark. In this case, the issue before the court seems to have been an assault against an unpopular master by both other masters and journeymen.[37]

The fear of rebellion was expressed in various ordinances, like that of 1326, to the effect that apprentices, journeymen and servants

---

[35] Thomas, ed., *Mayor's Court Rolls*, pp. 25, 52; *Plea and Memoranda Rolls 1364–1381*, pp. 291–2.
[36] Thomas, ed., *Plea and Memoranda Rolls 1323–1364*, pp. 108, 231–2; *ibid., 1364–1381*, p. 264.   [37] *Ibid.*, p. 54.

should work hard, and if rebellious, should be reported to the mayor. In a curious case in 1364, a group of textile craftsmen and a chaplain were imprisoned for demanding an interview with the king, outside London. On the king's instructions they were to be released, provided they gave information about confederacies and conspiracies in taverns.[38]

Illegal journeymen fraternities were also found at Coventry. A journeymen's fraternity of St Anne was founded in 1401, then suppressed, refounded in 1414, and suppressed again. In 1434, another fraternity, of St George, was founded and also suppressed. In Coventry, as in London, journeymen's fraternities and associations continued to be outlawed, unless permitted by the masters and controlled by them. The fear of subversion was rife in fifteenth-century England. In Bristol in 1450, the borough government even ordered the masters of crafts to exclude journeymen, servants and apprentices from their gild halls. If they did enter, they were to be sent before the king and his council as rioters and conventiclers against the king's peace and laws.[39]

There is evidence of similar conflicts over wages and working conditions in French towns, again mainly from the late thirteenth century onwards. As one might expect, the length of the working day featured more prominently than wage claims in the pre-Black Death period. Fullers and cloth finishers (laineurs) at Provins, who had already in 1305 manifested discontent over apprenticeship conditions, were in rebellion in 1324 against the length of the working day, and refused to work overtime. Journeymen in Amiens were in dispute over a long period, from the 1330s to the 1350s, over their hours of work, in spite of attempts by the échevins to play off those paid by the piece against those paid by the day. In 1335, they protested in particular against the installation of a municipal clock to measure their working time. Already in the middle of the thirteenth century, journeymen fullers in Paris, among other grievances which included the dilution of the labour force, demanded that the customary hours of work should be observed. After 1331, as a result of currency changes, an attempt by the crown to adjust Paris wage rates resulted in strikes (taquehans), which took the form of journeymen adjusting the hours of work according to wages received. Currency changes also led to craft-organised riots in 1306

[38] Ibid. 1323–1364, pp. 16 276.
[39] Harris, Life in an Old English Town, pp. 276–7; E.W.W. Veale, ed., The Great Red Book of Bristol, pp. 138–46.

against the effective tripling of rents – a problem which continued until the 1340s.[40]

Wage demands, as well as demands for the control of the working day, were made. Tanners, roofers, sawyers and others made claims at Amiens in 1351 for increased wages. The town authorities sought royal intervention, and the journeymen were punished by the pillory and by branding. Even before the problems caused by the Black Death, the crown was intervening generally to suppress wage claims. A royal ordinance of 1330 prohibited *alliances* aimed at raising wages. Coornaert suggests that before the fifteenth century there was little solidarity among journeymen because of corporate feelings about the craft and loyalty to their masters. However, the ordinance of 1330 does suggest a fear of common action among journeymen. It is also of interest in this context that in a fourteenth-century act of foundation of an artisan fraternity, quoted by Geremek, it was necessary to specify that the fraternity should not be used as a cover for strike action.[41]

I have quoted evidence concerning protest and rebellion in medieval towns, triggered off by unjust tax demands, when the bulk of a town's population would be led by the organised crafts including the craft masters; and lesser protests by journeymen concerning wage rates and the length of the working day. This evidence does not support the view that social discontent, sometimes leading to violence, was irrational, aimless or without class basis. It is possible that some historians, in so far as they are not ideologically motivated to deny the existence of classes and class motives in medieval society, place too much emphasis on the part played by the marginal elements of urban populations in riot and rebellion. It is very difficult to quantify or classify the various elements among the marginals. No doubt they would include unemployed rural immigrants, possibly also casual workers of urban origin. But might they not, for example, include those poor journeymen who could not afford decent clothes, whom the Parisian journeymen fullers wished to exclude (together with women and too many apprentices) from the masters' workshops? Whatever the answer, there can be no doubt that the medieval towns contained many very poor people, living in wretched conditions, who would be very willing to support

---

[40] Chapin, *Les villes de foire*, pp. 216 ff.; E. Maugis, *Recherches*, pp. 343–53; Cazelles, Paris, pp. 84–5; see also Geremek, *Le salariat dans l'artisanat parisien aux XIIIe–XVe siècles*, chapter 5.

[41] Maugis, *Recherches*, p. 353; Geremek, *Salariat*, p. 109.

any riots against the rich. Their presence, however, does not permit the historian to interpret urban popular protest simply in terms of the poor against the rich, without examining the specific concerns of the solid core of protesters. Nor, indeed, without examining the political expression of class divisions in the towns, as between the ruling mercantile oligarchies with all power in their hands, the master craftsmen represented in toothless councils or assemblies, with at most an advisory role, not to speak of the overwhelming majority with no voice and no representation.

Towns in England and France in the middle ages were ruled by narrow oligarchies representing mercantile interests with, in France towards the end of the middle ages, a strong penetration of officialdom. Although, in the earlier phase of European urbanisation, towns, led by the mercantile communities, put forward demands for varying degrees of autonomy from the feudal power, whether monarchical or seigneurial, their aim was to establish a place within the feudal order, not to challenge it, and this was accepted by those feudal powers. The mercantile oligarchies and the feudal powers had compatible economic interests and were indeed interdependent. If, however, I have questioned the concept of the urban element in feudal society as conflicting with the essential class formation of feudalism, I am not attempting to support the theory of feudal society as one of mutually interdependent and supportive orders. Town governments, dominated by mercantile interests, may well have sought to live in harmony with the feudal monarchies and the lay and ecclesiastical potentates, even while supporting their own specific interests. But English and French feudal societies were, nevertheless, class-divided societies, the most important class division necessarily being that between the landed aristocracy and the peasants. Towns, too, were class divided, and, as I have attempted to demonstrate, conflicts occurred at several different levels. Naturally, they do not simply mirror conflicts between peasants and lords. But, admitting the extra dimension of the division between employing craft masters and journeymen, the principal source of urban discontent was the appropriation of surplus from the basic producers, masters and journeymen alike, through a manipulated tax system. This appropriation, significant though it was, did not contribute as high a proportion to the incomes of the urban ruling class as did rents from the peasantry to the feudal landowners – though we should not forget the role of merchants who rented out urban property, such as Boinebroke of Douai.[42] Nevertheless, the tax harvest also represents a form of appropriation characterised, as was feudal rent, by non-economic compulsion.

[42] G. Espinas, *Les origines du capitalisme I: Sire Jehan de Boinebroke, patricien et drapier douaisien.*

Conclusion

I have attempted in this book to study various aspects of English and French towns during the middle ages as necessary features of the feudal society in which they existed. In so doing, I have not accepted interpretations of the medieval town which over-emphasise its rural nature, almost obliterating the distinction between town and country. The undoubted presence, within even quite large towns, of garden plots, vineyards, perhaps some arable and meadowland, not to speak of some inhabitants who were peasants and agricultural workers, is partly responsible for this view. But if occupational heterogeneity is accepted as one of the main determining features of an urban entity, with cultivators absent or constituting only a minority of the town's population, then the importance of the urban component of medieval society must be recognised, even from the earliest post-Roman period onwards.

It follows that one should beware of assimilating the medieval town or city into *agrarian* feudalism. The argument of this book started from the view that feudal society was not essentially based on a 'natural economy' in which everybody, from aristocratic land-owners to peasants, produced their own means of subsistence, whether from the demesne or from rent in labour or kind, in the case of the landowner, or from their family holding, in the case of the peasants. The specialisation of produce and the exchange of various manufactured goods for agricultural produce precedes not only the feudal era, but even so-called 'ancient society'. Clearly there have been periods when the exchange process was in a low state, as in the period of the 'barbarian' invasions in post-Roman Europe. Commodity production at the grass roots of society was, however, an important component of the early medieval economy, and money as the functional necessity of this commodity production was only rarely absent, if often scarce.

152

My stress on the importance of the small market town as an essential component of medieval urbanisation fits in with this emphasis on the early development of simple commodity production. As I have shown, many quite small towns had populations with a minority of cultivators and a heterogeneity of non-agricultural occupations. Nevertheless, given the tendency for medieval households to be multi-occupational rather than specialist – even in the bigger towns – the small market towns, especially if developing organically from a rural settlement, would have a rural feel about them because of the cultivatable plots in the possession of artisans and traders. It is this aspect of small towns which has led some historians to separate them from true urbanisation.

This separation is perhaps understandable if one approaches the phenomenon of urbanisation from a social rather than from an economic standpoint. Even if a small town, on the basis of an analysis of its occupational structure and market function, merits inclusion in the urban network, social existence and the way of life might be nearer to that of a big village than of a larger town.

In feudal society, life in towns with more than three or four thousand inhabitants must have had aspects which differentiated it from life in the small market town. Even if there were important resemblances between certain structures of village, small, and large town, resulting from them all being based on the family household unit of production, there would also be strong contrasts. These would, in the first place, result from a denser population settlement in the large towns. For example, the artisan workshops and retail shops selling foodstuffs, such as bread, would, in the bigger towns, probably be packed closer together than in the village or market town. The street might be a focus of sociability, hardly to be found in the rural context. It is true that this possibility could be complicated by the fact that in some urban streets, houses of three or four storeys would accommodate well-to-do townspeople as well as poor tenants living up towards the roof. Perhaps this division would be reflected in the social composition of the clienteles of different local taverns, which are well known to have been centres of urban sociability. The parish and its church would also have a social function, though this would not be peculiar to the town, except that urban parishes were often – though not invariably – very small.

There were, of course, religious gilds and fraternities in both towns and villages, in England and France alike. But in many of the bigger towns, the linking of the religious gilds and fraternities with the professional organisations of craftsmen must have created a climate which would not have been found in the market towns where craft gilds were unknown. As I have shown in chapter 3, some bigger towns did not have organised craft gilds, but a multiplication of social–religious fraternities, like the forty-three at King's Lynn, would give large-town life a special character.

Carnival, whether subversive or approved, was a peculiarly large-town phenomenon, as were the 'royal' and 'ducal' ceremonial 'entries', not to speak of mayoral processions and other forms of civic ceremony, as on Corpus Christi day. It is not that ceremony was absent from small towns, but tended, as in the villages, to be focussed on the patron saint (or saints) of the parish church. In the bigger towns, ceremony had its religious components, but also tended to have a more prominent secular element. This one would expect, since many of the ceremonies and processions were ritual expressions of secular power.

As I have already emphasised, another specific feature of large-town life was the presence of an incalculable number of people who were not integrated into those structures of medieval urban existence which, with some exaggeration, are thought of as essential, above all, the craft gilds and the fraternities. These unskilled labourers, marginals and transients certainly much pre-occupied urban rulers to the point of obsession. They must also have had their impact on the rest of the population, perhaps to some extent negatively, though it must be remembered that medieval town populations had to be constantly reinforced by rural immigrants. The hostility to 'outsiders' – 'forains' – certainly existed, not only among urban rulers, but also among established craft masters, as well as their journeymen. But medieval people were in general much more mobile than is sometimes supposed, and they themselves, even those whose families had been settled down for several generations (and there were not many), must have recognised the consequences of this mobility.

To emphasise the integration of towns into feudal economic and social structures is not to ignore the special features of urban existence. One must nevertheless be aware that these special features cannot be understood without also recognising the specific characteristics of the social formation of which they formed part.

Bibliography

Aers, D. *Chaucer, Langland and the Creative Imagination*, London, 1980.

Amargier, P. 'Autour de la création du conseil de communauté aux Saintes Maries de la Mer, 1307', *Bulletin philologique et historique*, 1965.

Ashford, L. J. *A History of High Wycombe from its Origins until 1880*, London, 1960.

Attenborough, F. L. *The Laws of the Earliest English Kings*, Cambridge, 1922.

d'Avout, J. *31 juillet 1358: le meurtre d'Etienne Marcel*, Paris, 1960.

Ballard, A., ed., *British Borough Charters, 1042–1216*, Cambridge, 1913.

Baratier, E. *La démographie Provençale du XIIIe au XIVe siècle*, Paris, 1967.

Barron, C. M. 'Richard Whittington: the Man and the Myth' in Hollaender and Kellaway, eds., *Studies in London History presented to Philip Jones*, London, 1969.

Bateson, M. *The Records of the Borough of Leicester*, 2 vols., London, 1899.

Benham, W. G. and I. H. Jeayes, ed., *Court Rolls of the Borough of Colchester, I. 1310–1352*, Colchester, 1921.

Beresford, M. *New Towns of the Middle Ages*, London, 1967.

Beresford, M. and H. P. R. Finberg, *English Medieval Boroughs: a Handlist*, Newton Abbot, 1973.

Berthe, M. *Le comté de Bigorre au bas moyen âge*, Paris, 1976.

Biddle, M., ed., *Winchester in the Early Middle Ages*, Oxford, 1976.

Bird, R. *The Turbulent London of Richard II*, London, 1949.

Birrell, J. 'Berre à la fin du moyen âge', *Cahiers du centre d'études des sociétés Mediterrannéennes*, Aix-en-Provence, 2, 1968.

Bland, A. E., P. A. Brown and R. H. Tawney, eds., *English Economic History: Select Documents*, London, 1933.

Bloch, M. *Seigneurie française et manoir anglais*, Paris, 1960.

Feudal Society, trans. L. A. Manyon, London, 1961.

'Le servage dans la société européenne' in Bloch, *Mélanges historiques*, II, Paris, 1963.

'From the Royal Court to the Court of Rome: the Suit of the Serfs of Rosny-sous-Bois' in S. Thrupp, ed., *Change in Medieval Society*, London, 1965.

Bloom, H. J. *Original Charters Relating to the City of Worcester in*

Possession of the Dean and Chapter, Worcester Historical Society, Worcester, 1909.

Bois, G. *The Crisis of Feudalism: Economy and Society in Eastern Normandy*, Cambridge, 1984.

La mutation de l'an mille: Lournand, village mâconnais de l'antiquité au féodalisme, Paris, 1989.

Bonnassie, P. 'The Survival and Extinction of the Slave System in the Early Medieval West (Fourth to Eleventh Centuries)' in *From Slavery to Feudalism in South-Western Europe*, Cambridge, 1991.

Bonney, M. *Lordship and the Urban Community: Durham and its Overlords 1250–1540*, Cambridge, 1990.

Bottomore, T. *et al.*, eds., *A Dictionary of Marxist Thought*, Oxford, 1983.

de Bouard, M. 'De la confrérie pieuse au métier organisé: la fraternité des fèvres de Caen (fin du XIIe siècle)'; *Annales de Normandie*, 7, 1957.

Boulet-Sautel, M. 'Les villes du centre de la France', in *Les villes*, I, Société Jean Bodin, 6, Brussels, 1955.

Bourde de la Rogerie, H. 'Les fondations de villes et de bourgs en Bretagne du XIe au XIIIe siècle', *Mémoires de la société d'histoire et d'archéologie en Bretagne*, 9, 1928.

Bourilly, V. L. *Essai sur l'histoire politique de la Commune de Marseille*, Marseilles, 1920.

Boussard, J. 'Hypothèses sur la fondation des bourgs et des communes en Normandie', *Annales de Normandie*, 8, 1958.

Bouton, A. *Le Maine. Histoire économique et sociale des origines au XIVe siècle*, Le Mans, 1962.

Braudel, F. *Capitalism and Material Life*, trans. M. Kochan, New York, 1974.

L'identité de la France, Paris, 1986.

Bridbury, A. R. *Medieval Clothmaking: an Economic Survey*, London, 1982.

Briers, P. M., ed., *Henley Borough Records: Assembly Books I–IV, 1395–1543*, Oxford Record Society, Oxford, 1960.

Britnell, R. H. *Growth and Decline of Colchester 1300–1525*, Cambridge, 1988.

Brooke, C. and G. Keir, *London: the Shaping of a City*, London, 1975.

Brooks, N. P. *The Early History of the Church of Canterbury: Christchurch from 597 to 1066*, Leicester, 1984.

Buffelan, J. P. *La noblesse des capitouls de Toulouse*, St Gaudens, 1986.

Butcher, A. F. 'The Decline of Canterbury 1300–1500', unpublished paper, n.d.

Cam, H. M. 'The Early Burgesses of Cambridge in Relation to the Surrounding Countryside' in Cam, *Liberties and Communities in Medieval England*, Cambridge, 1944.

Campbell, J., ed., *The Anglo-Saxons*, Oxford, 1982.

Carus-Wilson, E. and O. Coleman, *England's Export Trade 1275–1547*, Oxford, 1963.

Medieval Merchant Venturers, London, 1964, 1967.

Carver, M. O. *Medieval Worcester: an Archaeological Framework*, Worcester, 1980.

Castaldo, A. *Le consulat médiéval d'Agde. XIIIe–XIVe siècles*, Paris, 1974.

Cazelles, R. *Nouvelle histoire de Paris 1223–1380*, Paris, 1972.

Censier, F. 'Le patriciat lyonnais au début du XIVe siècle', *Colloque Franco-Suisse d'Histoire économique et sociale 1967*, Geneva, 1969.

Chapin, E. *Les villes de foire de Champagne des origines au début du XIVe siècle*, Paris, 1939.

Chédeville, A. *Chartres et ses campagnes XIe–XIIIe siècles*, Paris, 1973.

Chevalier, B. *Tours, ville royale 1256–1520*, Paris, 1975.

Les bonnes villes de France aux XIVe et XVe siècles, Paris, 1982.

Chippoleau, J. 'Entre le religieux et la politique: les confréries de St Esprit en Provence et Comtat-Venaisson à la fin du moyen âge' in Ecole Française de Rome, *Le mouvement confraternal au moyen âge: France, Italie, Suisse*, collection 97, Rome–Lausanne, 1987.

Cipolla, C. M., ed., *The Fontana Economic History of Europe: the Middle Ages*, London, 1972.

Clapham, J. H. 'A Thirteenth Century Market Town', *Cambridge Historical Journal*, 4, 1932–4.

Clarke, H. B. and C. C. Dyer, 'The Early History of Worcester', *Transactions of the Worcester Archaeological Society*, 1968–9.

Colloque Franco-Suisse d'histoire économique et sociale 1967, Geneva, 1969.

Consitt, F. *The London Weavers' Company, I, Twelfth to Close of Sixteenth Century*, Oxford, 1933.

Coornaert, E. *Les corporations en France avant 1789*, Paris, 1941.

'Les ghildes médiévales', *Revue historique*, 199, 1948.

Coss, P. R., ed., *The Early Records of Medieval Coventry*, London, 1986.

Coulet, N. 'Le mouvement confraternel en Provence et dans le Comtat-Venaisson au moyen âge', Ecole française de Rome, *Le mouvement confraternal au moyen âge: France, Italie, Suisse*, collection 97, Rome–Lausanne, 1987.

Aix-en-Provence: espace et relations d'une capitale, Aix-en-Provence, 1988.

Coville, A. *Les Cabochiens et l'ordonnance de 1413*, Paris, 1888.

'Cronica Maiorum et Vicecomitum Londoniarum' in *Liber et Antiquis Legibus*, ed. Thomas Stapleton, Camden Society, London, 1846, p. 98.

Crow, M. and C. Olson, *Chaucer Life Records*, Oxford, 1966.

Davies, C. S. *A History of Macclesfield*, Macclesfield, 1961.

Davies, H. W. C. 'The Liberties of Bury St Edmunds' and 'The Commune of Bury St Edmunds 1264', *English Historical Review*, 24, 1909.

Davies, N. Z. 'The Reasons of Misrule: Youth Groups and Charivari in Sixteenth Century France', *Past and Present*, 50, 1971.

Desportes, F. 'Le pain en Normandie à la fin du moyen âge', *Annales de Normandie*, 31, 1981.

Desportes, P. *Reims et les Rémois*, Paris, 1979.

Devlin, M. A., ed., *The Sermons of Thomas Brinton, Bishop of Rochester 1373–1389*, 2 vols., Camden Society, 1954.

Dobson, R. B. 'Cathedral Chapters and Cathedral Cities', *Northern History*, 19, 1983.

'The Risings in York, Beverley and Scarborough 1380–1381' in R. H.

Hilton and T.H.Aston, eds., *The English Rising of 1381*, Cambridge, 1984.

Dodds, M. H. 'The Bishop's Boroughs', *Archeologia Aeliana*, 3rd series, 12, 1915.

Dognon, P. *Institutions politiques et administratives du pays de Languedoc*, Toulouse, n.d.

Duby, G. *La société aux XIe et XIIe siècles dans la région mâconnaise*, Paris, 1953.

'Les villes du sud-ouest de la Gaulle', in *Settimani di studi sull'alto medioevo*, Spoleto, 6, 1959.

The Rural Economy and Country Life in the Medieval West, trans. C. Postan, London, 1968.

Le dimanche de Bouvines, Paris, 1973.

The Early Growth of the European Economy, trans. H.B. Clarke, London, 1974.

The Chivalrous Society, trans C. Postan, London, 1977.

Les trois ordres ou l'imaginaire du féodalisme, Paris, 1978.

Duby, G., ed., *Histoire de la France urbaine, I, La ville antique*, and II, *La ville médiévale*, Paris, 1980.

Dumézil, G. *Mythes et dieux des Germains*, Paris, 1939.

Duparc, P. 'Confréries du St Esprit et communautés d'habitants au moyen âge', *Revue de l'histoire du droit*, 1958.

Dupont, A. *Les cités de la narbonnaise première depuis les invasions germaniques jusqu'à l'apparition du consulat*, Nîmes, 1942.

Dyer, A. D. *The City of Worcester in the Sixteenth Century*, Leicester, 1973.

Ecole française de Rome, *Le mouvement confraternel au moyen âge: France, Italie, Suisse*, collection 97, Rome–Lausanne, 1987.

Ekwall, E. *Two Early London Subsidy Rolls*, Lund, 1961.

Espinas, G. *La draperie dans la Flandre française au moyen âge*, II, Paris, 1923.

Les origines du capitalisme I: Sire Jehan de Boinebroke, patricien et drapier douaisien, Lille, 1933.

Les origines du capitalisme III: deux fondations de villes dans l'Artois et la Flandre française. St Omer, Lannoy du Nord, Lille, 1946.

Favier, J. *Paris au XVe siècle*, Paris, 1974.

Favreau, R. *La ville de Poitiers à la fin du moyen âge*, Poitiers, 1978.

Fédou, R. 'Une révolte populaire à Lyon du XVe siècle: la Rébeyne de 1436', *Cahiers d'histoire*, 1958.

'Le cycle médiéval des révoltes lyonnaises', *ibid.*, 1973.

'Regards sur l'insurrection lyonnaise de 1269' in *Mélanges Perroy*, Paris, 1973.

Février, P.-A. *Le développement urbain en Provence de l'époque romaine à la fin du XIVe siècle*, Paris, 1964.

Fiétier, R. *La cité de Besançon*, Nancy, 1976.

Finberg, H. P. R. *Gloucestershire Studies*, Leicester, 1957.

Finberg, H. P. R., ed., *The Agrarian History of England and Wales*, I, Cambridge, 1972.

Fossier, R. *La terre et les hommes en Picardie jusqu'à la fin du XIIIe siècle*, Paris, 1968.

Fournial, E. *Les villes et l'economie d'échange en Forez aux XIIIe et XIVe siècles*, Paris, 1967.

Fournier, G. *Le peuplement rural en Basse-Auvergne durant le haut moyen âge*, Clermont Ferrand, 1982.

Frappier-Bigras, D. 'La famille dans l'artisanat parisien du XIIIe siècle', *Le moyen âge*, 1989.

Fraser, D. and A. Sutcliffe, eds., *The Pursuit of Urban History*, London, 1983.

Fulbrook-Leggatt, C. E. W. O. *Anglo-Saxon and Medieval Gloucester*, Gloucester, 1952.

Fuller, E. A. 'The Tallage of 6 Edward II and the Bristol Rebellion', *Transactions of the Bristol and Gloucester Archaeological Society*, 19, 1894.

Ganshof, F. L. *Feudalism*, trans. P. Grierson, New York, 1961.

Geremek, B. *Le salariat dans l'artisanat parisien aux XIIIe–XVe siècles*, Paris, 1968.

   The Margins of Society in Late Medieval Paris, trans. J. Birrell, Cambridge, 1987.

Goldberg, P. J. 'Women in Fifteenth Century Town Life' in J. A. F. Thomson, ed., *Towns and Townspeople in the Fifteenth Century*, Gloucester, 1988.

Gottfried, R. S. *Bury St Edmunds and the Urban Crisis 1290–1539*, Princeton, 1982.

Gouron, A. *La règlementation des métiers en Languedoc au moyen âge*, Paris, 1958.

Gouttebroze, J.-G. 'L'image de la ville dans l'œuvre romanesque de Chrétien de Troyes' in *Razo: Cahiers du centre d'études médiévales de Nice*, Nice, 1979.

Graus, F. 'Social Utopias in the Middle Ages', *Past and Present*, 38, 1967.

Green, A. S. *Town Life in the Fifteenth Century*, 2 vols., London, 1894.

Green, V. *History and Antiquities of the City and Suburbs of Worcester*, London, 1796.

Gretton, R. H. *Burford Records*, Oxford, 1920.

Grierson, P. 'La fonction sociale de la monnaie en Angleterre aux VIIe–VIIIe siècles' in Grierson, *Dark Age Numismatics*, London, 1979.

Grinberg, M. 'Carnaval et société urbaine, XIVe–XVIe siècles: le royaume dans la ville', *Ethnologie française*, 4, 1974.

Gross, C. *The Gild Merchant*, 2 vols., Oxford, 1890.

Guth, P., ed., *Le siècle de St Louis*, Paris, 1970.

Harris, M. D. *Life in an Old English Town*, London, 1898. (Coventry.)

Harris, M. D., ed., *The Coventry Leet Book: or Mayor's Register*, Early English Text Society, London, 1907.

Havighurst, A. F., ed., *The Pirenne Thesis. Analysis, Criticism and Revision*, Boston, 1958.

Hébert, M. *Tarascon aux XIVe et XVe siècles: histoire d'une communauté urbaine provençale*, Aix-en-Provence, 1979.

Hébert, M., ed. *Vie privée et ordre publique à la fin du moyen âge: études sur*

Manosque, la Provence et le Piémont (1250–1450), Aix-en-Provence, 1987.

Heers, J. *Fêtes, jeux et joutes dans les sociétés d'occident à la fin du moyen âge*, Montreal–Paris, 1971.

'Les métiers et les fêtes médiévales en France du Nord et en Angleterre', *Revue du Nord*, 55, 1973.

Hibbert, J. 'The Origins of the Medieval Town Patriciate', *Past and Present*, 3, 1953.

Higounet, C., ed., *Histoire de Bordeaux*, II, Bordeaux, 1966.

Higounet, C. 'Bastides et villeneuves' in *Paysages et villages neufs au moyen âge*, Bordeaux, 1975.

Higounet-Nadal, A. *Périgueux aux XIVe et XVe siècles: étude de démographie historique*, Bordeaux, 1978.

'Les jardins urbains dans la France médiévale' in *Flaran 9*, Auch, 1989.

Higounet-Nadal, A., ed., *Histoire du Périgord*, Toulouse, 1983.

Hill, D., ed., *Ethelred the Unready*, British Archaeological Reports, 59, Oxford, 1978.

Hill, J. W. F., *Medieval Lincoln*, Cambridge, 1948.

Hilton, R. H. *A Medieval Society: the West Midlands at the End of the Thirteenth Century*, London, 1966; Cambridge, 1983.

Bondmen Made Free, London, 1973.

The English Peasantry in the Later Middle Ages, Oxford, 1975.

'Lord and Peasant in Staffordshire in the Middle Ages' in Hilton, *The English Peasantry in the Later Middle Ages*.

'The Small Town as Part of Peasant Society' in Hilton, *The English Peasantry in the Later Middle Ages*.

Introduction in ed., *The Transition from Feudalism to Capitalism*, London, 1976.

The Decline of Serfdom in Medieval England, 2nd edition, London, 1983.

'Feudal Society' in T. Bottomore *et al.*, eds., *A Dictionary of Marxist Thought*, Oxford, 1983.

'Small Town Society in England before the Black Death', *Past and Present*, 105, 1984.

Class Conflict and the Crisis of Feudalism, London, 1985.

'Lords, Burgesses and Hucksters' in Hilton, *Class Conflict and the Crisis of Feudalism*.

'Some Problems of Urban Real Property in the Middle Ages' in Hilton, *Class Conflict and the Crisis of Feudalism*.

'A Thirteenth Century Poem on Disputed Villein Services' in Hilton, *Class Conflict and the Crisis of Feudalism*.

'Medieval Market Towns and Simple Commodity Production', *Past and Present*, 109, 1985.

'Pain et cervoise dans les villes anglaises au moyen âge' in *L'approvisionnement des villes, Flaran 5*, Auch, 1985.

'Révoltes rurales et révoltes urbaines au moyen âge' in *Révolte et société*, 2, Actes du XIVe Colloque d'histoire au présent 1988, Paris, 1989.

'Low Level Urbanisation: the Seigneurial Borough of Thornbury in the Middle Ages' in Z. Razi and R. Smith, eds., *The Manor Court and Medieval English Rural Society: Studies of the Evidence*, Oxford, 1992.

Hilton, R. H. and J. Le Goff, 'Féodalité and Seigneurie in France and England' in D. Johnson, F. Bédarida and F. Crouzet, eds., *Britain and France: Ten Centuries*, Folkestone, 1980.

Hodges, R. *Dark Age Economics: the Origins of Towns and Trade*, London, 1982.

Hodges, R. and B. Hobley, *The Rebirth of Towns in the West AD 700–1050*, Council for British Archaeology, 1988 (CBA Research Report, 68).

Hohenberg, P. M. and L. A. Lees, *The Making of Urban Europe*, Cambridge, Mass., 1985.

Hollaender, A. E. J. and W. Kellaway, eds., *Studies in London History presented to Philip Jones*, London, 1969.

Holt, J. C., ed., *Domesday Studies*, Royal Historical Society, London, 1987.

Holt, R. A. *Gloucester: an English Provincial Town during the Later Middle Ages*, unpublished Ph.D. thesis, University of Birmingham, 1987.

Holt, R. A. and G. Rosser, eds., *The Medieval Town: A Reader in English Urban History 1200–1540*, Harlow, 1990.

Horrox, Rosemary E. 'The Urban Gentry in the Fifteenth Century' in J. A. F. Thomson, ed., *Towns and Townspeople in the Fifteenth Century*, Gloucester, 1988.

Hoskins, W. G. *Local History in England*, London, 1959.

Hudson, W., ed., *Leet Jurisdiction in the City of Norwich*, Selden Society, 5, London, 1892.

Hudson. W. and J. C. Tingey, *Records of the City of Norwich*, 2 vols., Norwich, 1906, 1910.

Hunter, J., ed., *The Pipe Roll of 31 Henry I*, London, 1833, 1929.

James, M. 'Ritual, Drama and the Social Body in the Late Medieval English Town' in James, *Society, Politics and Culture*, Cambridge, 1986.

James, M. K. 'Gilbert Maghfeld, a London Merchant of the Fourteenth Century' in M. K. James, *Studies in the Medieval Wine Trade*, Oxford, 1971.

Jane, L. C., trans., *The Chronicle of Jocelin of Brakelond*, London, 1931.

John, E. *Land Tenure in Early England*, Leicester, 1960.

John, E. L. T., ed., 'Coventry Hundred Rolls' in P. R. Coss, ed., *The Early Records of Medieval Coventry*, London, 1986.

Johnson, A. H. *History of the Worshipful Company of Drapers of London*, I, Oxford, 1915.

Kimball, E. G., ed., *Rolls of the Warwickshire and Coventry Sessions of the Peace, 1377–1397*, Dugdale Society, London, 1939.

Kleinclausz, A., ed., *Histoire de Lyon*, 3 vols., I, Lyons, 1939.

Kowaleski, M. 'The Commercial Dominance of a Provincial Oligarchy: Exeter in the Late Fourteenth Century', *Medieval Studies*, 17, 1984.

Langlois, C.-V. *La vie en France au moyen âge. II, de la fin du XIIe au milieu du XIVe siècle d'après les moralistes du temps*. Paris, 1926.

Latouche, R. 'Un aspect de la vie rurale dans le Maine aux XIe et XIIe siècles: l'établissement des bourgs', *Le moyen âge*, 47, 1937.

    'La commune du Mans, 1070' in Latouche, *Etudes médiévales*, Paris, 1966.

Le Goff, J. 'Ordres mendiants et urbanisation dans la France médiévale. Etat de l'enquête', *Annales E.S.C.*, 1970.

'The Town as an Agent of Civilisation' in C. M. Cipolla, ed., *The Fontana Economic History of Europe: the Middle Ages*, Glasgow, 1975.

L'imaginaire médiéval, Paris, 1985.

Leguay, J. P. *Un réseau urbain au moyen âge: les villes du duché de Bretagne aux XIVe–XVe siècles*, Paris, 1981.

'Le rôle de la zone péri-urbaine dans l'approvisionnement des villes armoricanes au moyen âge' in *L'approvisionnement des villes, Flaran 5*, Auch, 1985.

Lermat, J. 'La ville dans *l'Escoufle* de Jean Renart' in *Razo: Cahiers du centre d'études médiévales de Nice*, Nice, 1979.

Lestocquoy, J. *Les dynasties bourgeoises d'Arras*, Arras, 1945.

Les villes de Flandre et d'Italie sous le gouvernement des patriciens, Paris, 1952.

'Le paysage urbain en France du Ve au XIe siècle', *Annales E.S.C.*, 8, 1953.

Lewis, E., ed., *Medieval Political Ideas*, I, London, 1954.

Lipson, E. *Economic History of England*, I, revised edition, London, 1937.

Lobel, M. D. *The Borough of Bury St Edmunds*, Oxford, 1935.

Lombard-Jourdain, A. 'Y-a-t-il une proto-histoire urbaine en France?', *Annales E.S.C.*, 8, 1953.

Aux origines de Paris: la genèse de la Rive Droite jusqu'en 1223, Paris, 1985.

Lorcin, M.-T. 'Une bourgade artisanale des Monts du Lyonnais aux XIVe et XVe siècles', *Le moyen âge*, 1973.

Lot, F. *Recherches sur la population et la superficie des cités remontant à la période gallo-romaine*, I and II, Paris, 1950.

Loyn, H. R. 'The Overseas Trade of Anglo-Saxon England' in Loyn, *Anglo-Saxon England and the Norman Conquest*, London, 1962.

'Towns in Late Anglo-Saxon England' in P. Clemoes and K. Hughes, eds., *England before the Conquest: Studies Presented to Dorothy Whitelock*, Cambridge, 1971.

Maitland, F. W. *Township and Borough*, Cambridge, 1898.

Mann, J. *Chaucer and Medieval Estates Satire*, Cambridge, 1973.

Maugis, E. *Recherches sur la transformation du régime politique et social de la ville d'Amiens des origines de la commune à la fin du XVIe siècle*, Paris, 1906.

May, P. *Newmarket, Medieval and Tudor*, Newmarket, 1960.

McClure, P. 'Patterns of Migration in the Later Middle Ages; the Evidence of Place-name Surnames', *Economic History Review*, 2nd series, 32, no. 2, 1979.

Metcalf, D. M. 'Continuity and Change in English Monetary History, 973–1086', *British Numismatic Journal*, 50, 51, 1980–1.

Miller, E. 'Medieval York' in *Victoria History of the County of York: the City of York*, I, London, 1961.

Mirot, L. *Les insurrections urbaines au début du règne de Charles VI, 1380–1383*, Paris, 1906.

Mollat, M. 'La draperie normande, moyen âge–XIVe siècle' in *Etudes sur l'économie et la société de l'occident médiéval, XIIe–XVe siècles*, Atti della IIa settimana di studio del Istituto Internazionale Economica Francesco Datini, Florence, 1976.

Mollat, M., ed., *Histoire du Rouen*, Toulouse, 1979.

Morris, J., general ed., *Domesday Book*, Chichester, 1982 *et seq.* (separate volumes for each county).

Morris, R. H. *Chester in the Plantagenet and Tudor Periods*, Chester, 1893.

Mousnier, R. *Les hiérarchies sociales de 1450 à nos jours*, Paris, 1969.

Moussot-Goulard, R. 'Les bourgeois de Condom, décimateurs au XIIIe siècle' in *Mélanges Perroy*, Paris, 1973.

Mundy, J. H. *Liberty and Political Power in Toulouse*, New York, 1954.

Musset, L. 'Peuplement en bourgages et bourgs ruraux en Normandie du Xe au XIIIe siècles', *Cahiers de civilisation médiévale*, 9, 1966.

'Foires et marchés en Normandie à l'époque ducale', *Annales de Normandie*, 1, 1976.

Nelson, A. H. *The Medieval English Stage: Corpus Christi Pageants and Plays*, Chicago, 1974.

Nightingale, P. 'Capitalists, Crafts and Constitutional Change in Late Fourteenth Century London', *Past and Present*, 124, 1989.

Noble, P. S. 'Knights and Burgesses in the Feudal Epic' in C. Harper-Bill and R. Harvey, eds., *The Ideals and Practices of Medieval Knighthood*, Woodbridge, 1986.

Otis, L. L. *Prostitution in Medieval Society: the History of an Urban Institution in Languedoc*, Chicago, 1985.

Owen, D. M., ed., *The Making of King's Lynn*, London, 1984.

Owen, H. and J. B. Blakeway, *History of Shrewsbury*, London, 1825.

Pape, T. *Medieval Newcastle-under-Lyme*, Manchester, 1928.

Pearsall, D., ed., *Piers Plowman by William Langland: an Edition of the C Text*, London, 1978.

Petit-Dutaillis, *The Feudal Monarchy in France and England*, trans. E. D. Hunt, London, 1936.

Les communes françaises. Caractères et évolution des origines au XVIIIe siècle, Paris, 1947.

Phythian-Adams, C. 'Ceremony and the Citizen: the Communal Year at Coventry 1450–1550' in P. Clark and P. Slack, eds., *Crisis and Order in English Towns 1500–1700*, London, 1972.

The Desolation of a City: Coventry and the Urban Crisis of the Late Middle Ages, Cambridge, 1979.

Pilette, F. 'Les bourgs du sud du Pays d'Auge du milieu du XIe au milieu du XIVe siècles', *Annales de Normandie*, 30, 1980.

Piponnier, F. *Costume et vie sociale: la cour d'Anjou, XIVe–XVe siècles*, Paris, 1970.

Pirenne, H. *Medieval Cities: their Origins and the Rebirth of Trade*, trans. F. D. Halsey, Princeton, 1949.

de Pisan, C. *The Middle English Translation of Christine de Pisan's Livre du Corps de policie*, ed. D. Bornstein, Heidelberg, 1977.

The Book of the City of Ladies, Foreword by Marina Warner, London, 1983.

Plaisse, A. and S. Plaisse, *La vie municipale à Evreux pendant la guerre de cent ans*, Evreux, 1978.

Platt, C. *Medieval Southampton: the Port and Trading Community, AD 1000–1600*, London, 1973.

The English Medieval Town, London, 1976.

Plucknett, T. F. T. 'Parliament 1327–1336' in E. B. Fryde and E. Miller, eds., *Historical Studies of the English Parliament*, I, Cambridge, 1970.

Poëte, M. *Une vie de cité. Paris, de sa naissance à nos jours*, I, Paris, 1924.

Poly, J. P. *La Provence et la société féodale 870–1166*, Paris, 1976.

Post, J. 'A Fifteenth Century Customary of the Southwark Stews', *Journal of the Society of Archivists*, 5, 1974–7.

Postan, M. M. *The Medieval Economy and Society*, London, 1972.

Razo: Cahiers du centre d'etudes médiévales de Nice, Nice, 1979, 'L'image de la ville dans la littérature et l'histoire médiévales'.

Reynolds, S. 'The Rulers of London in the Twelfth Century', *History*, 91, 1972.

An Introduction to the History of Medieval English Towns, Oxford, 1977.

'Towns in Domesday Book' in J. C. Holt, ed., *Domesday Studies*, London, 1987.

Rigaudière, A. *St Flour. Ville d'Auvergne au bas moyen âge: étude d'histoire administrative et financière*, Paris, 1982.

Riley, H. T., ed., *Munimenta Gildhallae Londoniensis I Liber Albus*, London, 1859.

Robertson, A. J. *The Laws of the Kings of England from Edmund to Henry I*, Cambridge, 1925.

Rogers, A. 'Medieval Stamford' in Rogers, ed., *The Making of Stamford*, Leicester, 1965.

Rogozinski, J. *Power, Caste and Law: Social Conflict in Fourteenth Century Montpellier*, Cambridge, Mass., 1982.

Rosser, A. G. 'Conflict and Community in English Medieval Towns: Disputes and their Resolution in Hereford 1200–1500', unpublished paper, n.d.

'The Essence of Medieval Communities: the Vill of Westminster 1200–1540', *Transactions of the Royal Historical Society*, London, 1984.

Medieval Westminster 1200–1540, Oxford, 1989.

Rotuli Hundredorum, ed. W. Illingworth, I, Record Commission, London, 1812.

Rotuli Parliamentorum, I, Record Commission, London, 1783.

Royal Historical Society, *The Handbook of British Chronology*, London, 1961.

Saint Léon, E. M. *Histoire des corporations de métier*, Paris, 1897 (4th edition, 1941).

Salter, H. E. *Medieval Oxford*, Oxford, 1936.

Sassier, Y. 'Une condamnation de la révolte au XIIe siècle. Hugues de Poitier et la commune de Vézelay' in *Révolte et Société*, I, Actes du IVe Colloque d'histoire au présent, Paris, 1989.

Sautel, G. 'Les villes du midi méditerranéen au moyen âge' in *Les villes*, II, Société Jean Bodin, 7, Brussels, 1955.

Sayles, G. O. 'Dissolution of a Gild in York', *English Historical Review*, 55, 1940.

Scattergood, V. J. *Politics and Poetry in the Fifteenth Century*, London, 1971.

Schneider, J. *La ville de Metz aux XIIIe et XIVe siècles*, Nancy, 1950.

'Note sur l'organisation des métiers à Toul au moyen âge' in *Mélanges Halphen*, Paris, 1951.

Shatzmiller, J. *Médecine et justice en Provence médiévale*, Aix-en-Provence, 1989.

Sjoberg, G. *The Preindustrial City*, New York, 1960.

Spufford, P. *Money and its Uses in Medieval Europe*, Cambridge, 1988.

Statutes of the Realm, I, Record Commission, London, 1810.

de St Blanquet, O. 'Comment se sont créés les bastides du sud-ouest de la France', *Annales E.S.C.*, 1949.

Stenton, D. M., ed., *Preparatory to Anglo-Saxon England* (F. M. Stenton's collected papers), Oxford, 1970.

Stenton, F. M. *The First Century of English Feudalism 1066–1166*, Oxford, 1932.

Anglo-Saxon England, Oxford, 1947.

Stockton, E. W., ed., *The Major Latin Works of John Gower*, Seattle, 1962.

Storey, R. L. *The End of the House of Lancaster*, London, 1966.

Stouff, L. *Arles à la fin du moyen âge*, 2 vols., Aix-en-Provence, 1986.

Stubbs, W., ed., *Chronica Magistri Rogeri de Hovedon*, IV, London, 1871, Rolls Series, pp. 5–6.

Select Charters and other Illustrations of English Constitutional History, 9th edition, Oxford, 1913.

Swanson, H. *Craftsmen and Industry in Late Medieval York*, unpublished Ph.D. thesis, University of York, 1980.

'The Illusion of Economic Structure: Craft Gilds in Late Medieval English Towns', *Past and Present*, 121, 1988.

Medieval Artisans, Oxford, 1989.

Sweezy, P. 'A Critique' and 'A Rejoinder' in Hilton, ed., *The Transition from Feudalism to Capitalism*, London, 1976.

Tait, J. *The Medieval English Borough*, Manchester, 1936.

Tanner, N. P. *Popular Religion in Norwich with Special Reference to the Evidence of Wills, 1370–1532*, unpublished Ph.D. thesis, University of Oxford, 1973.

Testut, L. *La bastide de Beaumont-en-Périgord 1272–1789: Etude historique et archéologique*, Bordeaux, 1920.

Thomas, A. H., ed., *Calendar of Early Mayor's Court Rolls of the City of London, 1298–1307*, London, 1924.

ed., *Calendar of Plea and Memoranda Rolls of the City of London, 1323–1437*, 4 vols., London, 1926–43.

Thomas, L. J. *Montpellier, ville marchande*, Montpellier, 1936.

Thrupp, S. L. *The Merchant Class of Medieval London*, Michigan, 1948.

Thrupp, S. L., ed., *Change in Medieval Society*, London, 1965.

Timbal, P.-C., 'Les villes de consulat dans le midi de la France' in *Les villes*, I, Société Jean Bodin, 6, Brussels, 1955.

Toulmin-Smith, L., ed., *English Gilds*, Early English Text Society, London, 1870.

ed., *The Maire of Bristowe is Kalendar by Robert Ricard*, Camden Society, London, 1872.

ed., J. Leland, *The Itinerary in England*, V, London, 1906.

Trabut-Cussac, J.-P. 'Bastides ou forteresses: les bastides de l'Aquitaine anglaise et les intentions de leurs fondateurs', *Le moyen âge*, 60, 1954.

Trénard, L., ed., *Histoire d'une métropole: Lille, Roubaix, Tourcoing*, Toulouse, 1977.

Tuetey, A. ed., *Journal d'un bourgeois de Paris*, Paris, 1881.

Unwin, G. *Gilds and Companies of London*, London, 1908.

Industrial Organisation in the Sixteenth and Seventeenth Centuries, 2nd edition, London, 1963.

de Valous, G. *Le patriciat lyonnais aux XIIIe et XIVe siècles*, Paris, 1973.

Veale, E. M. 'Craftsmen and the Economy of London in the Fourteenth Century' in Hollaender and Kellaway, eds., *Studies in London History presented to Philip Jones*, London, 1969.

Veale, E. W. W., ed., *The Great Red Book of Bristol*, I, Bristol Record Society, 1933.

Vercauteren, F. 'La vie urbaine entre Meuse et Loire du VIe au XIe siècle' in *Settimani di studii sull'alto medioevo*, Spoleto 6, 1959.

Vincent, C. 'La confrérie comme structure d'intégration; l'exemple de la Normandie' in Ecole française de Rome, *Le mouvement confraternel au moyen âge: France, Italie, Suisse*, collection 97, Rome–Lausanne, 1987.

Weber, M. *The City*, trans. D. Martindale and G. Neuworth, London, 1958.

Westlake, H. F. *The Parish Gilds of Medieval England*, London, 1919.

Whitelock, D., ed., *English Historical Documents*, I, London, 1955.

Wickham, C. J. 'The Other Transition: from the Ancient World to Feudalism', *Past and Present*, 103, 1984.

Williams, G. *Medieval London: from Commune to Capital*, London, 1963.

Wirth, L. 'Urbanism as a Way of Life', *American Journal of Sociology*, 44, 1938.

Wolff, P. *Commerce et marchands de Toulouse 1350–1450*, Paris, 1954.

Histoire de Toulouse, Toulouse, 1958.

'La draperie en Languedoc du XIIe au début du XVIIe siècle' in Wolff, *Regards sur le midi médiéval*, Toulouse, 1978.

'Les hostelleries toulousaines au moyen âge' in Wolff, *Regards sur le midi médiéval*.

'Les luttes sociales dans le midi français' in Wolff, *Regards sur le midi médiéval*.

'L'approvisionnement des villes en France au moyen âge' in *L'approvisionnement des villes*, Flaran 5, Auch, 1985.

Wormald, D. 'The Age of Offa and Alfred' and 'The Ninth Century' in J. Campbell, ed., *The Anglo-Saxons*, Oxford, 1982.

Zarb, M. *Histoire d'une autonomie communale: les privilèges de la ville de Marseille du Xe siècle à la révolution*, Paris, 1961.

Index

Past and Present Publications

General Editor: PAUL SLACK. *Exeter College, Oxford.*

Family and Inheritance: Rural Society in Western Europe 1200–1800, edited by Jack Goody, Joan Thirsk and E. P. Thompson*

French Society and the Revolution, edited by Douglas Johnson

Peasants, Knights and Heretics: Studies in Medieval English Social History, edited by R. H. Hilton*

Towns in Societies: Essays in Economic History and Historical Sociology, edited by Philip Abrams and E. A. Wrigley*

Desolation of a City: Coventry and the Urban Crisis of the Late Middle Ages, Charles Phythian-Adams

Puritanism and Theatre: Thomas Middleton and Opposition Drama under the Early Stuarts, Margot Heinemann*

Lords and Peasants in a Changing Society: The Estates of the Bishopric of Worcester 680–1540, Christopher Dyer

Life, Marriage and Death in a Medieval Parish: Economy, Society and Demography in Halesowen 1270–1400, Zvi Razi

Biology, Medicine and Society 1840–1940, edited by Charles Webster

The Invention of Tradition, edited by Eric Hobsbawm and Terence Ranger*

Industrialization before Industrialization: Rural Industry and the Genesis of Capitalism, Peter Kriedte, Hans Medick and Jürgen Schlumbohm*

The Republic in the Village: The People of the Var from the French Revolution to the Second Republic, Maurice Agulhon†

Social Relations and Ideas: Essays in Honour of R. H. Hilton, edited by T. H. Aston, P. R. Cross, Christopher Dyer and Joan Thirsk

A Medieval Society: The West Midlands at the End of the Thirteenth Century, R. H. Hilton

Winstanley: 'The Law of Freedom' and Other Writings, edited by Christopher Hill

Crime in Seventeenth-Century England: A County Study, J. A. Sharpe†

The Crisis of Feudalism: Economy and Society in Eastern Normandy c. 1300–1500, Guys Bois†

The Development of the Family and Marriage in Europe, Jack Goody*

Disputes and Settlements: Law and Human Relations in the West, edited by John Bossy

Rebellion, Popular Protest and the Social Order in Early Modern England, edited by Paul Slack

Studies on Byzantine Literature of the Eleventh and Twelfth Centuries, Alexander Kazhdan in collaboration with Simon Franklin†

The English Rising of 1381, edited by R. H. Hilton and T. H. Aston*

Praise and Paradox: Merchants and Craftsmen in Elizabethan Popular Literature, Laura Caroline Stevenson

The Brenner Debate: Agrarian Class Structure and Economic Development in Pre-Industrial Europe, edited by T. H. Aston and C. H. E. Philpin*

Eternal Victory: Triumphal Rulership in Late Antiquity, Byzantium, and the Early Medieval West, Michael McCormick*†

East-Central Europe in Transition: From the Fourteenth to the Seventeenth Century, edited by Antoni Mączak, Henryk Samsonowicz and Peter Burke†

Small Books and Pleasant Histories: Popular Fiction and its Readership in Seventeenth-Century England, Margaret Spufford**

Society, Politics and Culture: Studies in Early Modern England, Mervyn James*

Horses, Oxen and Technological Innovation: The Use of Draught Animals in English Farming 1066–1500, John Langdon

Nationalism and Popular Protest in Ireland, edited by C. H. E. Philpin

Rituals of Royalty: Power and Ceremonial in Traditional Societies, edited by David Cannadine and Simon Price

The Margins of Society in Late Medieval Paris, Bronisław Geremek†

Landlords, Peasants and Politics in Medieval England, edited by T. H. Aston

Geography, Technology, and War: Studies in the Maritime History of the Mediterranean, 649–1571, John H. Pryor

Church Courts, Sex and Marriage in England, 1570–1640, Martin Ingram*

Searches for an Imaginary Kingdom: The Legend of the Kingdom of Prester John, L. N. Gumilev

Crowds and History: Mass Phenomena in English Towns, 1780–1835, Mark Harrison

Concepts of Cleanliness: Changing Attitudes in France since the Middle Ages, Georges Vigarello†

The First Modern Society: Essays in English History in Honour of Lawrence Stone, edited by A. L. Beier, David Cannadine and James M. Rosenheim

The Europe of the Devout: The Catholic Reformation and the Formation of a New Society, Louis Châtellier†

English Rural Society, 1500–1800: Essays in Honour of Joan Thirsk, edited by John Chartres and David Hey

From Slavery to Feudalism in South-Western Europe, Pierre Bonnassie†

Lordship, Knighthood and Locality: A Study in English Society, c. 1180–c. 1280, P. R. Coss

English and French Towns in Feudal Society: A Comparative Study, R. H. Hilton

  * Published also as a paperback
  ** Published only as a paperback
  † Co-published with the Maison des Sciences de l'Homme, Paris